Lucretius I

An Ontology of Motion

Thomas Nail

D1612608

EDINBURGH
University Press

For Katie

Edinburgh University Press is one of the leading university presses in the UK. We publish academic books and journals in our selected subject areas across the humanities and social sciences, combining cutting-edge scholarship with high editorial and production values to produce academic works of lasting importance. For more information visit our website: edinburghuniversitypress.com

© Thomas Nail, 2018

Edinburgh University Press Ltd
The Tun – Holyrood Road
12(2f) Jackson's Entry
Edinburgh EH8 8PJ

Typeset in 10.5/13pt Monotype Baskerville by
Servis Filmsetting Ltd, Stockport, Cheshire,
and printed and bound in Great Britain.

A CIP record for this book is available from the British Library

ISBN 978 1 4744 3466 9 (hardback)
ISBN 978 1 4744 3468 3 (webready PDF)
ISBN 978 1 4744 3467 6 (paperback)
ISBN 978 1 4744 3469 0 (epub)

Contents

A Note on the Translation and Text

All quotations and citations from *De Rerum Natura* are cited from the Latin by book and line number. For English translations of the Latin I have followed Walter Englert's translation, *Lucretius: On the Nature of Things* (Newburyport, MA: Focus Publishing, 2003), sometimes modifying it slightly, and in some cases I have left the Latin words entirely untranslated. For example, in most places I keep the Latin word *corpora* instead of using the English translation 'atom'.

In my own translations and commentary I have followed P. G. Glare, *Oxford Latin Dictionary* (Oxford: Clarendon Press, 1982), and Charlton T. Lewis and Charles Short, *A Latin Dictionary: Founded on Andrews' Edition of Freund's Latin Dictionary* (Oxford: Clarendon Press, 1879).

This book is the first volume in a projected three-volume work on *De Rerum Natura*. The aim of this ambitious project is to bring Lucretius back into serious conversation with the contemporary world and provide a historical foundation for a new philosophy of movement. Each volume is structured as a close reading and commentary on two books from *De Rerum Natura*. Volume I focuses on Books I and II; volume II focuses on Books III and IV; and volume III focuses on Books V and VI. Each volume builds on the previous ones and together they provide a new materialist and kinetic theory of a range of areas including ontology, physics, epistemology, aesthetics, politics, ethics, history, and meteorology.

Acknowledgements

I am indebted to a number of people for their support and encouragement of this project. Before writing this book, I had read a number of scholars who referenced Lucretius as an important historical figure in relation to movement and new materialism, but the first true believer I actually met was Ryan Johnson. He was the only person I knew personally who was as excited as I was about the importance of Lucretius, and he generously shared, and continues to share, a number of excellent resources including an early draft of his own book, *The Deleuze-Lucretius Encounter* (Edinburgh University Press, 2017). He also introduced me to the work of Brooke Holmes, whose inspiring scholarship on Lucretius set a very high standard for further scholarship in the field.

Without the support and encouragement of a number of my close colleagues in Denver – particularly Josh Hanan, Chris Gamble, and Robert Urquhart – I would not have felt bold enough to write this book. In a world in which Lucretius is rarely taught in philosophy, and largely thought to have nothing of much importance to say about contemporary philosophy or physics, this group made me feel sane.

The year I wrote this book I taught a class at the University of Denver entitled 'Philosophy and Fiction', which, much to the students' surprise, consisted entirely of a close reading of Book I of *De Rerum Natura* . . . in Latin! By week three we had only read the first fifteen lines, and the group of students in our classroom was significantly smaller. I am absolutely grateful to all the undergraduate and graduate students who rose to the challenge, trusted this crazy idea, were patient, studied the Latin, and ultimately contributed to the ideas in this book.

In the publication of this book I am grateful to the extremely detailed and generous feedback given to me by my anonymous reviewers. They helped make this book better than it was. I thank Edinburgh University Press, and in particular Carol Macdonald for her support and excitement about this daring project, as well as for her kindness, to which everyone who has worked with her can attest.

Finally, I would like to thank my family and especially my wife, Katie, for her continued support, feedback, and editorial direction on parts of this project. They are the material conditions without which this work would not have been possible. I am also grateful to Kim and Lane Riddle for taking us to the South Carolina coast, those other material conditions, on whose shores I first read *De Rerum Natura*: a book best read on the beach in the wind.

Introduction

> The ancient atom is entirely misunderstood if it is overlooked that its essence is to course and flow.[1]
>
> Gilles Deleuze

The time has come for a return to Lucretius. A text that was lost for over a thousand years is today once again collecting dust on the bookshelves, read only as a historical document that once inspired an outdated scientific revolution.[2] The first-century Roman poet, whose famous didactic poem *De Rerum Natura* was single-handedly responsible for the reintroduction of Greek atomism into Western thought and its influence on the modern scientific revolution, has now decidedly fallen out of favour. The present book is the first attempt in a long time to reinterpret this classical text as an absolutely contemporary one: a Lucretius for today.

The Decline of the Atom

De Rerum Natura has been abandoned as a contemporary text because a number of key modern atomist tenets have now been proven scientifically and philosophically untenable in light of twentieth-century discoveries in physics.[3]

First, and most importantly, the core atomist thesis that all of reality is made up of discrete, indestructible, and indivisible atoms can no longer be upheld. Beginning with the discovery of electrons in the late nineteenth century and culminating with the discovery of other subatomic particles, the splitting of the atom, and the discovery of quantum fields in the twentieth century, it is no longer possible to maintain a philosophical or scientific belief in the core tenet of Greek atomism. The twenty-first-century scientific consensus is now that of quantum field theory: that all particles are fluctuations or effects of more primary field processes.[4] For all its historical influence and prescience regarding the discovery of the atom, the ontological core of modern atomism remains fundamentally mistaken about the nature of reality as we know it today.

Secondly, and correlatively, the modern atomist commitment to materialism remains fundamentally flawed. The modern interpretation of Greek atomism, primarily based on Lucretius' *De Rerum Natura*, remained committed to a version of materialism defined by at least three core aspects: discreteness, observability, and mechanistic causality.

Discreteness. For modern materialism, all of being is made of matter and all of matter is defined by discrete particles of three-dimensionally extended physical stuff. The particles of matter move around, but with respect to their own self-identity they remain unchanged. Matter can be divided up into smaller and smaller particles, but matter will always be nothing other than the sum total of divided discrete particles with extension in space.

Observability. All of these discrete particles are defined by their observability and measurability. According to classical physics, if something cannot be observed or measured with accuracy then it is not material. Discreteness and observation are thus related. A non-discrete body will not yield to the totality of presence required by a total observation of the body, but only a partial and thus incomplete observation. Furthermore, discreteness is also the precondition of completely accurate measurability. Without the discreteness of atoms, measurements or quantification become stochastic or chaotic, changing in character by virtue of being measured. If the act of measurement or observation modifies the object of measure, then a completely accurate measurement becomes impossible. Today, such simple scientific empiricism has become a deeply flawed methodology.[5]

Causality. Based on the intrinsic discreteness and measurability of corporeal matter, classical physics believed that the causal connections between discrete bodies could be mechanically broken down and made predictable. If the measure of one body could be determined, its relation to other bodies could be determined by the observation of patterns and so-called 'forces' between them. Matter, in this interpretation, behaves according to fixed laws, which are, in principle, rational, calculable, and predictable. 'The great book of nature', as Galileo says, 'can be read only by those who know the language in which it was written. And this language is mathematics.'[6]

Flux. Contemporary physics, however, has rendered these three features of modern materialism, inspired by Greek atomism, absolutely outdated.[7] Einstein's famous discovery of mass–energy equivalence ($E = mc^2$) fundamentally transformed our understanding of matter as some reified, discrete body. Discrete matter is essentially equivalent or trans-formable back and forth between continuous fluctuations of energy and discontinuous bodies of matter. Following the basic insights of quantum field theory, one can no longer maintain any such definition of matter as fundamentally discrete or reified.

Interaction. Furthermore, since the movement of quantum fields has been found to be fundamentally stochastic, one can no longer maintain a philosophical or scientific commitment to the necessarily observable or measurable nature of matter. One can observe and measure the energy and momentum of a quantum field only with respect to the particle it generates. The direct observation and measurement of quantum fields is further complicated by the fact that they are in constant motion and superposition. The act of measurement interacts with the field itself and gives determination to the indeterminate fields. Prior to this interaction or measurement there is no objective discrete state or states, only an indeterminate flux.

Pedesis. Finally, in quantum field theory matter cannot be understood causally or mechanistically. Since matter is fundamentally stochastic, the connections between motions are never absolute or predictable with certainty in advance. So-called immutable laws of nature are now mutable. We can no longer speak of absolute causality, but only prob-abilities of constant conjunctions between fields and particles. Fields are not discrete mechanisms with billiard-ball-like effects. Subatomic parti-cles can 'tunnel' through solid physical barriers and become 'entangled' over distances, duplicating the movement of the other and responding instantaneously to changes in motion. In short, the modern interpreta-tion of Greek atomist materialism, from the fifteenth through the nine-teenth centuries, can no longer seriously be entertained and has no place contemporary philosophy or science, except perhaps as a historical relic.

Given the failure of the core ontological and scientific tenets of modern atomism, it is not surprising that their textual origin, Lucretius' *De Rerum Natura*, has suffered the same fate. Atomism, materialism, clas-sical physics, and Lucretius all rose and fell together in the same great revolution. Thus, by tying *De Rerum Natura* to its modern interpreta-tion we have both elevated it as a historical document of the greatest revolutionary importance but also bound it to a very specific historical interpretation of atomism and materialism, which is far from the final word on the text. Like all great works of art, *De Rerum Natura* gains new salience as the historical conditions of reading it change.

The argument of this book is that another Lucretius is possible beneath the rubble of its modern interpretation. In light of contemporary physics it is possible again to return to Lucretius and find in his work fresh philosophical insights that provide a poetic and theoretical coherence to the philosophical and scientific discoveries of *our time*. Beneath the paving stones of atoms, the sandy loam of flux!

The Underground Current of Materialism

The return to Lucretius is not an isolated effort. It is part of a much longer tradition which the French philosopher Louis Althusser has called the 'underground current of materialism'.[8] This tradition, according to Althusser, began with Lucretius' Greek inspiration, Epicurus, and can be traced all the way up through Marx to the present. However, while Althusser defines this 'materialism' by a purely 'aleatory encounter', or swerve of contingency, I trace out in this book a different but related *current*: the actual material current or flow of matter itself, which has been covered over by the atomist, materialist, and even aleatory interpretations of *De Rerum Natura*. In other words, for this book, the emphasis is placed on the underground *current* of materialism as the *motion* of matter itself.

In this brief introduction I would like to argue that the history of *De Rerum Natura* is part of a subterranean current of philosophy that has been systematically decimated throughout Western history. People have been burned alive for reading this book. Copies of it have been destroyed and its ideas denounced as heretical, communist, atheist, hedonist, and materialist. It is not at all by accident that the writings of Epicurus and Lucretius were destroyed and those of Plato and Aristotle preserved. For all the diversity of the ancient philosophers, only one tradition was courageous enough to deny the existence of God and the immortality of the soul, and to reject the politics of the state and the aesthetics of representation: atomism. The fact that the writings of atomist philosophers, and therefore the robust legacy of their philosophical interpretation and development, have been destroyed and misinterpreted is a direct expression of a certain Graeco-Judaeo-Christian will to destroy their ultimate philosophical enemy. The current of materialism is underground, not by necessity, but by force of oppression. Like the damming of a flood, the primacy of matter in motion has been blocked up and systematically denied throughout Western philosophy.

There are, however, three great historical moments when this current has risen from its subterranean trajectory and burst forth like a volcanic eruption in the philosophical tradition.

The First Revolution: The Vortical Revolution

The first revolution occurred in fifth-century BCE Greece with the writings of Leucippus, Democritus, and Epicurus. According to Aristotle, one of the primary ontological tenets of atomism for Democritus and Leucippus is that 'there is always motion'.[9] With the exception of Parmenides, all pre-Socratic philosophers accepted the thesis of continuous motion,[10] but none of them accepted the idea that there was always motion without a static first cause of that motion. At the centre of Greek philosophy has always been the eternal, the God, the One, or the first mover and cause of all motion. Leucippus, Democritus, and Epicurus alone rejected the idea of a static or eternal origin. 'The atoms', Epicurus writes, 'move continuously for all time.'[11] Their movement has no origin and no end, no God and no immortal soul. There is only matter in motion. There are no static phenomena to appear to a stable observer but only *kinomena*, or bodies in motion.[12] All of being is produced by a curvature in the flows of this motion that subsequently generates a series of spiral vortices that appear as solid discrete material. Stability and stasis are therefore products of a more primary vortical movement of atoms.

It is no surprise that Plato and Aristotle despised Greek atomism. Every major tenet was against Greek philosophy in general, and against Platonic idealism and the primacy of ontological stasis or eternity in particular. According to Diogenes Laertius, 'Aristoxenus affirms that Plato wished to burn all the writings of Democritus that he could collect, but that Amyclas and Clinias the Pythagoreans prevented him, saying that there was no advantage in doing so, for already the books were widely circulated.'[13] Out of spite, Plato never once alludes to Democritus in any of his texts; Diogenes writes, 'not even where it would be necessary to controvert him, obviously because he knew that he would have to match himself against the prince of the philosophers'.[14] Given this bit of testimony, which is not unlikely, even if not entirely demonstrable, it is reasonable to infer that philosophical battle lines began to be drawn up around this time, each philosopher with their followers and bodies of written work in circulation. Plato's intense hatred, seemingly reserved only for Democritus, 'the prince of philosophers', reveals both the power and influence of atomism as well as its intense and fundamental incompatibility with Platonism and its Western legacy.

Arguably there have only ever been two real trajectories in Western philosophy: idealism and materialism, Plato and Democritus, Hegel and Marx. The first, in one form or another, has been and continues to be the dominant philosophical position in the West. The second, through a long and bloody history, has been systematically misinterpreted and crushed alongside the parallel historical subordination of movement to stasis, female to male, body to mind, and so on. The legacy of Platonism is the legacy of the subordination of the underground current of kinetic materialism.[15]

By the fourth century the Emperor Constantine had made Christianity Rome's official religion. With the reign of Theodosius the Great began the destruction of all pagan rituals and the closing of cultic sites. Christian mobs were unleashed on the great ancient libraries, including the library of Alexandria, and their books and art burned. Plato finally got his wish. If there were any works of Democritus left, they were burned in libraries across the Empire. When the Roman Empire finally collapsed, the books salvaged by the Christians were rarely pagan ones, and even when they were, only pagan texts that might contribute to the theological positions of Christianity were chosen: deism, idealism, the immortality of the soul, and so on. The rest were left to rot. 'Compared to the unleashed forces of warfare and of faith, Mount Vesuvius was kinder to the legacy of antiquity.'[16]

The first revolution of Democritus and Epicurus was thus crushed, burned, buried, and dammed up by the powers of Plato, Aristotle, and Christian theologians for the next thousand years, until 1417, when one of the last texts of one of the last faithful militants of atomism was discovered deep in a German monastery.

The Second Revolution: The Atomic Revolution

The second revolution of the underground current of materialism began in 1417 when the Italian humanist book hunter Poggio Bracciolini discovered and copied the last surviving and most complete existing manuscript of Lucretius' *De Rerum Natura*, which he sent back to Italy. All the odds were against this discovery, and yet this text remains the last, only, and longest ancient text on atomism; without it one can hardly speak of an atomist philosophy at all.

Monks in monasteries collected all kinds of crumbling ancient books and often did not know exactly what they had. Only an expert with a classical training in the humanities would be in a position to know the status of these kinds of works. Furthermore, after over a thousand years, many of the books were eaten by worms, decomposed, and illegible. Monks would then scrape a layer off the vellum (animal skin) and copy a new book over the first in a palimpsest. Additionally, these libraries were not open to the public, and pagan outsiders looking for texts would not be welcome. Luckily, Poggio Bracciolini had the right training, time, money, and the Christian prestige to get into these libraries and to know what he was looking for.

By the end of the fifteenth century, the recirculation of *De Rerum Natura* had spread around Italy, and atomism had become a definitively heretical position. By the end of the sixteenth century, word of atomism had spread all through Europe, and the book had been translated and printed in a number of languages. It would never be destroyed again.

The impact of the book on the budding scientific revolution was enormous. It gave a coherent philosophical account of the natural world and a non-theological explanation of a number of important natural processes well before many of them could have been experimentally proven. The influence of *De Rerum Natura* can be seen across the greatest minds of the humanities and sciences up to the beginning of the twentieth century: Giordano Bruno (1548–1600), Francis Bacon (1561–1626), Michel de Montaigne (1533–1592), Thomas More (1478–1535), Galileo Galilei (1564–1642), Pierre Gassendi (1592–1655), Molière (1622–73), Michel de Marolles (1600–81), the mathematician Alessandro Marchetti (1633–1714), Thomas Hobbes (1588–1679), Baruch Spinoza (1632–77), René Descartes (1596–1650), Isaac Newton (1642–1726), Charles Darwin (1809–82), Thomas Jefferson (1743–1826), William Thomson (Lord Kelvin) (1824–1907), and Albert Einstein (1879–1955).[17]

A full account of the impact and influence of *De Rerum Natura* on Western thought is impossible to give here, as to demonstrate it would effectively be to recount the entire history of Western thought during the scientific revolution.[18] In short, however, the reintroduction of Greek atomism through *De Rerum Natura* gave rebirth to an atomism, materialism, and naturalism that had been buried for over a thousand years. Being was no longer subordinate to eternal forms or essences, but to natural materials and motions. All of nature became matter in motion again.

Unfortunately, the counter-revolution did not take long to appear. In the first revolution, the enemy came from outside in the form of a direct attack by idealists, who destroyed the books and followers of atomism. In the second revolution, however, the counter-revolution came from within in the form of the discovery of *idealism within materialism*. In addition to the modern interpretation of atoms as discrete, observable, mechanical particles which reduced the vortical and turbulent movement of atoms to predictable mechanisms caused by so-called forces of nature, there was an attempt to redefine the stochastic nature of vortical motion in the idealist terms of 'freedom'.

The swerving stochastic movement of atoms in the work of Epicurus and Lucretius was given a transcendent determination, despite the explicit prohibition of such a determination in *De Rerum Natura* (see Chapter 6). Lucretius insisted that the spontaneous swerve of moving matter is contained entirely in the materiality of the movement itself and does not come from outside. In contrast, modern atomism introduced the metaphysical concept of 'force' and the idealist concept of 'mind' in order to give a causal explanation for why the movement of matter might appear stochastic in its swerve.[19] The motion of matter was thus explained by something else: force, mind, and God. At the heart of this counter-revolution was a deep fear and suspicion of the contingency and chaos at the heart of matter. By re-yoking the movement of matter to metaphysical forces, ideation, and freedom, modern atomism attempted to regain control, predictability, and causality in the otherwise chaotic natural philosophy of Lucretius.

And so it was that the eruption of kinetic materialism was again subordinated to the metaphysics of force, thought, and causal laws. Nature was again subordinated to human rationality.

The Third Revolution: The Kinetic Revolution

The third revolution in the underground current of materialism has only just begun. So far, there have been only tremors and rumblings to suggest a volcanic return of Lucretian materialism to philosophy. The first in a long time to utter such a possibility was Gilles Deleuze in an appendix to his *Logic of Sense* (1969). In a chapter of this appendix, entitled 'The Simulacrum and Ancient Philosophy', Deleuze outlines the challenge of the reversal of Platonism and inaugurates this reversal by showing the true chaos repressed within Platonism itself in the form of the simulacrum or pure dissimilitude, or difference, which is the condition for the division between model and copy.

In the following section, Deleuze continues this history by showing the similar status of the concept of the simulacrum in Epicurus and Lucretius. Whereas Plato tried to repress the simulacrum, Epicurus and Lucretius were the first to affirm it and make it the foundation of a new theoretical framework. In particular, Deleuze emphasises that to return to Epicurus and Lucretius today means not only rejecting the mechanistic view of atoms, their discrete observability, but also rejecting the reintroduction of transcendence into the immanence of moving atoms in the form of an idealist or humanist 'freedom' or a transcendent 'force' beyond the movement of material bodies. In a mere thirteen pages, Deleuze's suggestion for an immanent reinterpretation of atomism has had an incredible influence on all subsequent philosophical interpretations of Lucretius.[20]

In 1977, this influence became a sustained effort to return to the physics of Lucretius on the part of the French philosopher of science, Michel Serres, in his book *The Birth of Physics in the Text of Lucretius*. This is currently the only and most sustained philosophical attempt to reinterpret *De Rerum Natura* with respect to some of the problems of contemporary physics. In particular, Serres argues that one of the most profound and contemporary ideas in *De Rerum Natura* is the idea of the turbulence of fluid motion. Serres argues that the idea of stochastic movement and turbulence was not a nineteenth- or twentieth-century discovery, but was rather discovered first by Lucretius.[21] If Serres is right, any such discovery or theory in *De Rerum Natura* would be enough to undermine any attempt at a second internal idealist counter-revolution. If turbulence and chaos are fundamental aspects of matter itself, then there would be no need for the introduction of any additional metaphysical 'forces' or 'freedoms' to be injected back into matter to explain the cause of its motion or composition. It would be self-compositional. If movement were enough to organise matter, it would be possible to re-explain all of ontology and physics with respect to the movement of matter alone. *The Birth of Physics* does not attempt to develop an entire systematic reading of all aspects of *De Rerum Natura*, but focuses primarily on the description of vortical and turbulent motion in the text. More than Deleuze, it is the historical intuitions of Michel Serres that have inspired the present work.

In 1986, Louis Althusser traced this Epicurean idea of the contingency within matter itself through a number of figures in the history of philosophy including Lucretius, Machiavelli, and Marx, identifying them as thinkers of 'aleatory materialism', that is, philosophers who believe that matter itself is spontaneously creative and that this creativity is fundamentally stochastic. Althusser identifies the heroes of this tradition as well as the counter-revolutionary attempts to interpret it as identical to the mental freedom of human beings. Althusser thus provides an interesting historical lineage for the idea, even though he ends up oddly emphasising the 'aleatory' over the 'materialist' implications of atomism more than is accurate for Lucretius.

Today, the echoes of a return to Lucretius can be heard in the footnotes of 'new materialist' philosophers, such as Jane Bennett's *Vibrant Matter: A Political Ecology of Things* (2010), William Connolly's *A World of Becoming* (2011), and Levi Bryant's *Democracy of Objects* (2011), among others.[22] All of these works emphasise the original Deleuzean imperative to reinterpret Lucretius according to the creative and immanent power of matter itself against the modern atomist interpretations of mechanistic particles and psychological freedom. However, limitations notwithstanding, none of these thinkers develop a full-fledged reinterpretation of *De Rerum Natura* along these lines.[23]

What this book adds to the long tradition of underground materialism in general, and to the recent interest in materialism in particular, is precisely such a full-fledged reinterpretation of the founding document of Western materialism: *De Rerum Natura*. In other words, the point of departure for this book is to produce a new reading of Lucretius' revolutionary text based on the single most primary, but unappreciated, ontological feature of Greek atomism: movement. Greek atomism espoused a number of philosophical positions, but all are derived from the rare and radical ontological thesis that being is in motion. Even among today's atomist and materialist sympathisers, no one has dared to utter such a thesis, opting instead for theories of becoming, immanence, force, or neo-Spinozist vitalism. Being, for Lucretius, however, is nothing other than matter in motion.

This book is thus opposed to the modern atomic interpretation of Lucretius in three ways, following the triple failure of classical materialism and physics: discreteness, observability, and mechanistic causality. First and most importantly, instead of positing discrete atoms as ontologically primary, as in the ancient and modern interpretation, this book argues that Lucretius instead posited *the flow of movement as primary*. The difference between Lucretius and the earlier Greek atomists is precisely that – the atom. For Leucippus, Democritus, and Epicurus, atoms are always in motion, but the atom itself remains fundamentally unchanged, indivisible, and thus internally *static* – even as it moves. Thus instead of positing discrete atoms as ontologically primary as both ancient Greek and later modern theories do, one of Lucretius' greatest novelties was to posit the *movement or flow of matter as primary*.[24] Lucretius did not simply 'translate Epicurus', he transformed him.

For example, although the Latin word *atomus* [smallest particle] was available to Lucretius to use in his poem, he intentionally *did not use it*, nor did he use the Latin word *particula* or particle to describe matter. The English translations 'atom', 'particle', and others have all been added to the text based on a particular historical interpretation of it. The idea that Lucretius subscribed to a world of discrete particles called atoms is therefore both a projection of Epicurus, who used the Greek word *atomos*, and a retroaction of modern scientific mechanism on to *De Rerum Natura*. As such, Lucretitus' writings have been crushed by the weight of his past and his future at the same time.

In this book I argue that Lucretius *rejected entirely* the notion that things emerged from discrete particles. To believe otherwise is to distort the original meanings of the Latin text as well as the absolutely enormous poetic apparatus he summoned to describe the flowing, swirling, folding, and weaving of the *flux* of matter. Although Lucretius rejected the term *atomus*, he remained absolutely true to one aspect of the original Greek meaning of the word, ἄτομος (*átomos*, 'indivisible'), from ἀ- (a-, 'not') + τέμνω (témnō, 'I cut'). Being is not cut up into discrete particles, but is composed of continuous flows, folds, and weaves. Discrete 'things' [*rerum*] are composed of corporeal flows [*corpora*] that move together [*conflux*] and fold over themselves [*nexus*] in a woven knotwork [*contextum*]. For Lucretius, things only emerge and have their being within and immanent to the flow and flux of matter in motion. Discreteness is a product of continuous, uncut, undivided motion and not the other way around.

Secondly, for Lucretius, the material flows of being are *not necessarily observable* as such. Material flows never appear as discrete, observable or empirical particles. Material flows [*corpora*], he writes, are always just below the level of observation. This is because observation only notes discrete composites [*rerum*] and not the constitutive flows that produce the discrete product. Since material flows are fundamentally immanent to the constitutive kinetic flow which produces things, in principle one never finds a *corpora* but only an infinite *corporeal flow* as the material condition of any discrete composite or thing.

Thirdly, instead of a mechanistic causality between atoms, we find in Lucretius a theory of stochastic or pedetic motion inherent in matter itself. Matter is not moved by an external will or force, but by itself. It is the source of its own motion. Matter by its very nature is not a predictable mechanism. It is fundamentally turbulent, disordered, and chaotic. But from this turbulent motion it also produces order and stability through the folding, circulation, and knotting of flows. Matter is therefore onto- and morpho-genetic.

Method

Following this triple rejection of the atomist interpretation of Lucretius, this book is structured along four methodological lines.

Close Reading
First and foremost it is structured by a close reading of Books I and II of *De Rerum Natura* – in which Lucretius puts forward his core physical and ontological theses. Given the sheer poetic density of the text, the range of topics, and the enormous consequences of his arguments, a close reading is necessary to demonstrate the full *systematic primacy of motion in his work*. The status of Lucretius as the first philosopher of motion is not a dispute over a line or two of the text. It is something completely integral to the core of his thought and touches upon every aspect of it. It is what makes Lucretius' work and methodology so absolutely original in the history of Western philosophy.

Translation
This leads to our second methodological line: translation. This book offers not only a fresh interpretation of *De Rerum Natura* but also a few novel interventions regarding its English translation. Translators often introduce their own interpretations and assumptions about 'Lucretius the Epicurean atomist' in their translations. Occasionally they explain or justify this with quotes from Epicurus in the footnotes, but just as often they do not. It is therefore important to take issue on a few points of translation that have too readily merged Lucretius' original ideas

with those of his master, Epicurus. One of the most important is the difference between the Latin word for matter [*corpora, semina primordia*] and things [*rerum, rebus, res*], which are often conceptually and termi-nologically conflated, in even some of the best translations, with the English translation 'atom', borrowed of course from the Greek word *atomos* used by Epicurus. This is not trifling issue – it dominates and defines the modernist reception of Lucretius. It is thus impossible to overestimate the philosophical importance of this under-attended dis-tinction in Lucretius' work, as well as other related atomist translation issues. This book defiantly and systematically maintains the controver-sial thesis that there are no discrete atoms or anything like them in Lucretius.

Argumentation
This second line in turn leads to a third argumentative line followed by this book. This book argues that Lucretius was not an obedient translator of Epicurus, but an original thinker in his own right. More specifically, he was the first great philosopher of motion. He was the first to give the movement of matter ontological primacy, untethered by the static con-straints of Greek atomism.[25] Such a controversial thesis, I admit, is not immediately transparent and will entail more than a few battles with the prevailing atomist paradigm. This book therefore contains a number of argumentative lines of reasoning alongside its more poetic close readings and translation interventions, not from a love of polemic, but to show at each step the novelty and force of the readings and translations that support the larger thesis of the book.

History
The fourth and final methodical line of the book is historical. Following the argumentative thesis above will allow us to demonstrate a new his-torical resonance that has recently emerged between Lucretius and con-temporary physics. Every new epoch changes the conditions in which the past is understood – new lines and legacies are drawn up constantly. In particular, the current historical conjuncture at the turn of the twenty-first century makes it possible for us to see something we had not seen before: the ontological primacy of motion. Well before the discoveries of quantum field theory, which places the motion of fields at the founda-tion of reality, Lucretius had already developed a similar theory of mate-rial flows *consistent with*, although obviously not identical to, this theory.

This new historical resonance has also been discussed at length by the famous Italian physicist Carlo Rovelli.[26]

To be clear, my claim here is not that Lucretius' kinetic theory of matter was a necessary precondition for, or the genetic origin of, contemporary quantum field theory. Nor is my claim that Lucretius was retroactively right because we are scientifically right today, or vice versa. Rather, my thesis is *strictly historical* insofar as the present and the past are mutually illuminating. They tell a similar and compatible story from two different perspectives. The past allows us to reinterpret the present with a new lens, while the present allows us to newly reinterpret the past at the same time. The Lucretian past and the quantum present thus form a feedback loop or resonance like two aspects of the same event – the primacy of motion. They express the same thesis metonymically in two different languages: poetry and science. Both are appreciable in their own terms.

Thus my thesis here is not that Lucretius' theory of matter and the quantum field theory of matter are strictly identical, or that one is derived from or legitimated by the other, but that they are *historically compatible* and mutually illuminating in the way that atomism once was with classical physics. We are quite familiar with the modern atomic Lucretius, but we are only just beginning to discover the contemporary one.

Conclusion

Thanks to the systematic counter-revolutionary forces of modern atomism, *De Rerum Natura* has been buried for a second time. It has become a mere relic of history. Nothing appears left to be done but to eulogise it like the great city of Pompeii, where it has been frozen and preserved in the volcanic ash of classical physics and mechanistic materialism. It is now time to return the text to the surface and allow the underground current of materialism to erupt again with renewed movement.

Notes

1. Gilles Deleuze and Félix Guattari, *A Thousand Plateaus: Capitalism and Schizophrenia*, trans. Brian Massumi (Minneapolis: University of Minnesota Press, 1987), 489.
2. See Stephen Greenblatt, *The Swerve: How the World Became Modern* (New

York: W. W. Norton, 2011). This book is a historical celebration of atomism that marks less the return of interest in Lucretius than a testament to his death, his anachronism as an historical artefact of the past.

3. On several of these points and others, see Duncan Kennedy, *Rethinking Reality: Lucretius and the Textualization of Nature* (Ann Arbor: University of Michigan Press, 2002).

4. Lee Smolin, *The Trouble with Physics: The Rise of String Theory, the Fall of a Science, and What Comes Next* (Boston: Houghton Mifflin, 2006); Sean Carroll, *The Big Picture: On the Origins of Life, Meaning, and the Universe Itself* (New York: Dutton, 2017).

5. For a detailed critique of naive scientific empiricism, see Karen Barad, *Meeting the Universe Halfway: Quantum Physics and the Entanglement of Matter and Meaning* (Durham, NC: Duke University Press, 2007), ix: 'To be entangled is not simply to be intertwined with another, as in the joining of separate entities, but to lack an independent, self-contained existence. Existence is not an individual affair. Individuals do not pre-exist their interactions; rather, individuals emerge through and as part of their entangled intra-relating.'

6. Quoted in Keith Devlin, *The Language of Mathematics: Making the Invisible Visible* (New York: W. H. Freeman, 1998), 152.

7. For a highly accessible theory and history of quantum field theory, see Carlo Rovelli, *Reality Is Not What It Seems: The Elementary Structure of Things*, trans. Simon Carnell and Erica Segre (New York: Penguin Random House, 2017).

8. Louis Althusser, *Philosophy of the Encounter: Later Writings, 1978–1987* (London: Verso, 2006), 163.

9. Aristotle, *On Generation and Corruption*, 324b35–325a6, a23–b5.

10. See Thomas Nail, *Being and Motion* (Oxford: Oxford University Press, under review), chs 3 and 19.

11. Epicurus, *Letter to Herodotus*, in Diogenes Laertius, *The Lives of Eminent Philosophers Volume II*, trans. Robert D. Hicks (London: Heinemann, 1925), X.43, p. 573.

12. Epicurus, *Letter to Herodotus*, in Diogenes, *Lives*, X.40, p. 451.

13. Diogenes, *Lives*, IX.40–2, p. 451.

14. Diogenes, *Lives*, IX.40–2, p. 451.

15. For an excellent survey of Lucretius' enemies and influences, see David Sedley, *Lucretius and the Transformation of Greek Wisdom* (Cambridge: Cambridge University Press, 2009), 62–93.

16. Greenblatt, *The Swerve*, 94.

17. Karl Marx (1818–83) and Henri Bergson (1859–1941) are the only two philosophers to have remained committed to the fundamentally stochastic nature of matter and the ontological primacy of motion.

18. Greenblatt, *The Swerve*, 242–64.

19. See Nail, *Being and Motion*, Part III.

20. This gesture has been developed at length in Ryan Johnson, *The Deleuze–Lucretius Encounter* (Edinburgh: Edinburgh University Press, 2017). Unfortunately, in my opinion, Deleuze's interpretation of Lucretius remains fundamentally limited by its explicitly idealist character when he says that 'The atom is that which must be thought, and that which can only be thought . . . it is the object which is essentially addressed to thought.' Gilles Deleuze, *Logic of Sense*, trans. Mark Lester and Charles Stivale (New York: Columbia University Press, 2009), 268. 'It is a kind of conatus – a differential of matter and, by that same token, a differential of thought' (p. 269). For a more detailed account of the limits of Deleuze's ontology of becoming, see Nail, *Being and Motion*, ch. 3.

21. See Brooke Holmes, 'Michel Serres's Non-modern Lucretius: Manifold Reason and the Temporality of Reception', in Jacques Lezra and Liza Blake (eds), *Lucretius and Modernity: Epicurean Encounters across Time and Disciplines* (Basingstoke: Palgrave Macmillan, 2016), 21–38.

22. Jane Bennett, *Vibrant Matter: A Political Ecology of Things* (Durham, NC: Duke University Press, 2010); William Connolly, *World of Becoming* (Durham, NC: Duke University Press, 2010); Levi Bryant, *The Democracy of Objects* (Ann Arbor: Open Humanities Press, 2011); Peter Merriman, *Mobility, Space and Culture* (London: Routledge, 2013), 3–5; Ilya Prigogine and Isabelle Stengers, 'Postface: Dynamics from Leibniz to Lucretius', in Michel Serres, *Hermes: Literature, Science, Philosophy* (Baltimore: Johns Hopkins University Press), 135–58; Tim Cresswell and Craig Martin, 'On Turbulence: Entanglements of Disorder and Order on a Devon Beach', *Tijdschrift Voor Economische En Sociale Geografie*, 103.5 (2012): 516–29.

23. For a more detailed account of the limits of the Deleuzean ontology of becoming that is adopted by these scholars, see Nail, *Being and Motion*, ch. 3.

24. The Epicurean ethos of 'katastemic pleasure' [standing still] or 'ataraxia' based on stasis is thus transformed in the hands of Lucretius into something quite different.

25. This thesis is historically defended in Nail, *Being and Motion*.

26. A similar thesis about the renewed importance of Lucretius and his

resonance with quantum field theory has recently been put forward by the well-known Italian physicist Carlo Rovelli in his international best-seller, *Reality Is Not What It Seems*, 32–40.

Book I

1. The Birth of Venus

The return to Lucretius is a return to the most maligned idea of Western philosophy: movement. Mechanistic materialism has continually submitted motion to various metaphysical 'forces' or 'laws' that aim to restore causality. In Lucretius' *De Rerum Natura*, however, we find at the very heart of materialism a stochastic or turbulent theory of matter in motion that undermines all the classical ideas of discrete, observable, mechanistic atoms.

We begin this book with a close reading of the first twenty-five lines of Lucretius' breathtaking 'invocation of Venus', at the beginning of *De Rerum Natura*. In many ways these opening lines, which have inspired generations of great artists and thinkers, provide a microcosm of the poem itself and thus offer a perfect introduction to the primacy of matter, motion, pedesis, and continuum at the heart of the work as a whole.

In his praise of Venus, the inspiration for his poem, Lucretius gives us a threefold account of her conception, birth, and attributes which he relates directly to the being, genesis, and appearance of nature itself as a process of elemental materialisation. In particular, Lucretius describes a fluid ontogenesis in which all four elements are defined primarily as stochastic flows and fluxes which begin to curve with desire [*inclination*] and become increasingly composite bodies. The flows of air begin as wind, then fold into clouds, then into flying creatures. The flows of earth begin as seeds, then fold into flowers and plants, which turn into wild animals, nourished by the plants. The flows of water begin as the sea, then fold up into waves, and then into rushing rivers. The flows of fire begin as light, then fold into a glittering light, then finally into the shoreline itself as an illuminated surface. In short, the argument of this chapter is that Lucretius offers us here, in a mere twenty-five lines of hexameter, a whole theory of material ontogenesis, a Venusian ontology – and importantly one which has *nothing to do with atoms*.

Venus: Ontogenetrix

For Lucretius, first philosophy begins not with the idealist contemplation of immutable truth, but with the material conditions of nature itself. *De Rerum Natura* thus begins with an invocation of Venus, the mother goddess of all matter (1.1–2):

> *Aeneadum genetrix, hominum divomque voluptas,*
> *alma Venus*

> Mother of the descendants of Aeneas, desire of humans and gods
> life-giving Venus

The Immanence of God
But for a heretical and atheistic text to begin with an invocation *to a god* is surely a provocation! For what good is a sarcastic praise to a non-existent deity? Lucretius' invocation therefore must be of a different sort. It cannot be a praise of a transcendent god beyond nature, since there is nothing beyond the materiality of nature itself. Instead, a genuine praise, for Lucretius, must be praise to an immanent and material god *of this world*. Fittingly his praise is directed to the most corporeal and material of all the gods: Venus. Venus, for Lucretius, is not beyond the world, but of the world, identical with its self-generation or birth. Aeneas may have been the patriarch of the Roman people, but Lucretius' praise is not for Aeneas, or if it is, it is only secondarily. Venus is the mother of Aeneas and therefore the more primary condition of Aeneas himself.

Aeneas. Aeneadum, the first word of the poem, marks the genetic, political, and historical foundations of Rome and its legacy. But the invocation of this empirical foundation is immediately shown to have a more primary ground in the body of Venus herself. Aeneas derives his name from the Greek adjective *ainos* [unspeakable] 'since it was an *ainos* [unspeakable] *akhos* [grief] that took hold of me [Venus] – grief that I had fallen into the bed of a mortal man'.[1] Aeneas, like *De Rerum Natura*, is a speaking of the unspeakable, a name for the unnamable and invisible structure of nature. In other words, from the very first word of the first line it becomes apparent that Lucretius' philosophical poem is an ontological description of the *nature* of things, not the nature *of things*. Nature is not made of things, like Aeneas and the Roman legacy, but things themselves are made of a more primary nature which is irreducible to the sum total of invisible things.

Venus thus appears mortally and visibly on Earth in her son, Aeneas, but in-appears as the material condition of this appearance. Aeneas therefore appears as the visible marker of matters unseen and unsaid [*ainos*]. From the first word of line one, the poem thus invokes the challenging philosophical task of describing the material and natural conditions (Venus) of things (Aeneas), even though such conditions are themselves ultimately unspeakable [*ainos*]: a fine definition of both philosophy and poetry – a speaking of the unspeakable.

First philosophy, for Lucretius, thus begins not from dialectic, logic, reason, knowledge, truth, and so on, but from the generative and material conditions of the philosopher as a material being. The philosopher shares these same conditions with all other natural things. Before all else, being is creative and created through continual birth: the genetic line of the *Aeneadum* (1.1). Before philosophy and thought there is nature, birth, and generation, which conditions and makes human thought itself possible. First philosophy begins therefore with the realisation of the ontological primacy of a creative movement that is one with what it creates: Venus. The goddess creates, but is not divided from or beyond that which she creates. She is fully immanent.

The Mother of Matter

The *genetrix* (1.1) of Aeneas is the mother [*māter*] of Aeneas, from which the Latin words *māteriēs* [material] and *māteria* [matter] also come. *Māter* is also the tree or *matrix*, the source of the tree's growth, whose Indo-European root is described by the Greek word *hūlē*, meaning tree and matter. First philosophy, for Lucretius, begins with the mother, with matter itself, with the creative power of matter itself to produce all beings, the *aeneadum*.

This first invocation of the primacy of the creative mother [*māter*] by Lucretius is no coincidence. Numerous goddesses appear as privileged figures throughout Book I and II, as we will see. Furthermore, the Latin word *māter* is the root from which Lucretius derives his primary names for material nature: *māteriēs* (matters). Instead of using the Latin word *atomus* or the Greek word *atomos*, which have no etymological or theoretical resonances with the rest of the poem, we see instead that his choice of the word *māteriēs* is directly and immediately related to the primacy of the material mother-goddess who inspires the poet, Venus.

But the resonance goes both ways. The concept of *māteriēs* both maternalises matter and materialises the mother at the same time. In other words, the mother of all creation is herself made of the same matter that she creates. Her materiality is the same materiality of the world. The mother of matter is the matter of the mother. Her creation is therefore the process of matter's own process of materialisation. Maternalisation is materialisation.

Venus' creative power is therefore neither technological nor biological. Since the mother is not separate from her creation, she does not create technologically from her mind or craft outside her, like Zeus, Yahweh, or Ea, but she creates from the matter that she is. Her generation is thus ontogenetic or autopoetic, insofar as matter creates matter. Matter is self-creative. However, if maternal matter is ontogenetic, it therefore cannot be strictly biological. For example, inorganic matter is itself creative and does not depend on the vitalism of biological life for its movement. The mother of matter therefore creates neither technologically nor biologically, but ontogenetically: materially.

Voluptas

Venus is the desire of gods and men (*hominum divomque voluptas*) (1.1). The double genitive here is critical. Venus is not only the external object of desire *of* the other gods and of men, but she *is* the desire itself. She is therefore both the *process* and the *object* of desire. She is the object of pleasure [*voluptas*] and the subject of desire [*voluptas*] at the same time. In other words, Venus is the immanent process of desire/pleasure which desires itself. Gods and men are therefore unified by the *voluptas* that moves through them equally, as expressed in the beautiful Homeric *Hymn to Aphrodite*:

> Muse, sing to me the deeds [*ergon*] of golden Aphrodite
> of Cyprus, who roused sweet longing in the gods
> and overwhelmed the tribes of mortal men
> and the birds of the air and all the beasts . . .
> for the deeds of fair-wreathed Kytherea are a care to all.[2]

The transcendence of the gods and the immanence of men is instantly toppled by the double genitive of desire which is immanent in both and therefore produces both as immanent expressions of a single process of desire. In this sense, gods and men are themselves already expressions of a more primary process of desire within them. Their will [*voluntas*] is nothing other than the immanent desire of Venus expressed in and through them.

It is therefore a mistake to think of Venus as a mere object of desire, as if desire were cut off from its object and defined by a lack or negativity. The subject of that desire already presupposes a more primary constitutive flow of desire: the creative power of mother Venus herself. Venus is thus the creative desire that moves through and produces the subject and the object, and the desire/pleasure between them. The notion that desire is a lack or negativity is only a regional determination from the limited perspective of the divine or earthly subject, when in fact the desire of Venus is already the ontogenetic precondition for the production of the desiring subject *in the first place*. The subject and object of desire are therefore co-constituted in the same immanent material flow of desire. Here, Lucretius could not be farther away from the Platonic negativity of desire as a lack. Desire, here, lacks nothing. Desire desires itself in a purely positive feedback or fold.

Alma Venus
Life-giving, nurturing, bountiful Venus (1.2). She not only gives life, but nurtures that which she gives life to. What she creates by desire does not lack anything but is defined by a bounty [*alma*] and excess of her nurturing desire. The problem of bountiful desire is therefore not how to attain what one lacks but how to distribute the excess or bounty; how to absorb, make use of, and waste the nourishment and constant excess produced by desire.

Alma Venus creates life by materialisation and distributes life through cycles of eating, nourishment, and growth. Desire flows from the earth in the form of a life-giving food, and a pleasure or desire in the consumption of that food. The nourishment of the earth then allows for an excessive growth and further increase in pleasure.

The flows of life-giving desire, like Venus herself, are born from the ocean. In the beginning, before anything else, according to Homer, there is water. It is Oceanus, the spiralling and chaotic waters that encircle the world, and Tethys, the rounded and delimited mother ocean goddess, from whom all of creation and the other gods originate (γένεσιν). In Hesiod, it is Chaos, or space, that is first and is ontologically primary, but through a centripetal ontogenetic concentration of chaotic space come the broad curved breasts of Gaia [Γαῖ' εὐρύστερνος], Mother Earth; the 'solid foundation' upon which all other gods are birthed. The rounded, ovoid, cosmic breasts of the earth shelter and nourish creation like a womb, egg, bowl, or vessel, gathering all the flows of chaos into her 'broadpaths' [εὐρυόδεια], or 'tracks', through which it circulates as the internalised process of ontogenesis.

According to Hesiod, from Mother Earth (Gaia) came Father Sky (Ouranos), and together they produced all manner of monstrous off-spring, whom Ouranos hid away. In revenge Gaia persuaded her son Cronos to castrate Ouranos with a curved knife or sickle. After Cronos performed the deed, he threw Ouranos' genitals into the ocean (Tethys), which then produced a foam (*aphros*); this foam gathered together in a scallop shell and washed up on the shore of Cyprus and gave birth to Aphrodite (Venus).

Water. Being begins in watery chaos (Fig. 1.1). It flows and moves without predetermined order or direction. In Homer, the chaos of the ocean is folded or curved into the watery circle of the goddess Tethys. In Hesiod, the chaos is curved and folded into the rounded breasts of Mother Earth. In these accounts, the sky is a product of the earth, *not the other way around.* As if to remind the sky god Ouranos of this fact, Gaia has him castrated. Venus is the product of the overthrow of the sky at the hands of the material Mother Earth. Venus is therefore the product

Figure 1.1 Venus of Lespugue. c. 23,000 bce. Photo prepared by the American Museum of Natural History and Alexander Marshack, California Academy of Sciences.

of an unnatural inorganic reproduction; the product of the materialist overthrow of the transcendent heavens and their masculinity. She is born of the removal of the rectilinear phallus by the curvature of the sickle, and declination of the flow of fluids.

Venus, however, is not the negation of the heavens, but their materialisation as air. She is the product of an indirect and homosexual copulation between two goddesses: the earth and the ocean, Gaia and Tethys, through the castration of Father Sky. The air is not so much negated as it is encircled, entered, and gathered together by the fluid medium of the ocean in the form of a thousand tiny bubbles. Venus is the watery encircling of the air. She is the revolutionary overthrow of the vast ethereal sky by the fluid multiplicity of foam.

Foam. Venus is the foam of the ocean. Bubbles and froth are produced when the continuous flows of the ocean fold back over themselves, trapping air within their pleat. The fold gives the flows of air and water depth, extension, and spatiality. The fold produces the appearance of unity, identity, and stability, grounded in the continuity of a heterogeneous flux – the 'Iridescent-throned Aphrodite' as Sappho writes. The Greek word ποικίλος (*poikílos*) expresses the changing, varying, multicoloured, intricate, woven, and iridescent shimmer of bubbled foam.[3]

Bubbles and foam presuppose a turbulent movement that dis*turbs* the laminar flow of the ocean current. What begins as the placid flows of Tethys becomes the turbulent folds of the bubbles [*aphros*] and from the bubbles come the spume or foam that washes up on the shore of the earth. As the ocean approaches the shore she makes waves that cause her flows to fold back over herself as they touch the earth. Venus is therefore defined by the haptic fold of flows as they curve back around on themselves on the shore: the lesbian offspring of Gaia and Tethys touching one another on the shoreline through the prosthesis of the castrated Ouranos. As the flow of water folds back over itself it captures the air and circulates around it in the bubble. Venus is Heaven on Earth. She is the sky captured by water, rained down, and bound to the earthen seashore as foam. In short, she is the fluid kinetic conditions for philosophy itself. She is the liquid materiality of the body on earth, made largely of water, which holds the possibility for the thought of the heavens above, the earth below, and the process of their mutual transformation.

Shell. According to Hesiod, Aphrodite is born in perhaps the most vulva-like of all seashells – the scallop shell. The scallop is an organism, like other seashells, that gathers in the liquid flows of calcium carbonate from the periphery towards a place of central condensation. The seashell is formed by gathering these pedetic mineral flows and folding them together and over one another again and again. The shell therefore introduces a *klin*, a curvature, inclination, or desire, into the chaotic flows of the ocean. As it continues to fold these mineral flows, it grows, but it is a crystalline growth. Calcium carbonate is a mineral and therefore not a biological material. It does not grow like a plant grows, but like a crystal. The pattern of the shell emerges in a certain crystalline pattern from the calcium introduced and by a small amount of protein from the organism.

Crystals have a kind of inorganic material growth. They are the growth of matter itself, not through DNA or biological development, but the growth of the mineral through accretion and self-organisation. The growth of the shell is therefore not reducible to organic or inorganic genesis. It is between nature and technology. The genesis of the shell is the fold of earthen minerals within oceanic flows: Gaia and Tethys. In the shell, natural growth occurs through artifice and artificial growth occurs through natural process. The distinction between nature and technology is exposed here as a false one. There is no nature and culture in the beginning. There is only the process of materialisation. Matter generating itself: Venus.

The spiral patterns of the nautilus and snail shells attest to the fundamental movement of the *klin* that centripetally curves the chaotic flows of the ocean back around itself in a fold. Without this initial curvature the flows of matter remain chaotic and uncreative. Creation thus comes from the *klin*, meaning both curve and desire: from the vortical and spiral movement that folds in and over itself.

Space. It is the *klin* or curve of desire in Venus' shell that introduces space into the chaos of flux. As strange as it may initially seem, for Lucretius, space, like everything else, is a product of matter in motion.[4] The process of internalisation, however, occurs only when these flows begin to curve and fold back around themselves to create a division between an interior and exterior of the fold. This closed loop or circle created by flows is thus a product of curved flows and not a pre-existing form. 'The very permanence of its form is only the outline of a movement', as Bergson writes.[5] In short, spatial form is a product of motion. This is possible precisely because of a very specific type of motion: centripetal motion. The centripetal motion of flows gathers and folds inward in the curved pattern of a spiral or vortex, first described by Democritus as the *dine*, δίνη. The figure of the spiral has no centre, only an infinite process of internalisation as each fold returns to itself deeper and deeper towards a centre without ever reaching it. Centripetal motion is thus centric without having a centre. The spiral also has no absolute periphery, only an infinite gathering inward. The inside of the spiral is thus also its outside; they are two sides of the same movement of internalisation or folding. Space, as a product of spiral motion, is thus without absolute centre, periphery, inside, outside, top, or bottom. This is why 'human knowledge', as Lenin writes in his *Notebooks*, 'is not (or does not follow) a straight line, but a curve, which endlessly approximates a series of circles, a spiral'.[6] This is not a metaphor. Human thought literally follows a spiral motion precisely because it *is* a spiral motion, because it presupposes the material condition of the centripetal motion that defines its body.

This does not mean that space is without the possibility of local or regional insides and outsides. Regional closures of the spiral arms can be formed by closing off loops within the spiral arms, like the many chambers of the nautilus. Space is thus both continuous and discrete. Space is smooth insofar as it is the product of a continuous and undivided centripetal movement of accumulation, gathering together various flows. However, it is also striated insofar as it brings these flows into regional junctions or closed circulations that subordinate the flows to a relative satiability and repetition.[7] This is not an absolute binary, opposition, or normative distinction. It is simply a description of two kinds of motion that mutually transform one another. In one movement a continuous centripetal motion accumulates flows towards a centre without dividing itself, and in another movement these flows are folded over themselves and bound into a circulation capable of stabilising, renewing, and extending them. These are the movements that produce space from the bubbling foam of Venus.

The Shores of Light

Lucretius' praise of Venus is not only a description of her qualities; it is a description of her genesis, and as such, a description of the genesis of nature itself. The opening invocation in *De Rerum Natura* should thus be read not only as an invocation but as a theory of ontogenesis defined by the fluid dynamics of elemental, natural, and animal flows.

Like Venus, being is first of all composed of elemental flows and fluxes, whose motion produces a curvature. This curvature or fold then results in a kinetic space that allows the flows to circulate and attain a relative stability. Being moves from chaotic flows to more discrete matters through curvature or desire [*klin*].

The aim of this close reading is to make quite plain the fact that Lucretius' praise to Venus, and his philosophy generally, in no way begins with discrete atoms, particles, transcendent gods, or eternal forms. Rather it begins with the materiality of flows as they move and produce bodies through motion. The praise of Venus as ontogenesis follows three types of flows, each building on the previous: elemental, natural, and animal.

Elemental Flows

In the first part of his elemental praise to Venus, Lucretius describes the elemental waves of Venus' materialisation (1.2–5).

> *caeli subter labentia signa*
> *quae mare navigerum, quae terras frugiferentis*
> *concelebras, per te quoniam genus omne animantum*
> *concipitur visitque exortum lumina solis:*

> it is you who beneath the falling stars
> of heaven makes the ship-bearing sea and the fruitful earth
> teem with life, since through you the whole race of living creatures
> is conceived, born, and gazes on the light of the sun.

Air. Venus is first of all constituted by the *labentia signa* [smooth falling stars] (1.2) of the sky which flow, glide, slide, sink, and fall down out of the air into the ocean like Ouranos' severed seed raining down.[8] Currents of air, the most turbulent and ethereal motions of the sky, become smooth and begin to decline [*klin*] towards the ocean.

Water. Once the flows of air fall down into the sea they begin to curve as Venus gathers them into herself in the form of a *mare navigerum* (1.3), a sea vessel, ship, or shell. The turbulent flows of air yield to the smooth decline and the curvature of the hollowed-out vessel: the ship or the seashell. They produce a flow of water folded over itself with a pocket of buoyant air trapped inside: a bubble-shell.

The basic form of the ship or shell is the curved bowl. According to the Greeks, the first bowl was made by moulding clay around Aphrodite's breast. The curve of the female breast, the belly, the bowl, and the but-tocks are all the subject of the very first human figurines ever made. The

Venus figurines of early humans express this primary kinetic pattern of nature in the rounded bulbs of her body as well as in the carved shells and pottery vessels that define the first stages of human life. Without the bowl or vessel there could be no civilisation. The bowl is the model for the house, the grave, and the process of birth and regeneration. The sea thus bears the ship [*mare navigerum*] *as itself – and as an offspring*. It introduces a curvature and interiority in the watery chaos.

Earth. By gathering water around air to produce the bubble-ship-shell, Venus brings forth a multiplicity of clamouring and striving [*concelebras*] (1.4) life forms. Through the encircling of air by water, Venus brings life on to the earth [*terras*] (1.3). Air, water, and earth: Ouranos, Tethys, and Gaia produce an elemental wave. As the ocean moves near the shore, its lower half begins to slow down as it touches the earth and its upper half begins to fold over the top. As it folds over itself it pulls down the smooth air of the sky into itself and envelops it. The wave of air and water crashes on to the earth and produces a thousand tiny bubbles on its surface like little fruits [*frugiferentis*] (1.3) of the sea, compiling in larger and larger heaps of bubbles or foam that remain on the seashore independent of the waves that made them. In Lucretius' invocation, Venus is all the elemental process of the waves and *that which the waves produce* through their materialisation: *aphros*. Life on Earth is a product of the oxygenation of the water by waves. The shoreline of the earth becomes the space where the ocean deposits its creations, its materialisation, its foamy matter, its cell-membranes, its little vessels adrift from the ocean coming home.

Fire. Being is thus conceived, born, and nurtured by Venus. She is the maternal-material condition of all being, the process of materialisation by which it emerges, and the material product of the creation itself: a triple genitive of illumination. She is, Lucretius writes, the *concipitur* (1.5) that 'takes in' to herself through the receptive and *perceptive* curvature or fold that surrounds the air; she is the *exortum* (1.5) that 'comes out' and rises up like a bubble, *appearing* in the light; and she is the *visitque* (1.5) that 'comes out to look' back upon *the light* itself. Venus is therefore a triple *lumina*: visibility, vision, and view all at the same time. The froth of matter floats ashore, like Venus, on a bubble, but the materiality of air, water, and earth only comes to appearance with the addition of the *lumina solis* [light of the sun], or fire (1.5). Air, water, earth, and fire thus form the elemental body of Venus.

*

The movement of the four elements forms a single continuous wave of materialisation: the falling of the flows of air into the ocean [*labentia*] (1.2); the floating of the ship-shell upon the sea [*navigerum*] (1.3); their emergence on to the shoreline [*concelebras*] (1.4); and finally their basking in and gazing at the light of the sun [*visitque*] (1.5). The process of materialisation, according to Lucretius' praise of Venus, is therefore like the process of waves upon the beach, bubbling up like foam in the glistening sunlight. Matter comes into being and passes away like bubbles on the shore. Matter emerges from the hidden to the visible and back again in continuous cycles of creation and destruction, as the elements themselves collide in the wave, materialise in the light, and then return. There is no division between being and non-being, only a pure becoming of matter in motion. All relatively discrete things are merely bubbles or froth in the more primary process of elemental flows that produce them.

Natural Flows

Venus, for Lucretius, is therefore first and foremost defined by a multiplicity of elemental flows that fold over themselves in an endless movement of composition and recomposition. But these elemental folds are in turn woven to produce larger natural composites like clouds, waves, and plants (1.6–9).

> *te, dea, te fugiunt venti, te nubila caeli*
> *adventumque tuum, tibi suavis daedala tellus*
> *summittit flores, tibi rident aequora ponti*
> *placatumque nitet diffuso lumine caelum,*

> You, goddess, you the winds flee, you the clouds
> of the sky flee at your coming, for you earth the artificer
> sends up her sweet flowers, for you the expanses of the sea smile,
> and the heavens, now peaceful, shine with diffused light.

Air. Venus moves the flows of air in the sky, which in turn generate turbulence and condensation into clouds, which in turn flee and disperse. The double genitive is active again. Based on the previous lines describing the elemental birth of Venus from the air, Venus is both the air that flees and the wind that is fleeing; she flees herself as wind. The air is thus not only filled with falling stars or signs from the heavens (1.2), but Venus disturbs these flows as well in order to produce the inorganic bodies of the sky: the clouds. The air is part of her but also flees her in the form of clouds. In other words, the flows of air in the sky are folded over one another and accumulated together to produce bodies of air, not just a sky of chaotic flows. The non-linear dynamics of flows becomes consistent in the form of clouds through their fleeing, pleating, and condensation. The fact that the wind flees first and then the clouds flee, according to the poem, is not redundant. The fleeing of the wind produces the formation of clouds. Both move as 'you' (*te*) (the goddess) and 'for you' (the goddess) (1.6). In other words, she moves and flees from herself for herself as herself.

Earth. The earth [*tellus*] (1.7) sends up [*summittit*] (1.8) the sweet organic flow of plant life. The flow of inorganic minerals folds itself up into organic plant life. It does so, according to Lucretius, through a strange form of creation – neither natural or artificial – but material. The earth materialises organic plant life as a skilful construction. This is surely a strange way to describe the earth as *artificially* creating organic life. Lucretius describes the earth as a female Daedalus, *Daedala* (1.7). This idea of the earth as Daedala is an interesting combination of the natural feminine creativity of Gaia and the artificial masculine creativity of the Greek inventor Daedalus, who built a pair of wings made of feathers and wax to escape his island. The description of the earth as 'natural artifice' serves to undermine any idea of a reductive natural (organic) or technical (inorganic) creation. The earth of the sandy shore, in particular, is the most fluid matter of the earth. Sand is essentially rock made liquid, made to flow in the water, blow in the wind, roll on the earth, and shimmer in the sunlight. In the shifting of sand on the shoreline we watch the rock cycle in miniature; rock is deposited by the water, eroded by the wind, sucked back into the ocean, and spat back again further along.

Water. The ocean shakes with Venus' laughter [*rident*] (1.8), producing a series of sea waves [*ponti*] (1.8) whose motion is at once disturbed, soothing, calming, and pleasant [*placatumque*] (1.9). The movement of the ocean is chaotic. Its flows are wild, but through the rhythmic laughter of Venus the disturbance is self-ordered and becomes metastable in the form of the wave. The wave is thus a soothing and synchronous pattern that has been folded over itself in the continuous pleasure of material self-affection. The wave is the water that touches itself and in touching itself brings sensation and pleasure to itself. The laughter of the crashing of waves is the sound of the genesis of life on the shores of light. It is the auditory expression of the excess of this haptic desire. Laugher is unnecessary for life or even happiness, and yet we laugh. Matter releases an excess of auditory turbulence or 'crashing' laughter on the shorelines of light.

Fire. Finally, the light of the sun [*lumine*] (1.9) pours out in flows over [*diffuso*] (1.9) the shore which glistens and reflects it [*nitet*] (1.9). In this way all of matter becomes both the object and subject of illumination as it reflects off itself on to itself. Not only does the sky illuminate the earth, but the earth in turn reflects this light and illuminates the sky. As the French poet Joachim Gasquet writes, 'The world is an immense Narcissus in the act of thinking about himself.'[9] The ponds and oceans are the world's mirror where it illuminates itself twice: once by the sun and again by the reflection of the sky in the waters.

Animal Flows

The elemental flows of air, earth, water, and fire are folded into the natural bodies of clouds, plants, waves, and sunlight; but these organic bodies are in turn further folded into the animal bodies of insects, birds, beasts, and fish (1.10–22).

> *nam simul ac species patefactast verna diei*
> *et reserata viget genitabilis aura favoni,*
> *aeriae primum volucres te, diva, tuumque*
> *significant initum perculsae corda tua vi.*
> *inde ferae, pecudes persultant pabula laeta*
> *et rapidos tranant amnis: ita capta lepore*
> *te sequitur cupide quo quamque inducere pergis,*
> *denique, per maria ac montis fluviosque rapacis*
> *frondiferasque domos avium camposque virentis,*
> *omnibus incutiens blandum per pectora amorem,*
> *efficis ut cupide generarim saecla propagent.*
> *Quae quoniam rerum naturam sola gubernas,*
> *nec sine te quicquam dias in luminis oras*

For as soon as the sight of a spring day is revealed,
and the life-bringing breeze of the west wind is released and blows,
the birds of the air are the first to announce you and your arrival,
O goddess, overpowered in their hearts by your force.
Next wild beasts and flocks prance about their glad pastures
and swim across rushing streams. So taken by delight
each follows you eagerly wherever you proceed to lead them.

Then through the seas and mountains and fast-clutching rivers,
through the leaf-thronged home of birds and the verdant plains,
you like, injecting sweet love into the hearts of all,
and make them eagerly create their offspring, each according to kind.
Since you alone guide the nature of things
and without you nothing emerges into the sunlit shores
of light . . .

Air. The bringing into light of created beings occurs through the
sudden flourishing and ebullient movement [*reserata*] (1.11) of a generative [*genitabilis*] (1.11) west wind. The west wind [*aura favoni*] (1.11) is the
wind of Favonius, the god whose wind brings the most pleasant spring
and early summer breezes. The *aura favoni* is the movement which stirs
[*viget*] (1.11) the creation [*verna*] (1.10) of the winged, flying creatures
[*volucres*] (1.12) (birds, bees, and pollenating insects), which in turn generate the birth of spring flora. The *aura favoni* repeats again the aerial
genesis of Venus by dropping seed [*genitabilis*] (1.11) from the wind, just
as Ouranos' air-seed falls from the sky [*labentia signa*] (1.2), and generates life through the fluid media of air and water. Ouranos creates, but
through castration, by falling from Heaven, just as Favoni creates only
through his falling from Heaven, ousted by the sky god Apollo, and
rescued by Eros on Earth. Favoni is thus swept up by desire (Eros) to
spread seed over the flows of the wind to Flora. Favoni, like Ouranos,
becomes a means to the end of a feminine reproduction between goddesses. Gaia and Tethys procreate through Ouranos' severed seed just
as Venus and Flora now procreate through Favoni's captured seed. The
flows of wind-seed become the flying creatures, insects, and birds that
pollenate the flowers. The *volucres* are moved by a turbulence or overturning [*perculsae*] (1.13) within them that spurs them on in their creation. Insect motion thus rides the turbulence of the wind to find flowers.

Earth. On the earth, wild beasts [*ferae*] (1.14) leap and dance [*persultant*] (1.14) against gravity, expressing an excess of desire that animates
them. Their movements are thus not pre-ordered or domesticated but
wild, stochastic, and pedetic. Pedesis, to leap, is from the Latin word *-ped*,
meaning foot; the *ferae* flow stochastically leaping against the confinement
of gravity, against the rushing river. Their leap is an expression of desire,
not as a lack or negativity for what is missing, but as a motion of excess
and surplus. To leap, in the Nietzschean sense, is to create in excess of
survival, to introduce motive creativity into matter against the prevailing

forces of gravity and necessity. 'One must still have chaos in oneself to give birth to a dancing star', Nietzsche writes.[10] The chaos of their pedetic motion gives birth to the dance of the *ferae* across the undivided pasture [*pabula*] (1.14). The *pabula* is the source of earthen nourishment, the unowned pasture land, countryside, *nomos*,[11] or χώρα, the *chora* that provides the material and nourishing condition for the life of the beasts.[12] The *chora* provides the nourishing countryside, but also the stage for a continually moving circulation or dance, upon which the *ferae persultant*. So captured by desire [*cupide*] (1.16) are the beasts that they follow the continuous movement [*pergis*] (1.16) of Venus wherever she goes.

Water. Flowing through the sea [*maria*] (1.17) and the quickly moving waters [*fluviosque rapacis*] (1.17), Venus also flows through the curved dome of the birds' nests [*domos avium*] (1.18), shaped like the bowl of her breast. She flows across the verdant plains [*camposque virentis*] (1.18) of uncultivated but fertile, undivided, choric pasturage and introduces a shaking, trembling, and turbulence [*incutiens*] (1.19) into the bodies of all living beings.[13] This turbulence introduces a curve, swerve, or desire into their hearts that brings about further creation [*propagent*] (1.20).

Fire. Venus is the only one who can pilot [*gubernas*] (1.21) this shell-ship along the turbulent flows of the ocean. She is the only one who can guide the ship of creation to the brilliant shores of light and appearance [*luminis oras*] (1.22). The shores of light are not only the shores of materiality and matter illuminated by light, but also the light illuminated by the shoreline itself as it reflects light from itself giving light back to the sky and giving itself to appearance and visibility. Thus, the flows of light are not only poured out [*diffuso*] (1.9) from the sun to the shore, but are also poured out from the shore of creation itself, redirecting the flows of light back up and around, making itself appear. Light is what is emitted, reflected, and absorbed by matter, but is also itself material. The permeating flow of light is the invisible material condition for visibility which all of matter partakes in and responds to as it receives and reflects its flows. The light given by the sun is thus re-given again and again on Earth, circulated and re-circulated. The flows of light are invisible but remain thoroughly material and visible through that which they illuminate.

In contrast to the primacy and uni-directionality of Platonic lighting and illumination, Lucretius describes light as the illumination of matter, by matter, through the materiality of light itself. In contrast to the Platonic neutrality of light, which illuminates all without leaving any material remainder, Lucretius describes a light which is material and multiply directed. Light no longer simply emanates from the sun downward, but reflects off the shores of light itself and around. When light becomes material, matter becomes self-illuminating. Light is no longer a transcendent source, but becomes an earthly flow as it touches the shoreline of air, earth, and water. When the flows of light mix with the shoreline they are taken up by the elements, reflected by the rocks, the waves, and the clouds. The light of Venus is therefore an elemental and material flow of light. The shores of light are the shores *of* light in the double genitive sense in which they are both the shores illuminated by light and shores that illuminate by reflecting light.

Conclusion

All of being begins with elemental flows, which become increasingly folded and composite without the introduction of any transcendence or formalism: a purely material ontogenesis. In contrast to the classical division between being and appearing, for itself and in itself, Venus introduces a continuity between the two. They become two dimensions of the same continuous folded flow. Being is the continuous process of composition and recomposition that occurs in the transformation of elemental flows. Being is neither created nor destroyed, only recomposed, sometimes on the shores of light where it *appears* and other times in the sky and deep ocean where it remains yet unfolded and uncirculated, but is none the less real. The difference between being and appearing is therefore not an *ontological difference* but a *topological or kinetic difference* having to do with the regional circulation and composition of matter.

But the birth of Venus is only the first half of her invocation – her ontological or ontogenetic invocation. Of equal importance is her political invocation, as we will see in the next chapter.

Notes

1. Sappho, *The Hymn to Aphrodite*, 198–9, in Susan Shelmerdine, *The Homeric Hymns* (Newburyport: Focus Information Group, 1995), translation modified.
2. Sappho, *Hymn to Aphrodite*, 1–6. *Ergon* is not just her action but her whole domain or sphere of influence and power.

3. Sappho, *Hymn to Aphrodite*, 1.
4. This claim is substantiated in contemporary physics in the theory of quantum gravity described by Carlo Rovelli, *Reality Is Not What It Seems: The Elementary Structure of Things*, trans. Simon Carnell and Erica Segre (New York: Penguin Random House, 2017).
5. Henri Bergson, *Creative Evolution*, trans. Arthur Mitchell (New York: Random House, 1944), 135. Emphasis in original.
6. Lenin, *On the Question of the Dialectic*, written in 1915, first published in the magazine *Bolshevik*, 5–6 (1925).
7. See Gilles Deleuze and Félix Guattari, *A Thousand Plateaus: Capitalism and Schizophrenia*, trans. Brian Massumi (Minneapolis: University of Minnesota Press, 1987), 474–500.
8. The idea that life on earth began with the introduction of interstellar bacteria, or 'panspermia', has been defended by B. Weiss and D. Warmflash, 'Did Life Come from Another World?' *Scientific American*, 293.5 (24 October 2005): 64–71.
9. Cited in Gaston Bachelard, *Water and Dreams: An Essay on the Imagination of Matter* (Dallas: Pegasus Foundation, 1983), 24.
10. Friedrich Nietzsche, *Thus Spoke Zarathustra: A Book for All and None*, trans. Adrian Del Caro (Cambridge: Cambridge University Press, 2006), 9.
11. The Greek word *nomos* comes from the Proto-Indo-European root word -*nem* meaning undivided pasturage. See Emmanuel Laroche, *Histoire de la racine NEM- en grec ancien* (Paris: Klincksieck, 1949), 255.
12. See John Sallis, *Chorology: On Beginning in Plato's Timaeus* (Bloomington: Indiana University Press, 1999).
13. Just as Timaeus in Plato's dialogue describes the *chora* in lines 52e–53c. Plato, *Plato's Timaeus: Translation, Glossary, Appendices and Introductory Essay*, trans. Peter Kalkavage (Newburyport: Focus Publishing/R. Pullins, 2001).

2. Love and War

The second half of Lucretius' invocation of Venus is political. Not only does Venus exemplify the ontology of motion that Lucretius aims to emulate in his work, but she also exemplifies a politics of motion which leads to the love, peace, and freedom that Lucretius thinks is essential to human flourishing. Through a close reading of the next ten lines of the poem this chapter demonstrates several social and economic dimensions of a Venusian politics. Here, as in the first half of the invocation, the kinetic and materialist language of Lucretius' political theory is important to attend to.

In this second invocation Venus is called upon as a protection against war. However, the kind of war that Lucretius seeks protection from is not the war of chaos or disorder, but a specific military form of contractual state warfare (1.29–30).

> *Effice ut interea fera moenera militiai*
> *per maria ac terras omnis sopita quiescan*

> Meanwhile, make it so that the savage claims of war
> are put to sleep and lie quiet throughout every sea and land.

The *moenera militiai*

The *moenera militiai* (1.29) is not just a 'claim of war', it is a duty or debt of military service with the state. The word *moenera* is a conjugation of the Latin word *munus*, meaning contract, duty, or debt. The word *munus* comes from the Proto-Indo-European word **moy-nós*, from the root **mey-* ('change, swap'). The Latin word *munus*, according to the Lewis and Short Latin Dictionary, thus has several interrelated meanings used around Lucretius' time by other writers: duty (*mūnia*), exchange, gift, contract, service, burden, obligation, or debt. From the word *munus* also come the words *communis* (community), *munitions* (weapons), and *remuneration* (to repay a debt).

Debt

Debt, credit, community, exchange, and military warfare are all tied together in the same logic of the state apparatus. The military warfare of the state is not chaos, but precisely the opposite. The military is a very specific form of social circulation or regime of ordered motion. The military state apparatus is, as Lucretius rightly observes, predicated on the idea that once it emerges it retroactively claims to have been the ontological and social origin of the very people that constituted it in the first place.

Historically, the emergence of the dual figure of the god-king or deified warrior accomplishes precisely this. Once the military state emerges historically, the centralised leader becomes *god-on-earth* and thus the retroactive creator of his people as well as their *military king* and leader in battle. Insofar as the despot becomes the centralised ontological and political origin of his people, his people owe both their existence and social mobility to him. Their being is in debt to his creation and their action is in debt to his military command.

Credit

Under this regime, social life becomes a credit granted by the state to the individual. One exists purely by virtue and on the condition of the military despot's protection. The military despot-priest gives life and takes it away. The form of social community invented by the state is thus a form of *munus* – debt, service, obligation, or burden – owed by virtue of the credit granted in the form of social security. In Ancient Mesopotamia the earliest states were military states in constant conflict, based on contractual military service and the enslavement of the captured, whose life was also a type of credit granted by the despot, and thus included a social debt in the form of military or social service.

The state community is based on the notion of a collective debt owed to 'the community' in the form of an adherence to a system of centrally ordered laws inscribed by the central priest-bureaucrats and directed centrifugally outward to the concentric order of periphery villages by the priest-king. Credit radiates centrifugally outward from the spiritual-military centre and returns centripetally to the centre in the form of a debt owed to the state. Historically, this takes the form of corvée: the repayment of one's social debt to the state in the form of manual labour, public works, community service, and the military contract (*moenera militiai*).

The Latin word *militiai* means not only military *warfare*, but an onerous service or debt to the state more generally. Military service includes not only battle and war, but also public works such as the digging of canals, and the building of roads and state buildings. Under the law of corvée all community members of the state are essentially potential slaves because all members owe a debt to the despot's credit of security. Corvée is thus a political and economic *moy-nós* or exchange. Even though the state also invents money and taxation, these concrete inventions are simply expressions of an even more primary system of general equivalence. The centre grants an ontological credit in the form of the securitised mobility of life itself that radiates outward from the political centre and returns in the form of an owed mobility in the form of a *moenera militiai* or corvée. The power of the sovereign is thus first and foremost to move and make stop: kino-power. To let live and make die is not enough; life must be directed and circulated in the proper relation of kinetic exchange between credit and debt.

Exchange

With the historical emergence of the state in the ancient world also comes the introduction of exchangeability or equivalence. Again, exchange-ability is not itself merely an effect of the introduction of money, tax-ation, writing, number, or something else; rather exchangeability or *moy-nós* is what defines the whole immanent regime or pattern of motion within which all these material technologies themselves move. When Lucretius identifies the *moenera militiai* as the fundamental danger from which Venus is to protect us, he is not just worried about people dying in war, he is worried about the very structure of social credit, debt, and exchange that makes military warfare and social servitude possible. He is worried about the existence of a system of social and economic equiva-lence. The very condition of money, taxation, writing, and the military itself is the idea that being is divisible into discrete unified bits which are fundamentally identical to themselves, and as such potentially identical with others, that is, exchangeable, *moy-nós*.

Without this very specific notion of equality of exchange in the *moenera*, coins cannot be exchanged for goods (money), letters cannot be exchanged for meanings (writing), and individuals cannot exchange their living motion in repayment of a military debt (corvée). Without credit there is no debt, and without debt no credit. The two rely on one another, but they also rely upon a more primary principle of exchangeability between the two that allows beings to move back and forth between discrete possessors in the debt–credit relation. For example, with respect to the state, individuals are exchangeable units; the debt of one's labour can be paid off by the credit of another's; the life of one may be exchanged for the life of another in sovereign punishment. It is no coincidence that debt, writing, cardinal number, the state, the military, taxation, money, and slavery all emerge together in Mesopotamia around the fourth millennium BCE.

The Circle

Debt and credit are grounded in exchangeability, but exchangeability is in turn grounded in the kinetics of the circle. Circular motion exemplifies the kinetic form by which all concrete techniques of exchangeability function. It is only with the circle that any point on the periphery of the circle is exchangeable and identical with any other point on the periphery. Each point of the periphery is identical to all the others because each point is the radius of the same centre. Without the identity and centrifugal radiation of the centre, the circle and the exchangeability of radii is impossible. As Euclid describes, the circle is created by putting down the point of the compass and rotating it around a centre. The centre remains fixed, eternal, and divine, while the periphery moves around it, because of it, in service to it, on condition of its ever-giving credit. The wheel spins by the fixity of its axle. The periphery owes its mobility to the stasis of its centre. The radii of the circle thus appear as so many exchangeable points because each is modelled and derived from the principle of identity found in the immobile centre.

The Primacy of Flows

The state only *appears* to have come out of nowhere and only *claims* (*moenera*) a retroactive capture of social motion by force. However, as we saw in the elemental ontogenesis of Venus, all things begin as flows. Before the circle, or even the curve of the spiral, there are flows. The circle does not arrive on the scene fully formed and eternal, but rather must be produced by the movement of material flows. The flows of matter, therefore, not only flow and curve, as described in the elemental invocation of Venus, they can also curve again and fold back over themselves in a relatively stable and circular motion. The centripetal motion of social accumulation that occurs in the village ends up producing a central stockpile. The mound turns into a mountain and the mountain becomes occupied by a god; the stockpile is seized by the warrior-king. The state always seems to come out of nowhere because it already pre-supposes a more primary centripetal agricultural accumulation of the village from which it draws its supplies and conscripts its slaves.

The kinetic paradox of the state is that the centre claims to have come first and to have created the periphery, but a centre without a periphery is not a centre and therefore could not have already existed without the presupposition of a village periphery that first generated it in the form of a centralised surplus. The circle is thus the product of flows, not the other way around.

This kinetic paradox is identical to the exchangeability paradox. The idea that individuals owe a debt to the state assumes that the state first gave us credit that we could pay back, when in fact the opposite is true. Village society gives the state a credit by accumulation. The formula of the state can now be revealed in all its absurdity; society produces the state as a form of credit that it gives to itself and to which it owes a debt. This is the duplicity and social stupidity of the state. The centre accumu-lates a stock by a more primary centripetal motion; but once this central accumulation occurs a new centrifugal motion appears which claims to have generated itself and the entire periphery out of nothing, *ex nihilo*. The state is defined at its very core by this kinopolitical absurdity that Lucretius critiques at length.

For Lucretius, the state, like all other material formations, is the product of a more primary elemental ontogenetic process. The flows of nature come first, and it is only on condition of their curvature and continual circulation that something like the circular accumulation of the state can stabilise itself.

The *moenera Mavors*

The *moenera militiai* is not only a debt to the state but a debt to Mars, the god of military battle – the founding father of Rome (1.32–3).

> . . . *quoniam belli fera moenera Mavors*
> *armipotens regit,*

> . . . since Mars, strong in arms, rules
> the savage claims of war.

Love and war, Venus and Mars, produce two different founding Roman children. Unlike the Greek god of war, Ares, defined by disorder and destruction, Mars is the hyper-ordered military god who brings peace to the centre on the condition of a military expansion and conquest over the periphery.

Romulus and Aeneas

Mars is the father of Romulus and Remus, twins mothered by Rhea Silvia, but taken and abandoned by the river and nursed by a she-wolf. When they grow up they decide to found a new city: Rome. But in a dispute over exactly where to found it, Romulus kills his brother Remus. Rome is thus founded on fraternal violence and war. Romulus is from the land, raised by its rivers, animals, as a nativist and pastoralist. Mars's legacy is therefore one of autochthony, pastoralism, patriarchy, and murder.

On the other hand, Venus is the more primary mother of Rome since she gives birth to Aeneas, who technically founds Rome before Romulus and Remus do. Aeneas is not a native pastoralist, but rather a refugee, a migrant, a wanderer, without a home but in search of one. Aeneas is the *fato profugus* who flees, but in fleeing finds a new home in Rome, not through murder and the *ex nihilo* founding of supposedly unoccupied pastoral land, but through love and marriage to Lavinia, a native woman. Venus and Mars, Aeneas and Romulus, present us with two different founding political figures: the migrant who founds from outside and through movement, love, and desire, and the native who founds from inside, by violence and refusing to move; Aeneas the refugee and Romulus the autochthonist, movement and stasis.

The story of Venus and Aeneas appears first in mythology because the centripetal movement of social accumulation comes before the centrifugal movement of radiation found in the myth of Mars and Romulus. In other words, Venus is the mythological, ontological, and social condition of the *moenera*. She can can bring peace [*pace*], tranquillity [*tranquilla*], and delight [*iuvare*] back to humans because she is the very condition upon and against which war takes place (1.30–2).

> *per maria ac terras omnis sopita quiescant;*
> *nam tu sola potes tranquilla pace iuvare*
> *mortalis,*

put to sleep and lie quiet throughout every sea and land.
For you alone have the power to bring aid to mortals,
with tranquil peace

As the *genetrix* (1.1) of all being and appearing, Venus is already the elemental flows that have been historically and kinetically consolidated and centrally redirected into the centrifugal *moenera* of the state apparatus. As such, she is both the condition of their persistence and capture by Mars, but also the condition for their overcoming and return to tranquillity and pleasure.

The Wound of Love
Venus is the kinetic condition for the overcoming of the *moenera* in the form of the wound of love [*vulnere amoris*] (1.34). Through the exposure of a double wound in both Mars and Venus, the spatial interiority of the state and its circulation of credit and debt is exposed as a product or fold of more primary kinetic flows (1.33–4).

in gremium qui saepe tuum se
reiicit aeterno devictus vulnere amoris,

and he often lets himself sink
into your lap, completely overcome by the unceasing wound of love.

Mars is continually [*saepe*] (1.33) sinking or falling into the lap or bosom [*gremium*] (1.33) of Venus. The central and immobile point of the circle is thus capable of falling or sinking back down from its holy mountain into the curved motion of the periphery. In this falling, the centre no longer commands the periphery but sinks or is dissolved back into its continuous and horizontal curvature, completely overcome by a perpetual and unhealable wound of love.

The *vulnere amoris* that causes Mars to fall into the curved bosom of Venus should be thought in the double sense in which the wound is said of both Mars and Venus, *in one and the same twofold sense*. For Mars the soldier, the wound is the flesh wound that has torn open the skin to reveal the interiority of the flesh. The flesh wound ruptures the membrane of the skin that divides the inside of the body from the outside. The enclosed circulatory system of blood flows has been cut, but not divided. The cut is not a binary division but a bifurcation of flows. The cut vein, for example, is not split in two without producing a flow of blood that bifurcates into two bleeding openings. The flesh wound is thus always double because the cut introduces a bifurcation into the flesh such that the same body now bleeds from two sides of the same surface. The continuous surface of the skin has now become a twofold bifurcation, a twofold that wants to be reunited through healing or love. Love is only possible between two. So in striving to heal, the body desires itself: a wound of love. For Mars, Venus is the healing [*iuvare*] (1.31) movement of desire that brings together the two without absolute unification in the one.

The wound is a cut or rupture in a regime of circulation that exposes the exteriority of interiority. The military body of Mars has captured a regime of flows into a body divided between the inside (*communis*) and the enemy (*hostis*). The wound disrupts this division by introducing bifurcation into the system of flows. The wound exposes the interior to the exterior and in doing so reveals the continuity between them. The interior centre was always already a fold or internalisation of the exterior periphery. Both become flesh. The military body of Mars functions only on the condition of the materiality of its corporeal flows of blood and flesh. The blood desires circulation, but the wound exposes the blood to the air, revealing the blood's desire to flee circulation as well. The binary division between the inside and outside upheld by the seal of the skin is broken, revealing that the inside is already the outside turned inside. Depth is already an effect of the surface folded over itself – and surface an effect of depth folded over itself. The wound exposes the truth of depth as a depth of surface and the surface as a surface of a depth.

In short, the *vulnere amoris* reveals that the military body of the state is not the primordial cause and origin of its own being, but rather a folded effect of the nourishing material periphery that provides it with pasturage (*chora*), space, and love (*amoris*) to reproduce and nourish itself. The wound is therefore not a negativity, absence, or lack, but a positive unfolding that reveals the true kinetic conditions of the centre as a product of folded flows. Nature flows and folds into the curved bosom of the periphery, which only then can support a centre – not the other way around. The body is not a sealed sphere, *moenera*, or circle of exchange; the wound reveals that the circle is already a folded flow whose interiority is said only of a more primary exteriority or periphery.

The *vulnere amoris* is also the vulva of Venus. While the wound of Mars is inflicted through violence, the wound of Venus is opened by love. Both expose the interior to the exterior and reveal the enfolded nature of the flows of being. The wound therefore makes possible a double exposure between Mars and Venus. Both are exterior to one another but through their mutual vulnerabilities [*vulnere*] are opened to one another. Their exteriors become continuous and their interiors become folds within this continuum. Together, in the act of love the two surfaces become one folded surface.

The circle of the *moenera* is ruptured in the wound and opened up. Venus' liquid words and body drip down into Mars's eyes, ears, and mouth and leave his body in the form of a breath [*spiritus*] (1.37). When the circle of the *moenera* is broken, the inside of the circle is exposed to the outside that flows in and transforms the inside of the circle into the folded or curved outside. The equality of exchange between debt and credit is ruptured, as is the identity and unity of the circle. Even as the wound heals it leaves a scar at the point of bifurcation and curvature where the flows return to fold back over themselves, marking both a point of return and a point of departure or escape from the circle (1.35–6) (Fig. 2.1).

atque ita suspiciens tereti cervice reposta
pascit amore avidos inhians in te, dea, visus

And so gazing upwards, bending back his smooth neck,
he gapes at you, goddess, and feeds his hungry eyes with love.

Mars's neck becomes smooth and curves back around the periphery, exposing the vulnerability [*vulnere*] (1.34) of his open neck. Verticality and hierarchy are laid down and spread out horizontally. The word *reposta* (1.35) not only indicates a calming or subduing but also a stationing of military troops. Mars feeds on Venus' love [*amore avidos*] (1.36) as the military troops feed on the countryside and its pasturage. The political division of the *chora* occurs only on the presupposition of a pre-existing

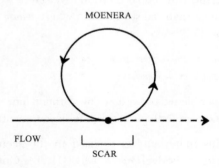

Figure 2.1 The *moenera*.

undivided continuum of the pasture which becomes divided. The nourishment of the countryside is what sustains the movement of troops. It
is their material condition. Even with the strongest walls, a city can only
withstand a siege for as long as it has nourishment.

Mars lies supine with his eyes open, feasting on Venus' love, but also
with his mouth open [*inhians*] (1.36). His gaping mouth forms another
opening or orifice [*vulnere*] (1.34) that opens up his interior to the exterior, revealing the folded or *interiorised* nature of his inside (1.37).

> *eque tuo pendet resupini spiritus ore.*

> And as he lies there, his breath hangs on your lips

Mars now sprawls out in a careless, effeminate, and desirous way [*resu-
pini*] with his very breath or spirit [*spiritus*] hanging [*pendet*] from Venus'
open mouth [*ore*] (1.37). The double wound of Mars and Venus is now
redoubled by their open mouths. Their mouths expose their interior to
the exterior, making both a continuous surface. The mouth reveals an
opening that runs all the way through the body, hollowing it out. That
which is interior is thus revealed to be only a fold of the exterior that
runs all the way continuously through the body. Their connected open
mouths thus redouble their enfolding in a kiss.

That which was previously above, ethereal, and transcendent, the
spiritus, now moves below and physically hangs supported by the material breath of Venus. Between their mouths, their vulnerable openings, hangs the materiality of the breath, the true corporeality of the
soul, *psuche*. Flows of air are mixed with water, swirling back and forth
between the openings of the body. The soul is thus revealed as immanent to its material conditions. It does not come from 'on high' but
from 'down low', and can return there in love. Here we see in the love
of Venus and Mars a materialist inversion where *natura* rises above and
spiritus drops below (1.38–9).

> *hunc tu, diva, tuo recubantem corpore sancto*
> *circum fusa super, suavis ex ore loquellas*

> Goddess, with your blessed *corpore* flow down around him
> as he reclines, and pour forth sweet words from your mouth,

The height of this materiality is realised in the seeming contradiction of Venus' sacred body [*corpore sancto*] (1.38). Christian theology
resolves the problem of the sacred body through the sacrificial son,

the God made man, and the Holy Trinity. But Lucretius takes a different and deeply heretical path. Rather than resolve the apparent paradox of the existence of a body which is also divine by multiplying it in the Trinity (and thus not actually solving it), Lucretius decides to collapse the distinction entirely in favour of a single folded flow of motion.

Venus is the immanent God, the God that flows through all other Gods, men, animals, and all of nature – as the bards sing. She is the body that by virtue of its ontogenetic power takes on a sacred status. However, at the same time, this sacred body becomes profane by its immanence to the body. The body is raised to the divine, crushing its divinity, and the divine is lowered to the corporeal, deifying matter. Matter becomes God and God becomes material. As Venus leans over Mars, her *corpore sancto* collapses the ontological division between transcendence and immanence as the two are folded over each other in a liquid flux. The sacred body becomes liquefied and the double exposure of their orifices enfold one another. Transcendence and immanence are collapsed into a single material flow that pours down from above like a waterfall, rain, or cataract, circulating and flowing around the body of Mars. The liquid pool supports him, floats him. He becomes a bubble in her foamy ocean and floats upward.

Venus is the *corpore sancto fusa super* (1.38–9), the super fluid sacred body. She is the liquefaction of the body and soul into a single stream that envelops and folds. All the great ontological binaries between the inside and outside, above and below, soul and body, male and female, are liquefied in Venus (the fluid goddess) and now flow pleasantly and smoothly [*suavis*] (1.39), pooling up at the bottom. Division and binarisation do not disappear, but rather emerge from the flow, like bubbles resulting from her *cataract*. They float to the surface and then pop or gather into foam. Her words are not divisions in being but flows that pour out of her mouth and produce pleasure [*suavis*]. In Venus, language is no longer a representation of being, but the immanent flow of sound waves that produces ripples of pleasure in the body.

The amorous scene between Venus and Mars already prefigures the ontological inversion that Lucretius puts forward in the next lines. The transcendent *spiritus* no longer explains the origin of *natura rerum*, but *natura rerum* explains the origin and material precondition of *spiritus* by the flow or cataract of matters [*corpora prima, materies, primera rerum*].

Ontology thus begins, not with God or discreteness, but with the cataract or *fusa super* of an excessive flow that continually flows and folds with desire and inclination.

Conclusion

In the opening invocation of Venus, Lucretius thus provides a robust theory of material ontogenesis and a critique of the transcendence of the state. The implications of this opening invocation now move us in two directions: the first towards a further criticism against religion [*religio*] as the fundamental error of Western thought and the second towards a materialist ontology of movement. The first direction will form the subject of Chapter 3 and the second direction the subject of Chapters 4 and 5. We now turn our attention to Lucretius' devastating critique of transcendence in all its insidious forms as *religio*.

3. Religion

The birth of Venus and her love of Mars shows us the primacy of material flows and the derivative nature of spirit and the state. The consequences of this thesis for philosophy are profound. *De Rerum Natura* calls for nothing less than a wholesale overturning of Western philosophy with its statism, logocentrism, idealism, patriarchy, and heteronormativity. For Lucretius, the lynchpin concept, the one that holds all these ideas together, is religion (in a very broad sense of the word) and its basic philosophical structure of transcendence in which the product of a process is mistaken as the origin of the process itself. This horrible delusion is the source of our suffering in all its diverse forms. To overturn religion, from the Latin words *religione* and *religio*, is to overturn the first and most basic misunderstanding of philosophy: that stasis comes before movement.

This chapter therefore continues its close reading with the aim of spelling out in detail the material kinetic conditions of thought, according to Lucretius, that both lead it to believe in religion and stasis but also free it from these self-imposed constraints.

Material Conditions

Just as Venus describes the material kinetic conditions for the emergence of elemental, natural, animal, and even political formations, so Lucretius further sets out to describe the material kinetic conditions of that which seems to exercise a power over us beyond all other matters: *religione* and the *caeli regionibus* (1.53–61).

> nam tibi de summa caeli ratione deumque
> disserere incipiam et rerum primordia pandam,
> unde omnis natura creet res, auctet alatque,
> quove eadem rursum natura perempta resolvat,

quae nos materiem et genitalia corpora rebus
reddunda in ratione vocare et semina rerum
appellare suemus et haec eadem usurpare
corpora prima, quod ex illis sunt omnia primis.

For I am beginning to set out for you the conditions
of the heavens and the gods, and to reveal the first beginnings of things
out of which nature creates all things, and increases and maintains them,
and into which nature dissolves them again once they have perished.
These we are accustomed, in setting forth our account, to call
'matter' and 'the generating bodies of things' and to name them
'the seeds of things', and to use the term 'first bodies' for them,
because all things exist from these first beginnings.

Ratione

The Latin word *ratione* (1.53) should not be interpreted strictly as
'reason', derived from the Greek word *logos*. *Ratione* is a key concept used
throughout *De Rerum Natura* and it is thus important to clarify it as soon
as possible. The Latin word *ratione* has a *double meaning*. It both refers
to the 'conditions under which something emerges' and 'an account
of their ordering'. It therefore describes both the conditions for the
emergence of order and the order itself. *Ratione* is therefore not simply
a rational account (*logos*), but more importantly a description of the
nature, way, method, or process by which that which is, comes to be.
For example, the *ratione* Lucretius gives of the heavens and gods cannot
coherently be understood to be simply a rational account or 'most high
system' of the heavens, as Rouse-Smith translates it. Lucretius is absolutely not describing the order or system of gods. Such a 'system' already
assumes the existence of that which is being ordered: the gods. Instead,
Lucretius offers us a *ratione* or account of the material *conditions* or *structure*
by which the gods and heavens came to be in the first place. This is not
cosmology, but naturalism.

The English translation of *ratione* as 'deepest workings', which Englert
uses, is much better than 'discourse', but neither are exactly to the point.
For Lucretius, the *ratione* is not simply the deep or inner workings of the
thing already presupposed to exist (gods), but rather the more primary
conditions under which a thing has come to be: its *natura*. The notion of
ratione as condition is much more fitting with Lucretius' general methodology, which sets out to re-explain the natural and material conditions

for all the events which we believe are caused by the gods (lighting, echoes, rain, and so on). To interpret or translate *ratione* as a 'discourse' on the gods would be to go against the explicitly stated goal of the entire text: to show how the gods and Heaven can be explained by purely material or natural conditions. The *ratione* is therefore a description of the *conditions* of the gods, not a mere discourse *about them*.

Rerum

Ratione as condition is also a more fitting meaning given the poetic context in which Lucretius describes his account as a taking into hand [*incipiam*] (1.54) of that which is to be distributed, described, or sown like seeds [*disserere*] (1.54).[1] Just as the seeds *of things* are the conditions of things (and thus different than things), so the *ratione* is a description or distribution of the seeds that is also different from the things it describes [*rerum*] (1.54).

In other words, the *ratione* is a description of the *rerum primordia* (1.54), or primary material conditions *of things*. Lucretius, of course, never uses the Latin word *atomus* or the Greek word ἄτομος to describe these material conditions, but instead uses a number of different related terms which are important to understand and distinguish from the notion of discrete atoms and things, from the Latin words *rerum, res, rebus* (all conjugations of the same root word). The first term he uses to describe these material conditions is *rerum primordia*. If the aim of the *ratione* is to describe the conditions (to sow the seeds), then *rerum primordia* is the name of the seeds [*semina rerum*] (1.58) that are being distributed/described by the *ratione*.

Thus, the word *primordia*, from the Latin *primus-ordior*, from *ōrdō*, meaning order, means the first or primary *process of ordering*. This definition is probably based on Cicero's use of the word '*ordo*' as 'ordered sequence' and on Horace's '*lucidus ordo*' meaning clarity of presentation.[2] For Lucretius, however, order is not reducible to temporal sequence, as it is for Cicero, but rather describes a more primary 'process of ordering' more generally. In other words, the ordered sequence of first, second, third already presupposes a more primary process of 'setting in order' of matters into sequence. The *rerum primordia* are therefore identical to the material conditions which are responsible for the first ordering of things. They are what produce the distinctness of things themselves, such that they can be sequentially ordered in the first place. Or more directly stated, the *rerum primordia* are the material conditions which are themselves both the process of ordering and that which becomes ordered through the process. This is the significance of the dual Latin meaning of *rerum* as both procedural material condition and concrete thing that is produced by the process. *Rerum* is both the active material condition for discrete things and that which comes about by this activity: the discrete 'things' themselves. There is no binary, negation, or opposition, but rather a phase transition of material like that from liquid to solid – from water to bubble.

The difference between *rerum* and *primordia rerum* is thus one of the most crucial terminological distinctions in the whole text, and we should take care never to conflate them or translate them equally as 'things', and above all not as 'atoms'. For example, when Lucretius uses the word *rerum* alone without any conditional modifiers such as *semina*, *corpora*, or *primordia rerum*, he is describing *rerum* as they *appear* as seemingly discrete 'things'. However, when he directly modifies the word *rerum* as with *semina rerum* (1.58), *corpora rebus* (1.196), or *rerum primordia* (1.55), as we will see, he is describing the active material conditions for the ordering and production of seemingly discrete things. This technical distinction between *rerum* and *corporea rerum* is crucial to understanding Lucretius' philosophical method. If the condition of discrete things (*primordia rerum*) is just other discrete things (*rerum*), we have explained nothing and precisely failed to give an account of the *nature* or *conditions* [*ratione*] by which discrete things themselves are produced. We have only presupposed precisely what we set out to explain: things. The conditions cannot resemble that which they condition. This is the fundamental thesis of Lucretian materialism. If they did then our explanations would be circular, mechanistic, and would uncover nothing about the *nature* of things.

His language of sowing seeds fits perfectly with this method. The play on the homology of *disserere* (1.54) as both 'discussion' and 'sowing' is rendered explicit by the word *pandam* (1.54), meaning to spread out, extend, unfold, but also to bend, or curve, from the Greek word πέταλον, *pétalon*, 'leaf'. Lucretius takes hold of the seeds or conditions of things [*semina rerum*] (1.58) that he will distribute and sow [*disserere*] (1.54) in the ground. He will unleash a flow of seeds which will grow and order themselves by curving and flowing upwards and downwards, unfolding and spreading out like the unfurling leaves of a plant [*pandam*].

Morphogenesis

The material conditions for the emergence of order [*rerum primordia*] flow, fold, and unfold out of the ground like the unfurling of a flower or leaf. The flow of the material conditions produces order out of itself in the form of a bend, curve, or fold in the flow [*clin*]. The flows create, expand, and continuously nourish the folds they sustain, like the leaves of a plant. The forms of the curve, the spiral, the circle, and all others emerge from the primacy and activity of the material flows themselves that generate and sustain them. The curve occurs in the flow, and the circle or fold occurs when the curve intersects with itself.

In short, the existence of what we call discrete things [*rerum*] with discrete forms are products of a more primary kinetic condition of distribution and folding that produces things by a process of self-ordering. Form emerges from matter. Lucretius emphasises the three core concepts of the process of morphogenesis:

1. Creation [*creet*] (1.56): Nature creates by material flows that expand and spread out [*pandam*] (1.55). As they expand, the flows also curve, bend, fold, and unfold over themselves, giving the appearance of relative discreteness [*creet res*] (1.56) in that which is fundamentally continuous with the seed-flow itself.
2. Increase [*auctet*] (1.56): Once the folds have been made, they increase in size and become composite, producing larger and more complex combinations of folds.
3. Nourishment [*alatque*] (1.56): Nourishment continuously flows through all the folds, repeating them, cycling through them, and sustaining them. The flow of nutrition does not happen once and for all but must be continually reproduced again and again with their limit cycles and periodicities. The material conditions are therefore defined by the continuous flow of nutrition.

Morphogenesis is thus the process by which the *rerum primordia* or material conditions produce order from within themselves and not from outside themselves. They are the ontogenetic condition for the ordering of being.

Just as form is created from these continuous flows folded into loops and sustained in cycles, the folds can also be untied, unbound, loosened, or opened [*resolvat*] (1.57). Nature is both the process by which being is created, increased, and maintained, but also the process by which it is dissolved or unfolded. When the folds of being are unfolded, it does not destroy the flows, because flows can neither be created nor destroyed. Folds can be unfolded [*resolvat*] back into their constitutive material conditions [*rerum primordia*], but composite things and their forms such as flowers, for example, are the beings that are destroyed. Form, for Lucretius, therefore has no existence independent from the kinetic activity of its material conditions or *rerum primordia*.

The *rerum primordia* are similarly described as *genitalia corpora rebus* (1.58), or corporeal conditions that are themselves creative or generative. Again, the idea is clear: the material conditions for the emergence of things are themselves *not things*. They are material; they have body [*corpora*]; and their bodies are onto- or morphogenetic insofar as they have a creative capacity, like seeds and Venus, to produce from themselves, out of themselves, and then continue to nourish that which they produce as a dimension of themselves. This is clearly opposed to the introduction of any transcendence into the creative process. Creation comes from matter, is birthed by matter, and is sustained by material processes [*materiem*] (1.58). *Rerum primordia* therefore cannot possibly mean, for Lucretius, separate discrete objects, since they are an *active* and *creative genitalia rebus* of seemingly discrete things in the first place. The form of things comes from the creativity of matter itself. Thus, for Lucretius, the division between organic and non-organic life is a false one. All matter is active, creative, self-organising, morphogenetic, *genitalia*.

The term *rerum* thus has two dimensions: a modified *rerum* qua active material condition and an unmodified *rerum* qua product of this condition. The term *semina rerum* should therefore not be thought exclusively as a discrete plant seed or even as a mobile human seed or semen, but more broadly according to the Latin infinitive from which it derives: as an act of sowing, spreading, leaving behind. If the term *rerum* has two senses, then so does the word *semina* that is tied to it. There are therefore two aspects of the same *semina rerum*: *semina rerum* qua active material condition of sowing and spreading and *semina rerum* qua discrete seed left behind by the process of sowing. If being is composed of nothing but *semina rerum* and thus creates on its own without the introduction of any divine transcendence, then *semina rerum* must have at least these three natural capacities: creation through the flow of throwing or distributing seeds, folding of these flows over themselves in increasing size, and the maintenance of these folds by the continuous circulation of flows through the periodic folds.

All this makes it clear that Lucretius is seeking to give us an account of the conditions for the emergence of things or the ontogenetic *nature of things*, and not simply an account of things as we already know them to be. Both are two dimensions of the same project. The *semina rerum* are also the *corpora prima*, or 'first bodies', which are the condition of all other composite or secondary bodies. The *corpora prima* are first bodies not in the sense that they are chronologically first (Cicero), since they themselves are neither created nor destroyed, but first in an ontogenetic sense in which they are the creative or fertile bodies that give birth to things. Again, we should not think of the term *corpora* as simply a 'discrete' body, as we often do in English. The Latin word *corpora* is much more general than this, as we can see from its usage by other ancient Latin writers,[3] that is, anything composed of active matter.

Since Lucretius uses the term *corpora prima* as a synonym for *semina rerum* and *genitalia corpora*, the meaning of the word *corpora* here is much closer to the meaning of 'flesh' as an active, living, creative bodily matter. However, the Latin word *corpora* can be used interchangeably with living and dead bodies,[4] again expressing the dual dimension of matter itself as folded sedimentation in one and the same process: life and death, creation and destruction, flows, folds, and unfolding.

In short, the *rerum natura* are the active material conditions or creative flows from which all of being is primarily composed [*quod ex illis sunt omnia primis*] (1.61), but also the seemingly discrete things which are produced as the products of this kinetic material process. The two must be said of *one and the same process*, but without conflating the difference between the conditions [*natura, semina, corpora*, etc.] and that which they condition [*rerum*]. Therefore the two co-present dimensions of *rerum* are like the two sides of the Möbius strip: where a single flow has produced a differentiation of itself by virtue of its own folding.

Epicurus

The man who first discovered the material kinetic conditions for all that is [*sunt omnia*] (1.61) was the Greek philosopher Epicurus. Before him, humanity appeared [*oculos*] as a foul and rotting form of life [*Humana ante oculos foede cum vita*] (1.62) which lay fallow, idle, and inactive [*iaceret*] (1.62) because it was crushed into the ground by the gravity and weight of religion [*in terris oppressa gravi sub religione*] (1.63), whose horrible head [*quae caput horribili super*] (1.64–5) stretched down from Heaven [*a caeli regionibus ostendebat*] (1.64) and stood upon mortals [*mortalibus instans*] (1.65).

Man the Maggot

The stench of rotting matter comes from anaerobic bacteria that thrive in environments without movement, circulation, and air. Foul and rotting life is life which has no access to the outside, to fresh air and movement. Nietzsche often describes human servitude to religion in similar fashion: as bad, foul, or rotting air. 'That [religion] I cannot cope with, that makes me choke and faint. Bad air! Bad air! The approach of some ill-constituted thing; that I have to smell the entrails of some ill-constituted soul!'[5]

When animals fail to digest and move their food along properly, the food rots in their bodies. When the human soul and mind become locked up in the body as forms of pure interiority, they rot and release a foul air. With religion and all other forms of idealism man becomes a 'maggot', Nietzsche says.[6] Maggots are the form of life proper to rotting, stagnant, uncirculated [*iaceret*] (1.62) matter. Matter without motion rots and foul forms of life emerge: maggots.

Religion therefore, like rot, is not death or stasis, but rather a form of minimal rotting life that feeds on dead matter, which has been sealed up in an enclosed circle without access to moving air. In this sense, religion becomes another dimension of the social *moenera* (1.29) which seals up the circular unity of exchangeability between debt and credit. Lucretius describes *religio* as *oppressa* (1.63), pressing down, but also a pressing together, closing off, or sealing up. *Religio* seals up the circle and closes it off and makes it separate [*sacer*] from life. The gods created beings and thus provided a credit which in turn had to be exchanged for a debt owed to them. Divine creation relies thus on a *moenera religione* between creator and created and the circularity of debt and credit, sin and redemption.

Gravity

We rot because we do not circulate freely, and we do not circulate freely because we have been crushed from above by a horrible head [*caput*] (1.64). We are crushed by our own ideas. For Lucretius, religion is something that emerges from matter (like all things), but stacks on top of matter, weighing it down, restricting its movement, as if it were some other being which had a force independent of the material conditions that made it. The weight of its ugly head is the weight of idealism that crushes the body. Active moving matter is the condition for the emergence of the mind or head, which continues to draw its nourishment from these same bodily flows. However, once the head emerges from its body, it tends to retroactively posit itself in the form of an immaterial and mental god, which claims to have created the body. The body then seems to owe a crushing debt to this gravitational weight that it has given itself to carry.

Religio thus stands [*instans*] (1.65) on life, for Lucretius, in the double sense in which it both requires the bodily frame [*corpora rebus*] (1.58) as its material condition to stand up, but also in the sense in which the dead tradition of religion 'weighs like a nightmare on the brains of the living',[7] as Marx writes. Every generation is capable of creating something new, but the persistence of tradition often appears as an inescapable weight that we must carry and reproduce but that restricts our movement. Nietzsche, too, describes religion in similar gravitational terms as a kind of kinetic restriction of movement and novelty. Nietzsche thus advises us to laugh at God, as Venus laughs [*rident*] (1.8) on the shore. 'Not by wrath does one kill but by laughter. Come, let us kill the spirit of gravity!'[8] 'Light feet', and 'dancing', 'ridicule of the spirit of gravity', he writes.[9]

It is crucial to note that the Latin term *religio* has as its primary meaning, and its chief use in ancient writers, not simply the belief in divinity, but very specifically 'a divine impediment to action, a prohibition, or obligation to law'.[10] It is therefore perfectly fitting for Lucretius to describe the primary problem of *religio* in kinetic terms. *Religio*, in Latin, is literally the restriction of motion through a *moenera religione* that binds [from the Latin root *lig-*] one's movement into the rotting circle of credit and debt. Lucretius' critique of *religio* should therefore be understood more broadly as a critique of the entire intertwined social, economic, religious, and political apparatus of kinetic binding [*lig-*] and *moenera*.

Resistance
However, Epicurus was also the first to teach us how to resist the horrible head of idealism, religion, and the state (1.66–71).

primum Graius homo mortalis tollere contra
est oculos ausus primusque obsistere contra;

quem neque fama deum nec fulmina nec minitanti
murmure compressit caelum, sed eo magis acrem
inritat animi virtutem, effringere ut arta
naturae primus portarum claustra cupiret.

It was a Greek man who first dared to raise his mortal eyes
against religion, and who first fought back against it.
Neither the stories about the gods, nor thunderbolts, nor the sky
with its threatening rumbles held him back, but provoked
all the more the fierce sharpness of his mind, so that he desired
to be the first to shatter the imprisoning bolts of the gates of nature.

Epicurus was the one who first stood up and abolished [*tollere*] *religio*
(1.66). The word *tollere* perfectly expresses the double kinetics of resistance. On the one hand it is defined as the movement of standing up
against a weight that has been accumulated on top of one, and on the
other hand it is an overthrowing or removal of the weight that held one
down. Since *religio* is not an external or transcendent entity, this is not,
for Lucretius, a simple reactionary struggle against some separate entity.
If that were the case none of his account here would make any sense.
Resistance, like *voluptas*, is not negation; it is a positive transformation
or redistribution of motion in a new direction. Since *religio* is something
composed of the same material process that conditions everything else,
it cannot be simply negated or destroyed. If we made *religio*, as Lucretius
argues, then it is a positive dimension of our living activity, which cannot
be destroyed *tout court*, but must be recomposed or redistributed into
something else which will allow us to move again.

Accordingly, Lucretius describes Epicurus' resistance as an *obsistere*
(1.67), or standing firm in one's place against the endless enclosed repetition of the circle. Resistance is thus kinetic. To resist we must stand
up against a weight we have created for ourselves, and in standing up
we must remove the weight from our backs and stand firm against its
attempts to trap us again in its circular enclosure.

The political connotations in this resistance to religion are explicit.
Lucretius says that Epicurus breaks open [*effringere*] (1.70) the gates of
the city [*portarum*] (1.71) and lets loose the captive [*cupiret*] (1.71) maggots
from inside the locked-up enclosure or military stronghold [*claustra*]
(1.71). He breaks the circle of identity, unity, and exchange that defines
the triple nightmare of centrifugal oppression: religion, idealism, and the
state. The Latin term *claustra* perfectly expresses the political, idealist,

and religious dimensions of this resistance in that it refers equally to the religious *cloister* of the monastics and to the military stronghold and walls of politics, which both express a certain model of the mind as enclosure, found in the tradition of Platonism.[11]

Ancient religion, idealism, and the state all follow the same kinetic model of the circle. The circle of the city walls, the circle of religious debt and credit, and the circle of idealist creation from the mind *ex nihilo* are all modelled on one another. It is not surprising that Athens, birthplace of Western philosophy and democracy, also gave rise to Socratic philosophers who often defined philosophy and wisdom itself as an 'impregnable walled stronghold'.[12] The mind is the citadel-wall of the city-body.[13]

Lucretius thus attributes to Epicurus a kind of philosophical and kinopolitical revolution and liberation of material flows. Epicurus shatters the enclosed interiority of the mind and the city that imprisons the body and lets loose again the flow of active matter [*semina rerum*] (1.59). He moves beyond the flaming walls of the world [*flammantia moenia mundi*] (1.73) in order to show us the unlimited nature of being [*omne immensum*] (1.74).

This thesis was denied by physicists, including Albert Einstein, all the way up to 1931, when Einstein was eventually convinced by Hubble's discovery that the universe itself was in motion and expanding. Even then scientific consensus took another twenty years to finally let go of the onto-theological commitment to a static and enclosed universe. Arguably, the Epicurean revolution in physics is a recent one. But the counter-revolution of onto-theology in cosmology persists in the form of a belief in a singularity at the beginning of the big bang. By holding on to the idea of a beginning of creation, even if it is not caused by a god, physicists still posit an *ex nihilo* creation that presumes the transcendence of creation itself. There are, however, loop quantum gravity physicists today who are looking to prove mathematically and empirically that the big bang was not the first, and that it is only part of a larger infinite and continuous process.[14] The Epicurean revolution against finitude continues today.

Pedesis

It is also important to note the type of movement made by Epicurus when he goes beyond the walls of the world [*flammantia moenia mundi*]: *peragravit* (1.74) – to wander or move through without precise direction. The movement of his resistance is not teleological. It does not have a specific goal posited in advance of its wandering or stochastic movement. Rather, the path of resistance and exploration is made by walking. Epicurus is therefore not offering a revolutionary programme given in advance of the movements that would be required to produce a philosophical and political alternative to the circular and centrifugal movements of the state, religion, and idealism. The movement of resistance to borders as *peragravit* is also a movement through the territory that does not go beyond it in the form of a new transcendence, but moves transversal to it, or through it. Epicurus shows us that there is always a way out of every confinement. Every fold leaks like an entropic escape hatch.

As such, Epicurus shows us [*ratione*] both the creative material conditions for all of being in the *semina rerum*, but he also shows us the material conditions or processes by which those same flows are damned up and folded into the crushing weights of *religio* and idealism that limit our motion by imposing certain deep set boundary stones [*atque alte terminus haerens*] (1.77) or limits to our wandering motion [*peragravit*] that lock it into circles of confinement and oppression.

Epicurus, Lucretius says, turns the tables and crushes *religio* under his feet [*pedibus*] (1.78) and raises us out of the rot. Lucretius again invokes the power of mobility by invoking the power of Epicurus' foot, not only to move across all limits [*peragravit*], but also to crush religion itself [*religio pedibus subiecta*] (1.78). The power of mobility is the power of the foot to run, dance against gravity, and to crush the horrible delusion of religion, which puts limits to action. The foot crushes the head; the power of revolution is thus a *pedetic* power (1.75–9).

Diana

The second materialist hero of movement against the negativity of religion introduced by Lucretius is Diana, known as Artemis to the Greeks. Diana has a special place among the gods because she exposed the structural evil and wickedness of religion from within. Diana was the virgin Roman goddess of the undivided wild forests (*nomos*), the hunt, wild animals, birth, and the moon. We have already seen the material kinetic importance of virgin creation (ontogenesis) the forests [*nomos*], wild animals [*ferae*], and birth [*genesis*] in Chapter 1.

Above all, Diana is the goddess of the moon. The moon is the moving curve that as it waxes brings life and light, until the crescent becomes saturated and completed in the circle, after which it then begins to wane until it dies and is reborn in the new moon. Diana exposes the lie that the circle is immortal and unchanging. The circle is a product of the curve or crescent, which itself is already the product of the movement of the orbiting moon itself. In short, movement secures the conditions for life, death, and rebirth. This movement is itself not a circle, but the circle is a product of this movement.

Diana is only one (Greek and Roman) incarnation of the moon goddess. The ancient moon goddesses of Neolithic Europe, for example, were portrayed as horned cow goddesses because of the curvature of the horns. The moon is thus historically and mythologically related to the privileged status of curves in goddess religions (breast, belly, womb, vessels, bowls, and so on), the fecundity of reproduction (menstrual cycles and childbirth), and the curved horns of large prey animals of the hunt. All three are brought together in the Roman goddess Diana, who was already a very old goddess, preceding the Greeks and Romans by thousands of years.[15]

In the more recent past (Ancient Sumer and Akkadia), the moon goddess went by the names of Inanna and Ishtar, respectively. In the myth, Nanna the moon god marries Ningal, the goddess of the moon; they have two children, Inanna, queen of the moon, and Utu, the sun god. As early as 3500 BCE, Inanna, or Ishtar as she was called in Akkadia, was elevated to the status of the Great Goddess of Sumeria under the name of the 'Virgin Queen of Heaven and Earth'.[16] As the queen of both Heaven and Earth, Inanna is still divided from her abyssal sister Ereshkigal. According to the 'The Descent of Inanna to the Nether World', the oldest ritual dramatisation of a lunar myth,[17] Inanna goes to visit her sister in the deep. As she descends, she is stripped of her jewellery and regalia at each of the seven gates of the underworld. When she reaches the deep, Ereshkigal fastens 'the eye of death' on her and Inanna hangs like a carcass on a hook. After three days, Inanna is released, and then forced to sacrifice someone else to take her place for half of the year. She chooses her husband, Dumuzi. Each year he dies and is resurrected. With this, Inanna 'places Dumuzi in the hands of the eternal'.[18]

In the Babylonian story, the goddess Ishtar's son-lover is mortally wounded by a wild boar and Ishtar descends into the underworld to wake him from his sleep in the dark. Ishtar also descends through seven gates (of the waning moon), and stays for three days (of the dark moon). While she is in the netherworld, the fertility of the earth is stopped. When she returns with her son-lover the earth blooms again.

The Roman goddess Diana is also a triple goddess called Luna in Heaven, Diana on Earth, and Proserpina in Hell. Like Innana and Ishtar, Diana moves between all three realms like the moon cycle itself, bringing life, death, and rebirth. The Roman story of Diana is almost exactly the same as that of Innana and Ishtar, as we will see.

The heroism of Diana, like Epicurus, also has a political dimension to it. Diana was goddess of the lower classes and of slaves. Her cult following, for a number of reasons, was always treated as a foreign one in Roman religion, like that of Bacchus. She was the patroness of the plebeians, proles, migrants, and refugees: the first goddess of the proletariat. Her temples were built deep in the undivided woods, the historical hiding place of runaway slaves and propertyless proletarians, and at crossroads, the borders between the political inside and outside. Diana appears at the social periphery and helps people escape from the crushing weight of social slavery. The temples of Diana and Artemis were considered asylums for refugees and those fleeing slavery. If Epicurus is the first revolutionary on the earth, Diana is the first revolutionary of the heavens.[19]

The Sacrifice of Iphigeneia

According to Lucretius, religious mythology exposes its own structural wickedness, cruelty, and evil in the sacrifice of Iphigeneia. According to Pseudo-Apollodorus, King Agamemnon went hunting in the sacred woods of Artemis, killed a sacred stag, and boasted that he was a better hunter than her. When the Greek fleet was departing for Troy to begin the Trojan War, a turbulent storm stopped the ships.

> Kalkhas [the seer] announced that they would not be able to sail unless the most beautiful of Agamemnon's daughters was offered as a sacrificial victim to Artemis; for the goddess was angry at Agamemnon because, after shooting a deer, he had boasted that 'not even Artemis' could have shot so well, and because Atreus [his father] had not sacrificed to her his golden lamb.[20]

At first, Agamemnon is horrified at such a wicked suggestion, but the debt of *religio*, according to Kalkhas, demands it. Aeschylus writes,

> But when he had donned the yoke [λεπαδνον] of Necessity [αναγκασ], with veering [τροπαιαν] of mind, impious, unholy, unsanctified, from that moment he changed his intention and began to conceive that deed of uttermost audacity. For wretched delusion, counsellor of ill, primal source of woe,

makes mortals bold. So then he hardened his heart to sacrifice his daughter so that he might further a war waged to avenge a woman, and as an offering for the voyage of a fleet![21]

Agamemnon is eventually convinced by the notion of religious debt described by the seer and decides to lure his daughter to the sacrificial altar with the promise of marriage.

> So Agamemnon sent Odysseus and Talthybios to Klytaimnestra and asked for Iphigeneia, saying that he had promised to give her in marriage to Akhilleus as payment for his military service. When his wife had sent Iphigeneia, Agamemnon placed her on the altar and was about to sacrifice her when Artemis spirited her off to the Taurians, where she set her up as her own priestess; she put a deer on the altar in the girl's place. Also, according to some, she made Iphigeneia immortal.[22]

What this myth demonstrates, for Lucretius, is that by thinking of weather patterns as punishments and rewards, debts and credits, in a system of religious exchange or *moenera*, humans are led to the most wicked conclusions.

Nomos. The undivided woodlands and mountains (*nomos*), which are the domain of Artemis, have always been the place of surplus which peasants, runaway slaves, and wild animals can draw on to survive outside the walls of the state. By hunting and gathering in the woods on the open and free periphery, the proletariat has been able to sustain itself. However, as Fernand Braudel writes, 'The mountains [have also] always been a reservoir of men for other people's use.'[23] Throughout history, states have raided the woodlands and mountains to gather more slaves, capture old ones, or go hunting.[24] The activities of hunting and the kidnapping of slaves in the form of man-hunting have always been structurally related within the logic of the state apparatus as a dual technology based on the exclusive political right over that which is wild and apolitical: wild animals and depoliticised men.[25] The technologies of the hunt remain the same because the state has a structurally similar relationship with its exterior as an open and unregulated zone of in-distinction.[26] By hunting in these forests and bragging of his superiority to the goddess who secures them, Agamemnon oversteps the power of the state, taking from the periphery without recognising the founda-tional role that the periphery plays in the support of the state itself, along with natural resources such as timber and food.

Aeschylus' text is clear: Artemis *does not* ask Agamemnon to sacrifice his daughter; Kalkhas does. In fact, such a request would be entirely unfitting to a goddess who protects women, virgins, and victims of injustice. Furthermore, had Artemis truly desired a sacrifice, she would not have prevented the very sacrifice she requested in the first place by rescuing Iphigeneia. Artemis is therefore not the perpetrator of the wicked sacrifice but the one who exposes the wickedness of the sacrifice as such.

Iphigeneia and Isaac. Compare the sacrifice of Iphigeneia by Agamemnon with that of Isaac by Abraham. In the case of Abraham, Yahweh explicitly requests the sacrifice of Isaac and only intervenes via the Angel Gabriel once it is clear that Abraham is going to obey the wicked request.[27] Yahweh draws on the infinite debt of religion to test the true depths of Abraham's obedient wickedness. Ultimately, the lesson is that God is the source of all truth and morality and as such can summon unimaginable wickedness in the name of the good with complete impunity and should be followed with total obedience. The fear of God is the truth of religion.

Artemis, however, exposes something else: that the truth of religion is the sanctification of wickedness. Instead of allowing Agamemnon to complete the presumed *moenera religio* of debt-credit-exchange through the sacrifice, she instead disrupts the sacrifice. In doing so, her disruption has the opposite effect to Yahweh's encounter with Abraham. Instead of affirming the faith of religion, it shatters it twice over.

First, the believers are confronted by the fact that Artemis would not have disrupted the sacrifice if she had wanted Iphigeneia to be sacrificed. This means that Agamemnon is forced to realise that he was going to sacrifice her out his own fear and delusion. The *moenera religio* is exposed as precisely what it is: wicked acts veiled by ignorance of the material conditions of the true nature of things.

Secondly, fitting to Artemis, she rescues the virginal victim (as a victim of patriarchy), and grants her priestess status and/or immortality. Agamemnon thus still loses his daughter because of his religious delusion. The victim (Iphigeneia) is rewarded and the perpetrator (Agamemnon) is punished. Justice is therefore done in the very port city of the goddess of justice herself (Aulis).[28] The fact that Artemis grants a reward to Iphigeneia in Aulis proves that she was the rescued victim of an unjust deed perpetrated by religious evil [*scelerosa*] (1.83). Yahweh grants no such status to Isaac precisely because Isaac is not and cannot be a victim of what was essentially a 'good' command given by God himself.

Lucretius now returns to the consideration of the material conditions that we began with in this chapter and under which this kind of structure can emerge in the first place [*ratione*].

Transcendental Materialism

Concluding this section on the critique of *religio*, Lucretius describes his methodology as one that provides the '*naturae species ratioque*' (1.148), or material conditions for nature as it appears. He explicitly contrasts this methodology with the classical metaphysical approach which claims to give an account of the nature of being qua being. For Lucretius, philosophy cannot have complete and total access to being, because being is not complete or total; it is continually moving beyond itself, surpassing one limit after another. Since there is no whole, there is no ontology of the one and thus no metaphysics of the nature of being in itself.

The terror and darkness of religion and idealism which assume a unity, totality, and identity of being must be shattered and dispersed [*discutiant*] (1.148) into the true multiplicity of the flow that it is. Lucretius says quite clearly that this *discutiant* cannot occur by the 'rays of the sun and the clear shafts of the day' [*radii solis neque lucida tela diei*] (1.147). The nature of things is not something that can simply be illuminated by an external transcendent light of pure clarity, as in Plato, which itself is not supported by the materiality of the light itself. There is no pure philosophical method or theological position from which being qua being can be illuminated without the process of illumination itself already altering the nature of being as it appears in the light. The light itself is already material and its position is already in the sensuous world, not beyond it. This is also a direct and explicit rejection of the enlightenment notion that truth is the shining of the independent light of the mind upon the passivity of inactive matter in nature. In this model, nature moves, but the mind, truth, beauty, and god remain static reference points for the description of being in its pure observed state.

Against this Platonic and enlightenment notion, Lucretius proposes an alternative methodology of lighting and philosophy, alluded to earlier in the idea of the shores of light [*luminis oras*] (1.22). Opposed to the *radii solis neque lucida tela diei* (1.147), Lucretius proposes to describe the *naturae species ratioque*, the material conditions [*ratioque*] for the appearance [*species*] of nature [*naturae*] (1.148). In other words, given the appearance of nature, Lucretius proposes to give us an account of the material conditions under which these appearances have come into existence. These conditions are not the universal or ontological conditions for all beings, since not all beings have appeared to us yet. This is the case in part because being or nature is constantly moving and changing. It is historical. At some times some beings appear, and at others, others appear. If being is non-whole and is in motion, then this means that our account of being, as beings, occurs under certain regional conditions.

This does not mean, however, that Lucretius' philosophy is anthropocentric or constructivist. Lucretius is offering a fully *realist* account of these conditions. The conditions are merely not universal. The nature of things is therefore transcendental in the sense that Lucretius offers an account of the conditions by which nature (and even gods and Heaven) appear. Unlike in Kant, these conditions are not of possible experience, but of the real empirical and material experience of nature as it appears. Instead of transcendental *idealism*, based on the limited anthropocentric conditions of the mind, ego, or subject, Lucretius offers us a transcendental materialism based on the wider material conditions that produce the mind (among other things) in the first place. The mind is one more material configuration, just like everything else. As such, the material conditions for the mind follow many of the same material conditions for other phenomena as well.

Lucretius therefore avoids the twin pitfalls of constructivism on the one hand, and naive metaphysics on the other. He rejects both the idea that we are confined to the realm of humanist idealism and that we can give a universal account of being in itself. Instead, his question is as follows: Given the appearance of nature in sensation, what must be the real conditions of its being, not as a phenomenon that appears only to humans, but as a kinomenon that moves and generates itself? Lucretius' method can therefore be described as a kind of transcendental realism, transcendental materialism, transcendental empiricism, or historical ontology of the present.

Conclusion

After his critique of *religio* by means of an exposure of its material conditions, Lucretius now moves on to a more detailed theory of these material conditions. He begins his account from the simplest and most profound feature of his materialism: the flows of matter, the subject of the next chapter.

Notes

1. There is a double etymology of the Latin word *disserere* that Lucretius is playing with here – 'to scatter seed, to sow' and 'to examine, argue, discuss, speak, harangue, discourse, treat'. From *dis-* + *serō*, 'I join, bind together', or from *dis-* + *serō*, 'I sow, plant.'

2. See Mary A. Grant and George Converse Fiske, 'Cicero's "Orator" and Horace's "Ars Poetica"', *Harvard Studies in Classical Philology*, 35 (1924): 1–74. Cicero's brief treatment of *ordo* illustrates the difference between the problems of the orator and those of the poetry. For the orator, *ordo* is a question of sequence and structural primacy, whereas for Horace, *ordo* is more a question of the text's essential quality of clearness (*lucidus ordo*). Well ordered, for Horace, means, clear and not necessarily, as for Cicero, sequentially structured around the strongest or primary terms first. For example: order = *right order, regular succession*: 'fatum appello ordinem seriemque causarum', Cicero, *De Divinatione* 1, 55, 125.

3. Charlton Lewis and Charles Short, *Harpers' Latin Dictionary: A New Latin Dictionary Founded on the Translation of Freund's Latin-German Lexicon*, ed. E. A. Andrews (New York: Harper & Bros, 1879).

4. Lewis and Short, *Harpers' Latin Dictionary*.

5. Friedrich Nietzsche, *On the Genealogy of Morals*, trans. Walter A. Kaufmann (New York: Vintage Books, 1967), 43–4.

6. Nietzsche, *On the Genealogy of Morals*, 43.

7. Karl Marx, *The Eighteenth Brumaire of Louis Bonaparte* (Moscow: Progress Publishers, 1869), ch. 1, p. 10.

8. Cited in Friedrich Nietzsche, *The Gay Science: With a Prelude in Rhymes and an Appendix of Songs*, trans. Walter A. Kaufmann (New York: Vintage Books, 1974), 257, n. 54.

9. Nietzsche, *The Gay Science*, 7.

10. See Lewis and Short, *Harpers' Latin Dictionary*. Lactantius (4, 28) and Augustine (*Retractations* 1, 13) assume *religare* as the primitive, and for this derivation Lactantius cites the expression of Lucretius (1.931; 4, 7): *religionum nodis animos exsolvere*.

11. See Thomas Nail, *Theory of the Border* (Oxford: Oxford University Press, 2016), 64–109.

12. 'Wisdom is a most sure stronghold which never crumbles away nor is betrayed. Walls of defense must be constructed in our own impregnable reasonings.' Diogenes Laertius relaying the thoughts

of Antisthenes, a rhetorician and student of Gorgia, in *Lives*, VI.1.13.

13. See John Protevi, *Political Physics: Deleuze, Derrida, and the Body Politic* (London: Athlone Press, 2001), 115–17.

14. See Carlo Rovelli, 'Loop Quantum Gravity', *Physics World*, 16.11 (2003); Carlo Rovelli and Lee Smolin, 'Loop Space Representation of Quantum General Relativity', *Nuclear Physics*, B 331.1 (1990): 80; and Lee Smolin, *Three Roads to Quantum Gravity* (Oxford: Oxford University Press, 2000).

15. See Anne Baring and Jules Cashford, *The Myth of the Goddess: Evolution of an Image* (London: Viking Arkana, 1991), and Marija Gimbutas, *The Language of the Goddess: Unearthing the Hidden Symbols of Western Civilization* (San Francisco: Harper & Row, 1989).

16. Baring and Cashford, *The Myth of the Goddess*, 176.

17. Baring and Cashford, *The Myth of the Goddess*, 216.

18. Baring and Cashford, *The Myth of the Goddess*, 220, n. 96.

19. Lucretius here is not suggesting that the myth of Diana is true, but is engaging in an immanent critique of religion itself, by turning it against itself through the figure of Diana.

20. Pseudo-Apollodorus, *Bibliotheca*, E3.21, in Apollodorus, *The Library of Greek Mythology*, trans. Keith Aldrich (Lawrence: Coronado Press, 1975).

21. Aeschylus, *Agamemnon*, 220–5, in Aeschylus, *Agamemnon; Libation-bearers; Eumenides; Fragments*, trans. Herbert W. Smyth and Hugh Lloyd-Jones (Cambridge, MA: Harvard University Press, 1999).

22. Pseudo-Apollodorus, *Bibliotheca*, E3.21.

23. Fernand Braudel, *The Mediterranean and the Mediterranean World in the Age of Philip II*, trans. Siân Reynolds (New York: Harper & Row, 1972), 51.

24. See Thomas Nail, *The Figure of the Migrant* (Stanford: Stanford University Press, 2015).

25. See Grégoire Chamayou, *Manhunts: A Philosophical History* (Princeton: Princeton University Press, 2012).

26. See Giorgio Agamben, *Sovereign Power and Bare Life*, trans. Daniel Heller-Roazen (Stanford: Stanford University Press, 1998).

27. Genesis 22:1–2, New International Version: 'Some time later God tested Abraham. He said to him, "Abraham!" "Here I am", he replied. Then God said, "Take your son, your only son, whom you love – Isaac – and go to the region of Moriah. Sacrifice him there as a burnt offering on a mountain I will show you."'

28. Aulis was a daughter of Ogygus and Thebe, from whom the Boeotian

town of Aulis was believed to have derived its name. Other traditions called her a daughter of Euonymus, the son of Cephissus. She was one of the goddesses who watched over oaths under the name of *praxidikai.* Pausanias, *Description of Greece*, IX.19.5, 6.

4. The Flows of Matter

The first and most important thesis in Lucretian materialism is that matter flows. Contrary to the prevailing interpretation of *De Rerum Natura* as an orthodox reproduction of a reified Greek atomism, lines 149 to 450 offer a clear and poetic description of the conditions of reality as material flows, fluxes, folds, confluences, and weavings. Not once in these lines where Lucretius articulates the five core principles of his materialism does he attribute discreteness or stasis to the fundamental processes by which things emerge. While Lucretius does describe things [*rerum*] as appearing to be discrete and limited, he never describes their material conditions [*corpora*] in the same way.

These lines are not only crucial for understanding Lucretian materialism on its own terms, but also for understanding its rejection of what most interpreters have understood to be a modern materialism associated with discreteness, observability, and mechanistic causality, none of which, as we will see, are positions held by Lucretius. It will become increasingly apparent over the course of the following chapters that *De Rerum Natura* was less the voice of the modern atomic counter-revolution and more a scapegoat that had to be sacrificed for its success. Lucretius was less a friend of modern materialism than he was a very close enemy who had to be held captive just long enough for the counter-revolution to succeed. Much has been said of Lucretius' influence on early modern science, but much less has been said of modern science's influence on Lucretius.

The following three chapters provide a close analysis of his first five theses on materialism in order to show the primacy of motion and continuum in each one.

First Thesis: Nothing Comes from Nothing

The first, and best-known, thesis of Lucretian materialism is that nothing comes from nothing. For Lucretius, there are two possible ontological starting points in philosophy: that all of being came into existence without any material conditions whatsoever, that is, by divine immaterial creation, or that there have always been material conditions which are combined differently to produce all that is. Lucretius affirms the latter (1.150).

> *nullam rem ex nihilo gigni divinitus umquam.*
>
> Nothing ever comes to be from nothing through divine intervention.

At first this thesis appears to be an exact repetition of the Epicurean thesis, but Lucretius has added something crucial: 'through divine creation' [*gigni divinitus*] (1.150). This is an important addition because the thesis 'out of nothing comes nothing' can be philosophically countered by simply positing that an eternal God, whose extended body is all of material being, has *always existed eternally*. There was never a point in which God did not exist, and therefore he did not come out of nothing, nor did his material body. Therefore, even if the rejection of *ex nihilo* creation is also a rejection of the Platonic and Christian creator God who created the world, it would not be a full rejection of a number of pre- and post-Socratic ontologies and mythologies that affirm the *non-created coexistence of God and matter*. God and matter are not created, one could reply, because they are *sempiternal*.

Lucretius' addition, however, allows him to reject these formulations because it rejects not only *ex nihilo* creation but also any form of divine immaterial creation [*gigni divinitus*] *tout court*. Even if one accepted a kind of sempiternal ontology of becoming which had no beginning or end, such a process of becoming or genesis, for Lucretius, could have absolutely nothing to do with any kind of immaterial becoming, divine, or eternal god, or else such a creation would violate the natural material emergence of things from matter. For example, ducks will never be born from cows. No divine or immaterial intervention can make this so. There is only a becoming of matter in motion and no other which could intervene upon it. Since we have never seen a duck born from a cow, no empirical evidence exists for such *ex nihilo* creation, but only for the contrary.

However, if we then replied that God was only able to create according to the natural order of material emergence (as Spinoza did), then God becomes immanent and identical with natural creation and thus superfluous to it, along with all his other attributes – which are only so many names, like God, for material genesis. In short, for Lucretius, there is no such thing as immaterial divinity or its activity. This thesis allows us to break through the walled *moenera* of *religio* and see the true material conditions of things, thus avoiding the idiocy and suffering of Agamemnon.

Seeds, Shoots, and Flows

If things simply came from nothing, then anything could come from any other thing, which is demonstrably not the case. Furthermore, things do not come from other things, because things [*res*] considered as discrete vacuum-sealed objects do not have the power to create or generate anything without seeds [*semine*] (1.156–7).

> *Nam si de nihilo fierent, ex omnibus rebus*
> *omne genus nasci posset, nil semine egeret.*

> For if things came to be from nothing, every kind of thing
> could be born from all things, and nothing would need a seed.

If we think of things as fundamentally distinct, discrete, or separate entities then there can be no connection, motion, or change between them. If the world is only discrete things then they cannot affect each other without changing one another, which would assume some commonality or interconnection between them and the violation of their vacuum-sealed nature. In other words, if the world is nothing but things then it is sterile, dead, and we must affirm the idealist principle of creation or change *ex nihilo*. If there were only things then there would be no efficient cause between them that would not be another self-enclosed thing. The world of things or discrete objects therefore requires a kind of divine or *ex nihilo* occasionalism that would allow things to seem causally connected.[1]

Accordingly, the first thesis of materialism is not only a rejection of *ex nihilo* cosmic creation but also a rejection of modern materialism itself, which views the world as made up of nothing but discrete things plus an immaterial principle of 'force' or 'causality' that connects those things together. The early modern notions of conatus, impetus, vis, endeavour, and others that multiply from Philoponus to Newton, are for Lucretius further examples of this same idea of *ex nihilo* creation and causation.[2] In its broadest interpretation the rejection of *ex nihilo* creation is synonymous with the rejection of all metaphysics *tout court*. This includes the notions of eternal forms, immaterial forces, and even theories of space and time as ontologically fundamental. What all metaphysical theories share in common is the notion that some ahistorical substance, which is not matter in motion, is responsible for the ontological origins of material motion.

Instead, Lucretius argues, all things [*rebus*] come from seeds [*semine*] (1.157). The word *semine*, however, should not be understood in terms of discrete homogeneous bits. In Latin the word was used to describe not only creative matter, but also origin, ground, and shoot.[3] The word *semine*, as Lucretius uses it here, should thus not be thought of as a *rebus*. He distinctly uses the word *rebus* in the lines above only to refer to discrete things *that emerge from seeds*. *Semine* are therefore not discrete things, but the origins of things in the shoots or flows of things. Nothing ever comes from another thing without there being a creative seed-flow from which it emerges and a seed-shoot that moves out of it. The thing [*res*], like an individual seed, is just one aspect within the flow of its sowing [*disserere*] (1.55), the fold of its matter, and the unfolding [*pandam*] (1.55) of its matter into another shoot-flow that emerges from it.

In other words, the fold of the thing always comes from a flow and grows out into a flow. It never comes from nowhere and it never comes from another thing. If there were not a creative material flow [*genitalia corpora*] (1.58) from which things come, there would be no consistent and certain [*consistere certa*] (1.168) source [*mater*] (1.168) that would shape how it came to be; then anything could come to be out of anything. Every fold must come from a flow [*enascitur*] (1.170) that precedes it.

That which is comes to be at certain times and places because of the distinct material flows from which it emerges (1.176–7).

> *si non, certa suo quia tempore semina rerum*
> *cum confluxerunt, patefit quod cumque creatur,*

> Is it not because whatever is created becomes visible
> in its own time when fixed seeds have flowed together,

Created things emerge only when certain [*certa*] (1.176) creative material flows [*semina rerum*] (1.176) begin to flow together [*confluxerunt*] (1.177) in a certain way. The creative flows of matter begin to cross and intersect and move together in an open and generative way [*patefit*] (1.177), from the Latin words *pateō* ('be open') + *faciō* ('make, construct'), in creation [*creatur*] (1.177). As we have seen and will see, the use of the term *confluxerunt* to describe the *semina* is not a one-off. The *semina rerum* are flux. They create and combine by flowing [*fluxerunt*] together [*con*]. The origin of the creation of discrete things [*res*] therefore occurs by matter in motion. In these lines we can thus identify three distinct kinetic moments in the creative process.

1. The seed-flows [*semina*] (1.176) are distributed and begin to unfold in their shoots.
2. The shoots then flow together [*conflux*] (1.177), entangle, and intersect with one another.
3. The resulting formation is a kind of open process of creation [*patefit*] (1.177) like a braid or weave that does not stop or close up, but continually opens up to the outside like a flower [*pelaton*].

Chaos

The first thesis of materialism is furthermore a rejection of the idea of pure randomness or chaos (1.180–3).

> *quod si de nihilo fierent, subito exorerentur*
> *incerto spatio atque alienis partibus anni,*
> *quippe ubi nulla forent primordia, quae genitali*
> *concilio possent arceri tempore iniquo.*

> But if they came to be from nothing, they would suddenly spring forth
> at random periods of time and during unsuitable parts of the year,
> seeing that there would be no first beginnings which would be able
> to be kept apart from generating union at an unfavorable time.

The movement of matter is pedetic and stochastic, but that does not mean that it occurs in isolation. In fact, being is stochastic *precisely because* it does not occur in isolation or abstraction. It is the interrelation and mutual influence of matter with itself that causes its unpredictable character. Lucretius makes clear here something that will be repeated later (2.220–5): that being is not capable of spontaneous *ex nihilo* action.

In contrast to the historical projection of Epicureanism on to *De Rerum Natura*, Lucretius never postulates that at one point being was nothing but atoms falling down like rain in a void, until one of them randomly swerved. *He says precisely the opposite!* What he explicitly says is that matter is simply 'accustomed to swerving' [*declinare solerent*] (2.221) and *if it were not* (*nisi*), 'all would fall like rain drops [*caderent*]' (2.222) Matter has always been stochastic. Lucretius could not be more clear on this point: there was no moment when matter was just a laminar rain and then swerved.

What is revealed in the passage above is Lucretius' rejection of the possibility of an isolated and completely random *ex nihilo* creation; no roses in winter. Movement is stochastic but there was no first movement that created it all. The Epicurean *cataract/clinamen* thesis contradicts the first principle of Lucretian materialism: nothing comes from nothing, movement does not come from stasis, and turbulent chaos does not come from absolute laminar order. Every laminar flow, like all matter, is already turbulent on the molecular level. Being has always been in motion and that motion has always been [*solerent*] (2.221) stochastic. Over a long period of time those movements combine [*conflux*] (1.177) and stabilise temporarily, giving the appearance of laminar stability, only to become turbulent later on.

The very idea of a purely homogeneous or purely random or chaotic motion presupposes that it was not affected by anything else previously, which presupposes that it was the first thing and that before it was nothing, which is *ex nihilo* creation, which is explicitly rejected by the first thesis of Lucretian materialism.

Elementa

Just as words are products of the more primary movements that inscribe them or speak and order them, so all things are composed of more primary processes that produce and order them (1.194–6).

> *ut potius multis communia corpora rebus*
> *multa putes esse, ut verbis elementa videmus,*
> *quam sine principiis ullam rem existere posse.*

> You should thus believe all the more that many bodies are common
> to many things, as we see elements are common to words,
> rather than that anything is able to exist without first beginnings.

In this passage Lucretius' use of the word *elementa* draws directly on the original Greek meaning of the word στοιχεία, *stoicheia*, used explicitly by Empedocles and Epicurus in the following threefold way as: 1) the most fundamental matter that makes up reality; 2) the natural elements: earth, water, air, and fire; and 3) the process of ordering or forming words by arranging sounds or inscribing letters.

Just as matter flows, confluxes, and folds into things, so sound waves flow and fold into phonemes [*verbis*] (1.195) and lines flow and fold into graphemes [*videmus*] (1.195). What is said and what is seen are only sensed under the condition of a more primary flux or flow of elements [*elementa*] (1.195) that produce them. In other words, discrete sounds [*verbis*] and sights [*videmus*] are the product of a more primary and continuous material kinetic process of sonic and graphic motions: flows of sound and flows of light.

The *elementa* should thus not be understood as the discrete letters that compose parts of the word, but should be understood in the proper Greek sense of the word in which Lucretius intends it: as *stoicheia*, the continuous and kinetic *process of ordering* of the flows of sound and light into words. To think of the *elementa* as discrete building blocks would be to ignore the Greek origin and use of this word in Lucretius' two main philosophical influences: Epicurus and Empedocles. It would be to conflate the terms *elementa* and *rerum*, and to reject the entire ontogenetic theory of elemental flows developed in the invocation of Venus and throughout *De Rerum Natura*. Just as the elements flow in the birth of Venus, so the *elementa* flow in the sounds and sights of words.

Second Thesis: Nothing is Destroyed into Nothing

The second thesis of Lucretian materialism is that nothing returns to nothing, but is simply folded and unfolded (1.219–24).

> *nulla vi foret usus enim, quae partibus eius*
> *discidium parere et nexus exsolvere posset.*
> *quod nunc, aeterno quia constant semine quaeque,*
> *donec vis obiit, quae res diverberet ictu*
> *aut intus penetret per inania dissoluatque,*
> *nullius exitium patitur natura videri.*

For no need would exist for a force that was able to arrange
  the destruction of the parts of each thing and dissolve its structure. But as it
    is, since
  each thing is composed out of eternal seed,
    until a force is present that hammers apart the thing with a blow

or penetrates within through empty spaces and dissolves it,
nature does not allow the destruction of anything to be seen.

Nexus

In this passage Lucretius introduces two more key kinetic processes by which being is not destroyed, but simply folded and unfolded. In the previous section, he described creation as a kind of conflux of flows. Matter flows, but when it flows together with other flows it intersects with them and produces something. This is the first creative motion: the conflux. In addition to this, Lucretius says matter can also fold back over itself and create a junction, joint, loop, bond, or clasp: a *nexus* (1.220). This is not the same movement as the conflux. Where the conflux was a mere flowing together or intersection of multiple flows, a *nexus* is stronger insofar as it joins together a flow with itself to produce a distinct junction, joint, or binding in the flow. The *nexus* produces the effect of a discrete loop or fold in the flow.

The third motion is that of the unfold. The flows of matter are never destroyed, instead they are simply unfolded or loosened [*dissoluat*] (1.216) from a *nexus* or fold. The flows of matter have no beginning or end [*aeterno*] (1.221). They are neither created nor destroyed. In this passage Lucretius is effectively stating the first law of thermodynamics over a thousand years before it could be experimentally confirmed.

The Fountain of Being

The first thesis of materialism proves the infinity of time [*aeterno*] (1.221) in the following manner. If time is infinite and matter could be destroyed, the world would have already destroyed itself. If there was an *ex nihilo* beginning of the world which itself was not created and did not become or change, but simply *was*, it would never be able to change or become different than it was. Alternately, if the world was becoming but had a final end and time was infinite, we would have already reached that end after an infinite time. Therefore being must have no beginning and no end.

The second thesis adds to this point the following: if time is infinite, that is, being has no beginning and no end, then matter cannot be destroyed. If being could be destroyed, it would already have been. Since it has not been, this proves that matter cannot possibly be destroyed.

Being is therefore an infinite fountain or source [*fontes*] (1.230) that flows continually without creation or destruction. Being flows, fluxes, folds, unfolds, and weaves, but is never destroyed (1.230–1).

unde mare ingenuei fontes externaque longe
flumina suppeditant? unde aether sidera pascit?

From where would internal springs and external, far-off rivers
supply the sea? From where would the sky feed the stars?

All of being flows like the elements: the source and matter of all things.
It empties itself like the springs, rivers, founts, and fluid sources [*fontes*]
into the ocean, which through evaporation and rain in turn resupplies
the springs and rivers. If being did not flow, from where would Venus
draw the flows of shining life [*generatim in lumina vitae*] (1.227)? Where
would the earth lead or conduct [*redductum*] (1.228) its movements? From
where would the flows of air [*aether sidera*] (1.231) come from to feed
[*pascit*] (1.231) the *nexus* of starry constellations? The Latin word *pascit*
means not only to feed or nourish, but to nourish specifically by driving
an animal flow to the undivided pasture with its flows of grass and
water.[4]

Contextum

If nothing could come from nothing and nothing could return to nothing
then anything and everything could be destroyed at any time (1.238–44).

Denique res omnis eadem vis causaque volgo
conficeret, nisi materies aeterna teneret,
inter se nexus minus aut magis indupedita;
tactus enim leti satis esset causa profecto,
quippe ubi nulla forent aeterno corpore, quorum
contextum vis deberet dissolvere quaeque.

Next, the same force and cause would destroy everything
indiscriminately, unless they were held together by an eternal stuff
entangled to a lesser or greater degree in its interconnection with itself.
Indeed a mere touch would undoubtedly be a sufficient cause
of death, especially seeing that there would be nothing with eternal *corpore*
whose texture a special force would be required to dissolve.

Unless the unlimited and indestructible material flows [*materies aeterna*]
(1.239) of being are capable of continually binding or joining together
[*nexus*] (1.220) in larger and smaller folds, then they could easily perish
and dissolve randomly. Since such dissolution is not the case, it follows
that being must be made of a tightly interwoven fabric [*contextum*]

(1.243). The *nexus* or folds of the flows would not be enough to preserve their integrity without the larger continuous interweaving that binds multiple *nexum* or *textum* (plaits or folds) together into a single *contextum* or multi-folded circulation. If the *nexum* and *textum* are the folds in the flows, the *contextum* is the continuous braiding or interweaving of multiple folds into a single fabric that brings together without imposing an order on them from beyond.

The *contextum*, however, is not a thing and it does not appear. Since the *contextum* is not a *nexus*, it has no affective capacity [*tactus*] (1.241), and thus cannot be a thing [*rerum*] or even part of a thing. The *contextum* is the continual flow that traverses the *textum*, binds them together, orders them, and conditions their co-motion and relation to one another. The *contextum* is nothing but a series of interwoven folds that connect with one another only indirectly through two or more related *nexum*/*textum*. The *contextum* is not an *a priori* order waiting to be filled with folds nor is it an *a posteriori* fiction that only seems to have ordered the folds. The *contextum* is the real and immanent constitution of order by the flows that traverse the folds. In turn, the *textum* are nothing other than the constitutive flows that fold themselves into these relations. *The whole process is one continual flow*. This is the incapacity of the *contextum*. Since it is nothing other than its *textum* it has only the capacities and effects of its folds. Therefore, the *contextum* is an incapacity in the dual sense in which it both has no effective capacities or qualities of its own and only has its capacities 'in' or through its constitutive conjunctions.

The *contextum* is not a negation or absence. It is a positive and immanent ordering that is entirely continuous with what it orders. It is not a negativity because it is not the opposite of the folds, but their support or coordination. The *contextum* has no positive or negative being independent of the *textum*, therefore it cannot be their opposite. It is not a thing, but an entirely positive no-thing that distributes and arranges things. The *contextum* is the flow of relations between and through things that is itself not a thing. It is the collective capacities of things that is itself neither a capacity nor a thing: an incapacity or nothing. It is what keeps things from randomly unfolding [*dissolvere*] (1.243).

The Rain of Matter

Matter flows [*semine*] (1.160), folds [*nexus*] (1.220), and is woven like a fabric [*contextum*] (1.243). Its flows are never destroyed but simply refolded and recirculated. The rain of matter falls but does not die. The rain of matter flows [*imbres*] (1.250) from the sky, as Lucretius says, folds up in the curved bosom of the earth [*gremium matris terrai*] (1.251), only to reconstitute itself into the composite flow [*manat*] (1.259) of glistening milk from the udders of cows. Nature remakes or reweaves [*reficit*] (1.263) things from the endless flows of matter.

But these are only the first two theses on materialism. In the next chapter we look more closely at the next two on the invisibility and porosity of matter.

Notes

1. This is precisely the ontology of becoming put forward by Whitehead and partially adopted by Deleuze. See Thomas Nail, *Being and Motion* (Oxford: Oxford University Press, under review), ch. 3.
2. See Nail, *Being and Motion*, Book II, Part III.
3. Charlton Lewis and Charles Short, *Harpers' Latin Dictionary: A New Latin Dictionary Founded on the Translation of Freund's Latin-German Lexicon*, ed. E. A. Andrews (New York: Harper & Bros, 1879).
4. Lewis and Short, *Harpers' Latin Dictionary*.

5. The Pores of Matter

Third Thesis: Matter is Invisible

Things [*rerum*] can be seen but matter [*corpora*] cannot. This is a fundamental distinction for Lucretius. The conditions of visibility [*rerum primordia*] are themselves not visible [*nequeunt oculis*] (1.268). They are what provides the condition of visibility but are themselves not reducible to what is visible. If they were, they would no longer be the conditions of the visible, but would fall back into identity with visible things and we would have gleaned nothing of the real conditions of visible things at all (1.267–70).

> *ne qua forte tamen coeptes diffidere dictis,*
> *quod nequeunt oculis rerum primordia cerni,*
> *accipe praeterea quae corpora tute necessest*
> *confiteare esse in rebus nec posse videri.*

> since you cannot see the first beginnings of things with your eyes,
> let me remind you besides that there are bodies which you must admit
> exist in things and yet are not able to be seen.

The third thesis of Lucretian materialism is in direct conflict with the basic principles of empiricism and modern mechanistic materialism. Empiricism denies the reality of anything which cannot be sensed. As such, a strict empiricist must reject the current scientific consensus regarding the existence and reality of quantum fields, since they cannot be observed directly or independently of the particles they produce.[1] Quantum fields have energy and momentum that can only be indirectly observed by their macroscopic visible effects, like the recently discovered Higgs-Boson particle.[2] Although the popular press fetishised the so-called 'god particle', the most important discovery for physicists was actually the Higgs *field*, not the particle. The visible particle only proved the reality of the more important and more fundamentally generative invisible field.

The version of modern mechanistic materialism that appropriated Lucretius for its own ends only accepted the third thesis of materialism in a *de facto* and not a *de jure* way. For example, the postulate of modern atomism was that the world was made of tiny particles that we could not see with our naked eyes 'right now', *a posteriori* but not *a priori*. Ultimately, the thesis goes, through modern experimental science we will be able eventually to observe the most fundamental matter of reality directly through technical instruments. Perhaps some contemporary physicists still hold this view today in a speculative way.

Lucretius, however, rejects this *a priori*. There is no textual support in *De Rerum Natura* to suggest that Lucretius ever thought we would eventually be able to directly see material flows [*corpora*]. 'The flows of matter are fundamentally invisible' [*nequeunt oculis rerum primordia*] (1.268), he says. The Latin word *oculis* does not strictly mean 'eyeball', but, more generally, visibility. Matter is an active and creative process which one can never see as a whole or in its most fundamental state. For Lucretius, matter is something that can only be known indirectly as the ontological condition of that which is. Physics will keep observing smaller and smaller processes, but they will never hit bottom. The visible will always have as its condition an invisible kinetic and processual substratum which distributes it.

In other words, in contrast to a naive empiricism or naive materialism, Lucretius adopts instead a transcendental empiricism or transcendental materialism which aims to discover the real conditions for the emergence of the empirical and visible material. Thus the conditions of the empirical can themselves not be anything empirical. This does not mean that the conditions are not thoroughly material; it only means that matter is not strictly empirical.

This position is consistent with contemporary quantum physics in two ways. First, quantum fields are in a state of superposition. Thus, empirical observation can only take place as a series of indirect and entangled observations, and not as a total observation.[3]

Secondly, quantum fields can only be observed through the visible effects they create and not in themselves. In order to generate mass and particles, quantum fields by necessity must have energy and momentum. Since, as Einstein showed, mass and energy are convertible, particles are born from and return to their quantum fields. Field energy becomes particle mass becomes field energy in a continuous momentum or movement. Matter-energy modulates between field and particle through a flow of movement or momentum. Therefore a quantum field is just as material as particles are because *particles are nothing other than folds or excitations in the flow of fields*. Matter is already a flow of matter that has simply folded up into a particle.[4]

The Fluid and Thermo- Dynamics of Matter

Lucretius gives several poetic examples of the relation between the invisible corporeal flows [*corpora*] and the things they produce [*rerum*], all of which follow the same relation established earlier in the poem between the *corpora* flow [*flux*], fold [*nexum*], and weave [*contextum*] into seemingly discrete *rerum*. Things are made from more primary invisible flows of matter.

Wind. Matter flows like the invisible wind flows [*rapido percurrens*] (1.273) and begins to curve into a vortex or spiralling, turbulent formation [*turbine*] (1.273) across the open fields [*campos/nomos*] (1.273) and sea [*ponti*] (1.8). As it moves it sweeps up matter [*verrunt ac subito*] (1.279) into a shaking [*vexantia*] (1.279), metastable, homeorhetic vortex [*turbine*] that carries it along in a held morphogenetic unity. We see the vortical form and visible effects of the flows as they emerge and produce metastable patterns, like dust in a dirt devil, even though the flows of matter themselves remain unseen.

Water. Water teaches us the same fluid dynamic lesson about the nature of corporeal flows, but more explicitly since we can see them directly. When the flows of rain fill the rivers [*imbribus*] (1.282) they become rapid [*aquae fertur*] (1.281) and turbulent [*turbidus*] (1.286). The flows begin to curve and roll up [*volvitque*] (1.288) into waves [*fluctibus*] (1.289), producing giant vortices [*vertice*] (1.293) of folded up matter. The flows of matter begin to twist [*torto*] (1.293) and interweave with each other, whirling around [*rotanti*] (1.294) in a metastable spiral pattern [*turbine portant*] (1.294).

Heat. Thermodynamic energy is also defined by its invisible flows. We feel heat and see its effects, but we do not directly see the flow of energy that produces them. However, insofar as we are able to sense their effects we can rightly infer that their flows (combustion, evaporation, and so on) are made of matter because nothing is able to touch or be touched except corporeal flows (1.302–4).

quae tamen omnia corporea constare necessest
natura, quoniam sensus inpellere possunt;

But it must be that all these things are bodily
by nature, since they are able to set the sense organs in motion.

Corporeal flows [*corporea*] (1.302) must necessarily be in motion such that they are capable of moving [*inpellere possunt*] (1.303) our senses [*sensus*] (1.303). All *corporea* consist necessarily and by nature in setting the senses in motion with their own motion.

Affect

Matter is unseen, but affective. The power [*potest*] (1.304) to touch [*tangere*] (1.304) and be touched [*tangi*] (1.304) is only the power of the body [*corpus*] (1.304) and not the power of the thing [*res*] (1.304).

tangere enim et tangi, nisi corpus, nulla potest res.

For nothing is able to touch or be touched except *corpus*.

The capacity to touch and be touched, to affect and be affected, is already assumed in the definition of the fold or *nexus*. Insofar as corporeal flows fold back over themselves and join to themselves, they have the capacity for self-affection or touch. The thing is composed of corporeal affective folds that make it a thing. Only *corpora* can touch *corpora*, but things are only the outward appearance of this more primary kinetic touching or self-affection of the *corpora* with themselves. The discreteness of the thing cuts it off from the world, but the affective continuity of the corporeal flows that compose the thing brings it back to the world.

Affection is the point where a flow folds back over itself and touches itself. This motion reveals an ambiguity in the *nexus*: that it is a single and same flow but also an intersection between two different points in the same flow. Affect is the ambiguity between sensibility and the sensed. The two are identical in the fold of sensation (the sensed) but differentiated in the continuous movement of the flow across its cycle (sensibility). Affect exposes the kinetic process which is the condition for tactility: a calm pool or eddy in the flows that makes possible the sensation and beauty found by Narcissus. As Baudelaire writes:

Là, tout n'est qu'ordre et beauté,
Luxe, calme, et volupté

There all is order and beauty,
luxury, calm, and sensuousness.[5]

Without the difference between one point in a flow and another, there would be no sensation, only logical static identity. However, if sensibility and the sensed were fundamentally discontinuous entities, they could not produce the same sensation of the sensed.

This later discontinuous formulation of sensation has given rise to the philosophical division between so-called primary and secondary qualities, from at least Locke onwards. Primary qualities inhere in things in themselves, as they are objectively in the sensed; secondary qualities appear in things only as they are subjectively sensed by the sensor. However, the mere continuity or discontinuity of being will never produce a single sensation. Sensation occurs only in the fold or periodic cycle of a flow returning to itself in the *nexus*: *sensing itself as an other*.

Touch is a receptivity, a capacity to be affected and to affect. In other words, a flow has the capacity of being receptive to other points in the same flow. Two different regions of the same continuous flux have the capacity to touch, intersect, and respond to one another. Sensation is the point at which they return to one another in a continual cycle, acting and reacting back on one another. Sensibility is the continuous flow itself that makes possible a given intersection of the flow with itself at a different point. It is the condition, limit, or receptive surface of sensation. The sensed is the exact point of intersection where the two different points become one in the auto-affection. Thus, the sensed being does not precede the process of sensation. The flow contains a great many possible capacities, but not every capacity is always expressed in action. Fish have the capacity to eat, but they are not always eating. Thus, sensation is actively expressed only in the fold between a receptive capacity and active redirection of the flow back over a point of reception. When they intersect, sensation occurs; when the junction unfolds [*dissolvere*] sensation does not occur.

The kinetic processes of sensation, therefore, have two distinct operations: receptivity and redirection. Sensation either allows flows to pass through or it delays them by redirection. It adds nothing to what it receives. In other words, sensation should be contrasted with representation. Representation is a duplication or mimesis of one discrete thing by another. Representation thus presupposes the existence of a distinct original that precedes the copy. Sensation, on the other hand,

is produced only at the unique point of intersection between two differentiated regions of the same flow. It is the repetitive intersection of
differences and not a replication of a previous point.

Sensation is a chiasma or crossing-over (from the Greek letter χ, *Chi*)
that combines the operations of receptivity and redirection at a single
point. The hand that touches is also touched back by what it touches.[6]
At the chiasma of sensation the flow that actively bends and returns back
on itself is also the same flow that receives this folded flow. At the point
of intersection the flow either passes across itself continuing elsewhere or
it is taken back up into a repetitive periodic cycle for a delayed release
later on (1.328).

> *corporibus caecis igitur natura gerit res.*

This is proof that nature conducts her business with invisible bodies.

Things [*res*] are therefore carried along and kinetically supported [*gerit*]
(1.328) by invisible corporeal flows [*corporibus caecis*] (1.328).

Fourth Thesis: Nature is Porous

When the flows of matter fold they produce a looped surface or space on
the interior of their fold. In folding and joining [*nexus*] with themselves
the flows of matter produce an interiority and an exteriority. In other
words, they produce the space required for the existence and extensive
movement of things (1.329–30).

> *Nec tamen undique corporea stipata tenentur*
> *omnia natura; namque est in rebus inane.*

But all things are not held packed tightly
together everywhere by the nature of *corporea* for there is void in things.

Since *corpora* are not completely enclosed in the total and closed bind
[*-lig*] of the *moenera*, they are mobile, and since they are mobile they can
flow and fold. Only on the condition of the flow and fold of the *corpora*
can things [*res*] exist in spatial extension and move. Because the flows of
matter cannot be held in a total unity, the flows always leak entropically.
But because they always leak, they can flow and curve into hollows,
eddies, or spaces.

The flows of matter do not flow in space, but space is produced by
flows. Space does not pre-exist matter in motion; it is created by matter

in motion at the same time as it flows. This is echoed at the macro and micro level of contemporary physics: cosmology and quantum gravity. In cosmology, for example, not only does the big bang require there to be an origin of space and time, or in other words an aspatial atemporal origin in a super-dense quantum matter, but even recent discoveries about the early nature of the universe reveal that in the beginning of the cosmos space-time was not a perfectly smooth, pre-formed background fabric. Rather, it had an extremely turbulent unfolding *when it was produced and unfolded by motion*, which only gradually settled down into what we now perceive as the relatively smooth background space-time of reality.[7] In short, kinetic turbulence is at the heart of the cosmic origins of space-time itself.

At the micro level of quantum field theory the fundamentality of space is now rejected by most physicists. According to physicists such as Carlo Rovelli and Lee Smolin, space is itself a product of quantum fields flowing and looping below the level of empirical observation (the Planck level). Loop quantum gravity theory demonstrates that it is mathematically possible (and experimentally verifiable, although not yet verified) for space itself to be a product of the more-primary process of the folding and bubbling of quantum fields. This theory is called the 'spin-foam' theory of space because the flows of quantum fields fold up into tiny bubbles that compose larger foam structures; these provide the seemingly smooth but actually quite folded and bubbly topology of space.[8] No matter which quantum theory of gravity wins out in the end, the next major move in physics will be to prove the unity of general relativity and quantum field theory – in other words, a quantum kinetic theory of gravity and space.[9]

Pores

The inside of a fold or *nexus* is not an absolute negativity, but only a relative hollow space or fold carved out by the flow of corporeal curvatures. The idea of the void [*inane*] (1.330) in *De Rerum Natura* has been wrongly understood as an absolute ontological nothingness, in part because the flows of matter [*corpora*] have been understood as absolutely positive discrete particles. For Lucretius, however, being is not a totality, unity, or One. Since the *corpora* are fundamentally in motion without absolute limit, there can be no ontological totality. Every limit or totality is instantly surpassed by the mobile expansion of the universe itself, described implicitly in 1.73 by Epicurus' constant moving beyond the flaming walls of the world, and explicitly in 1.970 with the infinite series of javelin throws beyond the limits.

There is matter and there is void, but always in an alternating relation at the macrocosmic level and never in their pure form. Every material limit produces a relative interior and exterior void which is soon limited again by another corporeal limit. Neither matter nor void ever finally totalise the other at the macro or micro level. Matter and void are only reciprocal expressions of the same kinetic process of folding and unfolding. *Corpora* and *inane* are therefore two sides of the same kinetic process which Lucretius literally defines as their twofold [*duplex*] motion (1.503). Both dimensions are produced by the same process of kinetic *folding*.

The primacy of motion in Lucretius' concept of space [*spatium*] (1.379), place [*locus*] (1.426), and void [*inane*] (1.330) is evident from their Greek origins. The Latin word *locus* is derived from the Greek word χορα, meaning an active and undivided distribution of nourishing movement or dance which produces an open place of motion.[10] The Latin word *inane* comes from the Greek word ιναω, 'to empty, purify', and ιναϲθαι, 'to be sent forth', from the Sanskrit word *isnati*, 'to bring in quick movement or spurt out'. *Inane* is therefore not just an abstract emptiness, but is the process by which something is emptied or hollowed out through motion. *Inane* is the process by which the movement of folding produces an opening. It is an active process of opening up and cleansing, also related to the Greek word ιαινω, meaning 'to heal and bring pleasure'.[11] The Latin word *spatium* comes from the Greek word ϲπαδιον, meaning 'racetrack', from the Proto-Indo-European root **speh₁-*, meaning 'to stretch, or pull'.[12] The conceptualisation of space or place as an absolute negativity or lack has been a long but consistent historical process of erasing the kinetic activity of space, historically associated with nature, women, and matter.[13] Therefore, one must keep in mind that the meaning of the Latin words that Lucretius uses to describe space should not be obscured by the counter-revolutionary interpretations foisted on them by modern notions of space as inert, inactive, abstract, and empty.

Corpora and *inane* are unlimited, but both limit the other. All matter contains and is contained by void and all void contains and is contained by material flows. Lucretius is therefore neither a monist, a dualist, nor a pluralist, but a thinker of multiplicity. The motion of matter makes nature an infinite sum without totality, a pure multiplicity.

Since every corporeal flow contains and is contained by another flow, there is only a positive continuum of nested folds all the way down. The difference between nested folds is unequal, but it is a positive inequality; it is a 'pore' [*foramina*] (2.386). A pore is not a lack, but something positive like the knothole of a tree formed by the spiralling flow of wood or the hollow of a bird's nest formed by the shape of the bird's body. On the surface of a given *nexus* everything appears perfectly flat. But since every *nexus* is nested in others, the difference between one surface and the smaller ones inside it appears as a pore or hole. But this is not a discontinuity. Just as skin appears flat and smooth to the naked eye but highly porous under a microscope, so junctions appear as simple unities on one level, but are filled with porous folds at another level. The skin is completely continuous with itself through all its folds and bifurcations. At each level it appears smooth, at the next level rough, but just like skin, there is a continuity between all the layers, all the way down. The porosity of the skin makes the whole body a fold between the exterior and interior.[14]

A pore is nothing other than the excess of the corporeal flows themselves that create hollows within and between each other like the tortuous folds of a continuous fractal pattern. Everything [*res*] is pockmarked with the pores and openings of the multiplicity of corporeal flows moving through infinite micro and macro levels. These pores are like so many eyes, ears, mouths, noses, and other orifices [*vulnere*] (1.34) that draw in a pool or flow through their opening and make possible sensation and touch through folding.[15] Pores are the knotholes of sensation embedded in the body of a thing that expose its inside to its outside and its outside to its inside. This double exposure is made possible by the process of folding, like 'Sierpinski's Sponge' or 'Menger's Cube', or the volcanic rock-foam (pumice) that buried *De Rerum Natura* at Pompeii. Being is continuous but infinitely folded and thus porous.

Intensive and Extensive Movement

Space is required for the existence and movement of things, but space is only made through motion and there are two kinds of motion: corporeal or intensive movement and reified or extensive movement (1.334–9).

qua propter locus est intactus inane vacansque.
quod si non esset, nulla ratione moveri
res possent; namque officium quod corporis exstat,
officere atque obstare, id in omni tempore adesset

omnibus; haud igitur quicquam procedere posset,
principium quoniam cedendi nulla daret res.

Therefore there exists intangible space, void, and emptiness.
If void did not exist, there is no way things
would be able to move. For that which is the natural role of *corporis*
to roll in the way and obstruct, would be present at all times
for all things. Therefore nothing would be able
to move forward, because nothing would provide a beginning of
yielding.

The two movements, like continuum and discreteness, are not opposed.
Rather, they are two aspects of the same process of kinetic materialisation. Corporeal flows cannot move without producing space, and things
cannot move without assuming it. Without movement there is no space
and without space there is no movement.

Extensive movement is the movement of things and is defined by
a change in discrete units of space-time. Things [*res*] are quantitative,
limited, and measurable. Extensive movement is a change of place,
or translation. Things [*res*] move from one discrete point to another
by changing places [*locus*], but places themselves never touch [*intactus*]
(1.334). If places themselves could touch they would no longer be discrete, measurable units, but continuous with other places and therefore
no longer different places. Extensive movement is thus the difference
between discrete *loci*.

The second kind of movement is intensive, corporeal, and qualitative.
It is a change in the whole or transformation. If we take the extensive
example of motion to be a change of place from point A to point B
along line AB, the line AB has already been drawn such that A and B
are points on the line that movement traverses. As Bergson says, it is
'already motion that has drawn the line' to which A and B have been
added afterwards as its end points.[16] A and B presuppose the movement
and continuity of the line on which they are points. The division into
A and B is always a division *of something* [*corpora*]: an attempt to impose
arbitrary divisions on to a continuous movement. The movement of
the *corpora primordia* is thus already primary, but we imagine it is not in
order to explain it later as derived from *rerum*. Bergson, who published
his first book as a close study of *De Rerum Natura*, similarly writes '[I]t is
movement which is anterior to immobility.'[17] 'Reality is mobility itself',
'If movement is not everything, it is nothing.'[18] Accordingly, when an

extensive movement occurs from A to B, the whole AB undergoes a qualitative or intensive transformation or change.[19] The line itself flows like the corporeal flows, leaving behind a continuum upon which A and B can be selected. Through a series of successive selections on the line a thing appears to move when it is actually a series of different dimensions of the line itself.

A similar distinction occurs in contemporary physics between quantum fields and particles. At the level of visible 'things', discrete particles appear to move from point A to point B in an electron microscope. However, these discrete particles are actually nothing other than the excitations in the flows and folds of continuous fields. What appears to be an isolated self-identical particle moving from A to B in 'empty space' is actually the modulation of the same wave in a series of successive patterns transforming itself continuously at one point and now another. At the level of visible things, there appears to be 'space' between A and B, and even spaces within the particle itself between component particles; but as we look closer and closer the space is increasingly filled with a continuous field, which in turn produces folds and pores at even deeper levels. Nature alternates between flows and pores, all the way down. Quantum entanglement, the simultaneous change in electron spins at great distances, only appears to be miraculous in the world of extensive motion. Intensively speaking, we are simply looking at two different topological regions of the same field. There is no 'action at a distance' or transfer of information because there is no distance and no external action in the first place.

Movement is therefore both extensive and intensive at the same time. They are two aspects of the same movement. But, for Lucretius, *rerum* are always derived from *corpora* and not the other way around. Every extensive movement or quantitative translation between two points also produces a transformation of the whole flow of which it is a regional point. The two are always present together, like the latitude and longitude of a materialist kinography.

Without the relative appearance of pores in the corporeal folds there would be no condition for the extensive motion of things [*nulla ratione moveri res possent*] (1.335–6) through 'space'. If *corpora* simply remained static [*exstat*] (1.336) and in place, obstructing [*obstare*] (1.337) motion, there would be no flow, and thus no fold and no movement of things. As the corporeal flow expands, it increases its capacity to modulate and wave differently and therefore makes possible the appearance of new extensive movement. The modulation of the flow-wave is the *cedendi* (1.339) that yields to motion and recedes into pores and vacuoles through which things move. Movement and space thus emerge at the same time, just like *corpora* and *inane*.

Without both, not only would things not be able to move, but without the movement of the flows to modulate and fold into loops, there would be no generative conditions for the existence of things at all [*omnino nulla ratione fuissent*] (1.344). The discreteness of things already presupposes the extension of space which they are in. If there were no extension of space there would be no extended things. But extension itself already presupposes the movement of the folding of flows within which the pores open up. In this sense, the corporeal flows limit things but also allow them to move; the flows are what things move in. The conditions of mobility are therefore the conditions of a relative immobility. By creating space they are also the very limits of that space, which always surpasses itself. If space were absolutely unlimited by corporeal flows there could be no things; likewise, if corporeal flows were absolutely unlimited there would be no folds to limit things and all of nature would be one solid undifferentiated block. Things move only under the ontological condition of alternating infinite multiplicities: flows and folds, matter and pores, *corpora* and *inane*, intensive and extensive motion.

Two Multiplicities

Every corporeal fold contains and is contained by at least one other fold. Between the containing fold and the contained fold is the place, space, or void [*locus, spatium, inane*]. Within every fold a space is opened up for other flows and folds. Things only appear to be solid, but they are all filled with pores through which flows move.

For example, water [*liquidus*] (1.349), Lucretius writes, trickles [*flent*] (1.349) through the seemingly solid ground into caves. Flows of food move and circulate [*dissipat*] (1.350) through the body. Water and nutrients flow [*diffunditur*] (1.353) through the trees. Sound waves flow through [*transvolitant*] (1.355) walls. Cold flows through our flesh [*permanat*] (1.355) to our bones. Lucretius is explicit here. Solid things [*res*] are filled with holes [*inane*] through which flows move. Those flows in turn fold and produce smaller things, which in turn are filled with holes, and so on (1.329–45).

Admixtum

Lucretius tells us that the two multiplicities, *corpora* and *inane*, alternate and mix [*admixtum*] (1.369) in things [*rebus*] (1.368–9).

> *est igitur ni mirum id quod ratione sagaci*
> *quaerimus, admixtum rebus, quod inane vocamus.*

> Therefore it is certain that what we have been searching for with keen reasoning, what we call void, exists, mixed in things.

However, the Latin word *admixtum* does not mean the static product of a mixture of discrete elements. *Admixtum* is not simply combination. It is a mixture made by mingling. It is a combination made by movement. In other words, the condition [*ratione*] of things exists only insofar as void [*inane*] is kinetically mixed [*admixtum*] into things [*rebus*] through the movement and flow of the *corpora*.

If all of being were full [*omnia plena*] (1.376) of nothing but things, Lucretius argues, there would be no intensive [*posse moveri*] (1.375) or extensive movement [*mutare locum*] (1.376). If there were only discrete things, they would form a solid and immobile unity. Nothing new could emerge and nothing in existence could die. This is the case because movement does not emerge from things, but things emerge *from movement* (1.370).

Lucretius is explicit: either we begin with motion or we never get it (1.381–3).

> *aut igitur motu privandumst corpora quaeque*
> *aut esse admixtum dicundumst rebus inane,*
> *unde initum primum capiat res quaeque movendi.*

> Therefore either all bodies must be deprived of motion,
> or it must be admitted that void is mixed in things, from which
> source each thing takes its first beginning of motion.

If we accept that there is nothing but things, then there can be no motion. If being flows then it cannot be first and foremost ontologically discontinuous or discrete being [*res*]. If being is fundamentally discrete there can be only a static difference between discrete objects or things and not real movement or continuity between them, since nothing would connect them. Motion cannot be derived from stasis and continuity cannot be derived from discontinuity. But the reverse is not true. Relative stasis and discontinuity can be derived from movement and continuity. If being is fundamentally flow (continuous movement), then the discrete would be simply a relative or regional fold of that motion. For example, point A and point B would not be fundamentally separate from one another, divided by an infinite series of midway points, but rather regional folds of space-time on and of the continuous line AB. In the same way that point A and point B presuppose the continuity of the line AB, discrete and static beings presuppose the flow of being of which they are a mere fold, like the foam of an ocean wave.

Here is the crux of the problem of movement: either we begin with it or we never get it. This is a fundamental question for philosophy. Either we begin with discrete and discontinuous objects and have to say that motion is an illusion, or we begin with flow and are able to explain both movement and stasis as a relative form of movement. All the discrete objects in the world will never give birth to a single motion, as Zeno demonstrated. They are nothing more than the 'dead and artificial reorganisation of movement by the mind', as Bergson writes.[20] Their bodies fill an ontological graveyard. Valéry writes,

> *Zénon! Cruel Zénon! Zénon d'Élée!*
> *M'as-tu percé de cette flèche ailée*
> *Qui vibre, vole, et qui ne vole pas!*
> *Le son m'enfante et la flèche me tue!*
> *Ah! le soleil . . . Quelle ombre de tortue*
> *Pour l'âme, Achille immobile à grands pas!*
>
> *Non, non! . . . Debout! Dans l'ère successive!*
> *Brisez, mon corps, cette forme pensive!*
> *Buvez, mon sein, la naissance du vent!*
> *Une fraîcheur, de la mer exhalée,*
> *Me rend mon âme . . . O puissance salée!*
> *Courons à l'onde en rejaillir vivant.*

Zeno, Zeno, cruel philosopher Zeno,
Have you then pierced me with your feathered arrow
That hums and flies, yet does not fly! The sounding
Shaft gives me life, the arrow kills. Oh, sun! –
Oh, what a tortoise-shadow to outrun
My soul, Achilles' giant stride left standing!

No, no! Arise! The future years unfold.
Shatter, O body, meditation's mould!
And, O my breast, drink in the wind's reviving!

A freshness, exhalation of the sea,
Restores my soul . . . Salt-breathing potency!
Let's run at the waves and be hurled back to living![21]

Only the flows of being's wind and water can save us from the grave-yard by the sea. In other words, *inane* must be kinetically mixed *through motion* into things [*esse admixtum dicundumst rebus inane*] (1.382), such that a vast mobile multiplicity is created. From the beginning, movement must do the mixing of void into things [*primum capiat res quaeque movendi*] (1.383). Void is not always already there pre-mixed, floating abstractly as the 'non-being' of things. Void is not non-being. Void is only a rela-tive difference between matters. It therefore must be *mixed* [*admixtum*] in through motion. Only on the precondition of motion can void appear mixed in things. Again, the sea provides a perfect example; the moving sea flows and folds over itself, mixing air into itself through waves, producing bubbles and foam that wash up on the shores of light. The corporeal flows fold up and introduce loops or pores that mix void into things.

Things

Things are an admixture. *Inane* is the difference between corporeal flows, but *rerum* are the exact outline of this difference. A thing is that which contains *corpora* and is contained by *inane*. But *inane* is already itself the product of corporeal folds [*nexum*] at a larger level, and so on. These are the two sides of the same process that defines the existence of a discrete thing. Corporeal flows and void alternate to infinity in a series of mutual self-limitations, where the *rerum* are only the exact spatial outline of a given relative difference between the two multiplicities. Things are thus the relative and continuous difference between what they contain and what they are contained in.

The discovery of the nature of these things is, as Lucretius describes, possible by a kind of transcendental empiricism (1.422–5).

corpus enim per se communis dedicat esse
sensus; cui nisi prima fides fundata valebit,
haut erit occultis de rebus quo referentes
confirmare animi quicquam ratione queamus.

For ordinary perception declares by itself that *corpus* exists.
Unless trust in perception is firmly founded and flourishes,

in the case of hidden things there will be nothing to which we can refer
to prove anything at all with the reasoning power of the mind.

We see only visible discrete things as the difference between *corpora* and
inane, but our senses also tell us that these things must be supported by
yet something else which the things contain and something else which
contains the things. Again, Lucretius is not seeking the nature of being
qua being, but rather the real (not possible or epistemological) conditions under which being occurs to our senses. Sensuous materialism
takes the senses as the starting point of philosophy and seeks to discover
the hidden natural conditions of those sensuous things or *ratione*. In other
words, given the sensuous appearance of things, we can discover the real
material conditions under which those things that exist can appear: the
real conditions for the appearance of that which is.

We will look more closely at this method in later chapters. However,
before doing so we need to complete our close examination of Lucretius'
fifth and final thesis on materialism in the next chapter.

Notes

1. Personal correspondence with the physicist Brian Skinner, PhD
   researcher in theoretical condensed matter physics at MIT. 'The way
   to see the energy/momentum of a field is to arrange some clever experiment in which a series of "microscopic" movements of energy and
   momentum in the field kick off a chain reaction of larger-scale movements of energy/momentum until a "macroscopic" thing is affected in
   a way that we can see. This is basically what designing an experiment is
   all about.'
2. See Sean Carroll, *The Particle at the End of the Universe: How the Hunt for the
   Higgs Boson Leads Us to the Edge of a New World* (New York: Dutton, 2012).
3. Karen Barad, *Meeting the Universe Halfway: Quantum Physics and the
   Entanglement of Matter and Meaning* (Durham, NC: Duke University Press,
   2007).
4. Carlo Rovelli, *Reality Is Not What It Seems: The Elementary Structure of
   Things*, trans. Simon Carnell and Erica Segre (New York: Penguin
   Random House, 2017).
5. Charles Baudelaire, 'L'invitation au voyage', in *Fleurs du mal / Flowers
   of Evil*, trans. William Aggeler (Fresno: Academy Library Guild,
   1954).

6. See Maurice Merleau-Ponty, *Phenomenology of Perception*, trans. Donald A. Landes (Hoboken: Taylor and Francis, 2013), 94. See also Maurice Merleau-Ponty, *The Visible and the Invisible: Followed by Working Notes* (Evanston: Northwestern University Press, 1968), 130ff.
7. See 'First Second of the Big Bang', *How The Universe Works*, Season 3, 2014, Discovery Science.
8. See Carlo Rovelli, 'Loop Quantum Gravity', *Physics World*, 16.11 (2003); Carlo Rovelli and Lee Smolin, 'Loop Space Representation of Quantum General Relativity', *Nuclear Physics*, B 331.1 (1990): 80; and Lee Smolin, *Three Roads to Quantum Gravity* (Oxford: Oxford University Press, 2000).
9. A more developed kinetic theory of time is developed in Thomas Nail, *Being and Motion* (Oxford: Oxford University Press, under review), Part IV.
10. F. E. J. Valpy, *An Etymological Dictionary of the Latin Language* (London: Baldwin and Co., 1828), 235.
11. Robert Beekes and Lucien Beek, *Etymological Dictionary of Greek* (Leiden: Brill, 2010).
12. Valpy, *An Etymological Dictionary of the Latin Language*, 439.
13. See John Sallis, *Chorology: On Beginning in Plato's Timaeus* (Bloomington: Indiana University Press, 1999).
14. See Jean-François Lyotard, *Libidinal Economy*, trans. Iain Hamilton Grant (Bloomington: Indiana University Press, 1993).
15. On John Stuart Mill's definition of matter as a 'permanent possibility of sensation', see Vladimir Lenin, *Materialism and Empirio-Criticism: Critical Comments on a Reactionary Philosophy* (New York: International Publishers, 1927), https://www.marxists.org/archive/lenin/works/1908/mec/three1.htm (accessed 29 July 2017).
16. Henri Bergson, *Matter and Memory*, trans. Nancy Paul and William S. Palmer (New York: Zone Books, 1988), 189.
17. Henri Bergson, *An Introduction to Metaphysics*, trans. Thomas A. Goudge and T. E. Hulme (New York: Liberal Arts Press, 1949), 53.
18. Henri Bergson, *The Creative Mind*, trans. Mabelle Louise Cunningham Andison (New York: Philosophical Library, Dover Reprint, 1946), 160, 155.
19. By 'whole', Bergson does not mean a 'totality', because a totality cannot change or become other than it is. Bergson means something like an open and vibratory whole.
20. Bergson, *Matter and Memory*, 193.

21. Paul Valéry, *The Graveyard by the Sea*, trans. C. Day Lewis, http://unix. cc.wmich.edu/~cooneys/poems/fr/valery.daylewis.html (accessed 29 July 2017).

6. The Event

Fifth Thesis: All Matter is Either Conjunctive or Evental

As we saw in the fourth thesis, all of nature is made of two kinds of multiplicities: *corpora* and *inane*. In this fifth and final thesis on materialism, however, Lucretius argues that these in turn can be distributed according to two different kinetic formations: conjunctions and events (1.449–50).

Nam quae cumque cluent, aut his coniuncta duabus
rebus ea invenies aut horum eventa videbis.

For all things that have a name, either you will find that they are
conjunctions of these two things or you will see that they are events.

Conjunction

The Latin word *coniuncta* is often translated into English as 'properties', but this is inconsistent with Lucretius' description of the flows of matter, which themselves have no properties and which are not discrete static things which could 'have' anything like properties at all. Furthermore, the Oxford and the Lewis and Short Latin dictionaries define *coniuncta* as 'to bind together, connect, join, unite'. The English translation of *coiuncta* as 'properties' thus refers less to the original Latin meaning, its historical usage, and Lucretius' philosophy, than to a projection of the Anglo-empiricist tradition of primary and secondary qualities on to the poem.

Furthermore, this translation, like the translation of *corpora* as 'atoms', explicitly ignores the fact that Lucretius actively chooses to avoid using the perfectly obvious Latin term to describe the properties of things, '*proprietates rerum*'. If he had meant to say 'properties' he easily could have.

Furthermore, the idea that *corpora* have 'properties' is confusing because it sounds as if properties are something other than the *corpora* and are added to them, which Lucretius explicitly denies.

The flows of matter do not have properties of any kind, as Lucretius argues at length in lines 1.730–1022. By simply translating *coniuncta* as properties we end up presupposing precisely what needs to be explained, namely: how the properties of things (hardness, texture, colour, and so on) are produced in the first place by things which themselves have no properties. How do flows that have no properties produce properties in the first place? If there are only *corpora* and *inane*, where do properties or qualities come from?

We should begin to answer this question with a closer look into the Latin meaning of the word *coniuncta*, from *con*, meaning 'with', and *iuncta*, meaning 'to join, connect or yoke'. The meaning of the Latin word *iuncta* by this definition and as used by Cicero[1] is almost identical to the word *nexus*, 'to connect or bind together', used by Lucretius throughout to describe the process by which the flows of matter fold over and join themselves to themselves and produce a haptic bond. *Iuncta* is even more explicit in that this junction or fold is produced by joining something to itself in a yoke, as a moving animal is bound to something else through the circular yoke around its neck. The yoke is the loop or fold that by curving back around itself, touching itself, captures or harnesses a flow of motion. In general, however, the *iuncta* is not conceptually dissimilar from the *nexus*; both terms describe the process by which flows are joined to themselves in a bond or yoke. *Coniuncta* are therefore the connection of two or more *iuncta*, *nexum*, or folds. But this still does not answer the question of how *corpora*, which are without qualities, are capable of somehow immanently producing qualities such as hardness, colour, and weight.

The Waveform Theory of Quality

When a corporeal flow folds back and intersects with itself in a junction [*iuncta*], it produces a sensation *of itself* both as sensed and as sensor. The sensed dimension of the *corpora* is not something which precedes or exceeds the process of sensation, but is rather an immanent product of it. The continuous process of sensibility occurs as matter flows and folds over itself. A 'thing' is thus nothing other than the conjunction of kinetic affects, folds, or *iuncta* that compose it. Things have no essence, only a conjunction of capacities to act and be acted upon: affects. Outside of this affective kinetic sensibility there is no transcendent essence of the thing.

The self-intersection of a flow [*iuncta*] is a point of sensation or auto-affection, but also a point of affection that defines the capacities and kinetic being of the thing. The *nexus* is the precise point where two different aspects of a flow become joined into one single loop. This point appears not as an abstract or logical identity but as a kinetically qualified identity: as a certain solidity, size, speed, colour, temperature, and so on. Depending on the way the flows are folded over one another they produce different qualities.

Kinetic theory in physics has elaborated a fairly robust account of many different qualities explained entirely by motion. For example, the kinetic *density* of folds determines the solid, liquid, or gaseous quality of the thing; the kinetic *speed* of the folds determines the quality of its temperature; the *frequency* of kinetic folds determines the wavelength across the electromagnetic and pressure spectrums, producing qualities of colour and sound. Even a quality such as sweetness is produced by a certain *density and movement* of carbohydrate-saturated saliva over an area of the tongue. It is therefore entirely consistent with contemporary physics to suggest that qualities are the result of kinetic affections; flows whose density, shape, speed, and frequency are receptive and directive. Quality is therefore the product of an auto-affection or fold in the flows where matter senses itself.

This affective kinetic quality produced by flows differs from classical ideas of quality in several ways. First, a kinetic quality is never a pure quality in isolation; it exists only through and immanent to sensation in relation to a fold or junction in a flow. Contrary to Plato, quality does not transcend its concrete manifestations in matter.[2] The same quality can appear in different things without there being an unchanging transcendent form of this quality, because flows are capable of being moved and affected in similar patterns in more than one place at a time. Furthermore, the same junction can be shared by more than one flow at a time as they converge and cycle around the same affective point or *nexus*. This movement does not require any immaterial form or idea.

Secondly, a kinetic quality is not an attribute of a pre-existing substance. Quality, contrary to Aristotle, is not a mere attribute of 'one and the selfsame substance' that 'while retaining its identity, is yet capable of admitting contrary qualities'.[3] A kinetic quality is not attributed after the fact to a pre-existing thing to which the quality is attached as something other than the thing. The quality and the thing are produced at the same time in the fold because the thing is nothing other than the conjunction of kinetic affects.

Thirdly, a quality is not an essence. An essential quality is a quality that a thing has independent of any observation of it and that must remain the same in order for that thing to be what it is. For example, a primary or essential quality of a book is that it must have pages. If we remove all but one page of a book, a single piece of paper is, by definition, no longer a book. However, the colour of the book is an accidental quality or property of the book. If a book is first white but is then painted black, it remains a book.

Kinetic qualities do not follow this opposition between objective essential and subjective accidental qualities because all qualities are affective functions of the same fluent process.[4] To say anything else would be to abandon Lucretian materialism entirely. What a thing 'is' changes what it is each time one of its qualities changes. For example, the 'book' with one page has a diminished capacity for being read, but an increased capacity for portability; the black book has a diminished capacity for reflecting light waves, but an increased capacity for absorbing them. There are no essential or accidental qualities, only diminished and increased capacities for specific material sensations. The *coniunctum* of affects has simply changed. *Rerum* can be destroyed, but *corpora* can only be disjoined [*seiuncta*] (2.648) and conjoined [*coniuncta*] (1.449).

Degrees of Quality. Material quality also admits of degrees: more or less solid, more or less large, more or less hot, more or less dark, and so on. This is because there can be larger and smaller intercalated junctions which all return to the same point of sensation [*nexus*]. A degree of a quality (more or less) is thus always relative to its *nexus* or point of sensation, through which all the intercalated cycles pass. One junction is 'more' than another the more smaller junctions it envelops with respect to the zero-point of intersection.

The point of sensation is the point of arrival (reception) and departure (redirection) for all the intercalated flows. Without this periodic structure of repetition that defines the *coniuncta*, a quality such as solidity would quickly dissipate if the flows did not return to one another in a certain density. If, for example, flows of magma disjoined all the silicon flows in a basalt rock and mixed them elsewhere with other metamorphic flows, the rock would lose its qualitative degree of solidity. In this case its flows would not return and cycle qualitatively. The rock, qua *rerum*, would be destroyed and would no longer exist since the identity function of periodicity is required for the existence of qualities.

The period or *nexus* of sensation is the self-intersection of intercalated qualitative cycles. Since each of these cycles is in continual movement, qualities are in constant but stabilised flux. Flows constantly move out and return back, like waves of light bouncing between things and our eyes, or waves of sound vibrating the tiny bones in our ears. These qualitative flows cannot be interpreted as quantities unless their continuity is treated as a numerically discrete particle. Since kinetic qualities are produced by processes of fluctuation, their movement is continuous and thus infinite and non-denumerable. However, this does not mean that there are not larger and smaller infinities relative to their periodicity or point of identity.

Just as it is possible to distinguish between larger and smaller infinities in mathematics without knowing the exact quantitative difference between these infinities, so it is possible to distinguish between more or less of a quality without considering the exact quantitative difference between them.[5] Something can feel more or less hot in relation to a point of sensation without considering the exact magnitude of the difference. As Nietzsche writes, 'We cannot help feeling that mere quantitative differences are something fundamentally distinct from quantity, namely that they are qualities which can no longer be reduced to one another.'[6] The differences between continuous flow cycles are not equal. Thus, in between these cycles there can be only a qualitative sensation of an intensive difference of more or less, and not a cardinal number.

Quantity

However, qualitative folds are also quantitive insofar as their continuous cycles are treated as numerically discrete unities. There is therefore no fundamental or ontological division between quality and quantity; there are only flows and folds; *corpora* and *coniuncta*. The Lucretian kinetic theory of folds thus allows us to go beyond the simple opposition between heterogeneous quality and homogeneous quantity. Quality and quantity are simply two dimensions of the same continuous movement of material folding.[7] While quality describes the period or *nexus* of sensation in the fold, quantity describes its periodicity as a whole, identical, and unified complete cycle. Greater or lesser quantities are determined by counting the smaller subcycles they contain (Fig. 6.1).

For example, ten degrees of temperature is hotter than at least nine

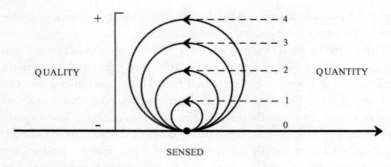

Figure 6.1 Quality and quantity.

other measurable qualitative subcycles or degrees. In this way a cycle can be counted as a quantitive multiplicity without presupposing an onto-logical division between the period and cycle of a fold. Contemporary physics, for example, accepts both the qualitative continuity of matter as quantum fields, but also the quantifications of those fields at different emergent levels: particles, atoms, molecules, cells, animals, plants, galax-ies, and so on.[8] This is possible only because quantity is nothing more than the cycle of a qualitative fold of motion, considered as a unity or 'one'. Quantity is therefore a movement of expansion or identification of the kinetic period to the whole unity of the cycle [*iuncta*], while quality is a movement of contraction of the unity of the cycle back to the single point of its self-sensation or affection [*nexus*]. The 'properties' of quantity and quality are in this way two dimensions of the same kinetic process of matter and motion.[9]

Coniunctum and seiunctum

Coniuncta is the connection between two or more junctions, which together produce the multiple, interconnected qualities we call things. *Seiunctum*, however, is the disjoining of junctions and the unfolding or unravelling of the qualities of things (1.451–4).

> *coniunctum est id quod nusquam sine permitiali*
> *discidio potis est seiungi seque gregari,*
> *pondus uti saxis, calor ignis, liquor aquai,*
> *tactus corporibus cunctis, intactus inani.*

A conjunction is that which is never able to be disjoined
and separated off without a fatally harmful disintegration,

as weight is to rocks, heat to fire, fluidity is to water,
tangibility to all bodies, and intangibility to void.

Junctions are connected together through one or more conjunctions. A conjunction arranges two or more distinct qualities and quantities, each with their own degree of intensity and number. A conjunction of sensate qualities produces what Lucretius will call an image [*simulacrum*] (2.112). A conjunction of numerical quantities produces an object. Together, a series of conjoined qualities and quantities is what Lucretius calls a thing [*rerum*].

Quality and quantity are two distinct but inseparable dimensions of the same thing. For example, a chair is a conjunction of qualitative sensations of a certain solidity, temperature, texture, colour, and so on that defines its sensory image. However, it is also a conjunction of certain determinate quantities: four legs, one seat, two arm rests, all of a certain length, width, and height that define its numerical objectivity. Together, the combination and arrangement of these qualities and quantities produces a relatively cohesive grouping that defines the thing: chair (Fig. 6.2).

While things may appear discrete or discontinuous from their surroundings, they are in fact relatively continuous with them. For example, living organisms are only relatively stable pools or junctions in a continuous flow of expenditure and transformation of energy moving from the sun, conjoined [*coniunctum*] by the organism, reproduced in its offspring, and disjoined [*seiungi*] in death. Life is only an eddy in a corporeal stream.

Even the inorganic bodies of minerals are nothing more than relatively stable combinations of junctions in the continuous transformation

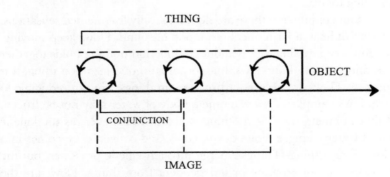

Figure 6.2 Conjunction, thing, object, and image.

of kinetic energy. Igneous, sedimentary, and metamorphic rocks are simply three relative stages of a continuous mutation and conjunction of the earth's liquid body: the rock cycle. Solid, liquid, gas; ice, water, and air are simply the three relative stages of a continuous conjunction in the earth's liquid body: the water cycle. At the microscopic level, all organic and inorganic bodies are conjunctions of smaller bodies and those of even smaller bodies, and so on, all of which are in constant motion at every level. Flows of molecules, particles, and subatomic particles are continually moving and conjoining with one another, resulting in all kinds of diffraction patterns.[10] Quantum fields ebb, flow, conjoin, disjoin, and collapse into particles on the shores of existence. As the Italian physicist Carlo Rovelli writes, 'The world is a swarm of elementary events, immersed in the sea of a vast dynamic space that sways like the water of an ocean.'[11] Even at the macroscopic level all these bodies do not produce a final stability. Everything is moving through an accelerating universe at incredible speeds. Since all things are products of kinetic conjunction they are metastable. Things are always supported by flows at a smaller level.[12]

So-called 'essential' qualities and quantities, such as a certain extension, volume, shape, [*pondus uti saxis, calor ignis, liquor aquai*] (1.453), are nothing more than the products of the process of continuous conjunction. It is only after a series of qualities and quantities have been added together in a conjoined structure that *rerum* come into being. Thus, it is only retroactively that they appear to have these qualities and quantities by necessity or essence. Necessity and essence are only kinetic effects produced by conjunction. They are retroactive tautologies. Therefore, it is only on this condition that disjunction [*seiunctum*] destroys things by unfolding them.

Without conjunction there are no things, only fragmented sensations, a degree of heat, a flash of colour, a pop of sound. Flows keep moving, junctions keep cycling, but without conjunction nothing holds together as a 'thing'. Everything flows, but corporeal motion is not a thing; it is a process. Flows are vectors or processes in things, but not reducible to them. For example, at a given time a body of water may not be frozen. At that moment, there is no thing called ice. However, as the kinetic flow of water changes, slows down, cools, and congeals, ice comes into existence as a thing. Things emerge through kinetic processes; but the processes are not separate or independent from things. Flows are the processes by which things come into and go out of existence. They are the warps, woofs, and vectors by which existence is woven [*contextum*] (1.243), folded [*iuncta*] (1.449), and unfolded [*seiuncta*] (2.648).

The conjunctive process is additive, 'one by one', not something attributed once and for all. This is the case because there is no single substance to which the conjunctive processes can be attributed. Since flows are multiplicities, being is a non-totality, and thus conjunctions can only be regional. The conjunctions that compose *rerum* are, like the flows themselves, in constant motion and can always undergo a change or recomposition. The determination of the qualities of a thing is thus never total, complete, or final because the flows that compose them always leak or connect to something else outside it. The kinetic thing as a process of flows is thus not reducible to any fixed set of qualities or quantities conjoined at a given moment.

Once a conjunction between two or more junctions has been produced and forms a thing, larger composites of conjunctions or things can be woven together [*contextum*] into larger systems that circulate through and sustain the conjunctions.

Events

Events, on the other hand, occur when corporeal flows cross or intersect with one another in a confluence [*conflux*] (1.177) without necessarily producing a fold [*iuncta*], conjunction [*coniuncta*], or disjunction [*seiuncta*] of folds. Once the motions of two or more corporeal flows intersect or connect with one another they create an event. An event is thus a singular point at which two or more flows cross. Again, the Oxford and Lewis and Short dictionaries do not define the Latin word *eventa* as 'secondary qualities or accidental properties', as it is often translated, but rather as a 'chance occurrence'. Events are not random or chance properties of pre-existing things. Again, this assumes precisely what needs to be explained: the existence and production of things from matter. Rather, events are occurrences or intersections between corporeal flows already in motion (1.455–8).

> *servitium contra paupertas divitiaeque,*
> *libertas bellum concordia cetera quorum*
> *adventu manet incolumis natura abituque,*
> *haec soliti sumus, ut par est, eventa vocare.*

Slavery, on the other hand, and poverty and wealth,
freedom, war, peace, and other things at whose
arrival and departure the nature of things remains unharmed,
we are accustomed to call, as is right, events.

According to Lucretius, events are produced when a corporeal flow [*manet*] (1.457) comes [*adventu*] (1.457) and goes [*abituque*] (1.457) without harming [*incolumis*] (1.457) the existing conjunction.

As such, an event is not a thing, object, or sensation. It is of another order altogether. It is what occurs in the *intersection between flows*. The intersection between flows is not the same thing as the flows that intersect, because in their crossing they are changed at that point, even if the point does not immediately harm [*incolumis*] an existing conjunction. Thus, between two or more heterogeneous flows the event is a singular point that changes the *possible* trajectories of their flow; it opens up a new world, a new region of possibility.

As a singular intersection, the event is also a fleeting moment. A new future or trajectory is glimpsed or opened in this moment. However, since the flows each continue on [*adventu et abituque*] (1.457), the event can also quickly disappear after the transformation. The event then can retroactively appear only as a trace of something that once occurred, but also something that made possible a potentially infinite new practical trajectory for movement. Novelty occurs when a flow is crossed by something from outside: another flow. In this way the event is fundamentally collective. It always requires more than one. It occurs through an unpredictable encounter with the other or outside, whereas the fold [*iuncta*] is defined by its intersection with itself.

The consequences of the evental encounter are only realised in motion: by following out the new vector opened up by this intersection. It is not enough for an event to simply occur; its region of kinetic possibility has to be developed and supported by a *contexum* of conjunctions if it is going to have a lasting effect.

In this sense, the event does not cause the flows and does not pre-exist or have any pre-existent characteristics independent of the intersections that constitute it. However, once the flows intersect, following their pedetic motions, the event appears retroactively as the destination of the preceding flows. From the evental point at least two infinite trajectories stretch out. The event is thus like a pivot, joint, or relay along a trajectory that makes possible a relatively stable position from which the intersecting flows can be interpreted and traversed and upon which folds can occur to sustain and reproduce the singularity. The point is a *conflux* of flows, the first bit of stability that makes possible a new world.

Furthermore, events do not happen in time, but *they produce time itself.* Just as corporeal flows do not occur in space, as we saw in previous chapters, but rather produce space through curvature and folding, the same is true of time. Time is the product of ordered sensations and not the fundamental or transcendental condition in which all sensations occur as such. Time does not exist in itself, as Lucretius says [*tempus item per se non est*] (1.459), but rather flows [*consequitur*] (1.460) from our sensation of things [*sed rebus ab ipsis consequitur sensus*] (1.459–60).

The affective sensations or corporeal folds that compose things and sustain events are already distributed by the evental *conflux* of a singular intersection upon which they produce a conjunction of sensations, things, and eventually a whole *contextum* of conjunctions or world. Events occur first as the intersection of flows; only afterwards can the flows begin to bifurcate from their trajectory and curve back around to the evental in order to sustain, support, and repeat it. These folds in turn make possible a sensation of temporality as the succession of folds; but the event itself is not temporal. Time, for Lucretius, is nothing apart from the relative motion, rest, and sensation of things [*tempus sentire fatendumst / semotum ab rerum motu placidaque quiete*] (1.462–3). The theory of the event is illuminated brilliantly in Lucretius' description of it in the Trojan War.

Helen and the Future Anterior of the Event
The Trojan War was one of the greatest events in the ancient world. The key to understanding it, for Lucretius, is to understand its material and evental structure (1.464–70).

> *denique Tyndaridem raptam belloque subactas*
> *Troiiugenas gentis cum dicunt esse, videndumst*
> *ne forte haec per se cogant nos esse fateri,*
> *quando ea saecla hominum, quorum haec eventa fuerunt,*
> *inrevocabilis abstulerit iam praeterita aetas;*
> *namque aliud terris, aliud regionibus ipsis*
> *eventum dici poterit quod cumque erit actum.*

Indeed when they say the daughter of Tyndareus was *raptam* and the Trojan peoples were subdued in war, we must beware that they do not

accidentally force us to admit that these things exist on their own
just because an age which is past and can't be called back
took away these races of men, whose events these were.
For whatever will have happened will be able to be called an event,
on the one hand of the lands, on the other of the regions of space
themselves.

Helen. The evental precursors of the Trojan War begin with Zeus's attempt to eliminate chaos and strife from love. The twin goddess of chaos in Greek mythology is Eris, who, according to Hesiod, is both destructive and creative in the same chaotic motion.[13] Zeus hosts a wedding party for Peleus and Thetis and everyone is invited but Eris. The implication here is that love and marriage should be a perfect *moenera* of unity and harmony, officiated and sealed by the Father God himself, without discord.

In retaliation, however, Eris throws a golden apple inscribed with the word *Kallisti* [For the fairest] into the party, thus provoking a strife between the three most beautiful goddesses: Hera, Athena, and Aphrodite.[14] They ask Zeus to judge, but in order to avoid the wrath of the other two, Zeus delegates the decision about who is the most beautiful to Paris. For Paris, each of the goddesses is ideally beautiful and he cannot choose. So each goddess offers him a gift. Hera offers property and power; Athena offers skill in battle and wisdom; but Aphrodite offers love. As the poet Ovid writes,

> 'Paris, let not these gifts move thee, both of them full of anxious fear!' she says; 'my gift shall be of love, and beautiful Leda's daughter [Helen], more beautiful than her mother, shall come to thy embrace.' She said, and with her gift and beauty equally approved, retraced her way victorious to the skies.[15]

Love and desire triumph over property, power, wisdom, and war. Helen, however, was already married to King Menelaus of Sparta, a marriage collectively arranged and agreed upon by the most powerful men in ancient Greece, who at Tyndareus' request, following Odysseus' advice, were required to promise to defend Helen's marriage to the man he chose for her. Helen effectively becomes the collective property of Greece and is bound into the *moenera amoris* of marriage to Menelaus.

In spite of this, Paris still goes to Greece to woo Helen. Ovid writes,

> 'Only give yourself to me, and you shall know of Paris' constancy; the flame of the pyre alone will end the flames of my love. I have placed you before the

kingdoms which greatest Juno [Hera], bride and sister of Jove [Zeus], once promised me; so I could only clasp my arms about your neck, I have held but cheap the prowess that Pallas [Athena] would bestow. And I have no regret, nor shall I ever seem in my own eyes to have made a foolish choice; my mind is fixed and persists in its desire.'[16]

Paris was offered a choice between the greatest gifts in the world and he has chosen the love of Helen. Upon hearing this story, Helen falls in love with Paris and runs away with him to Troy.

'My first pleasure, then, is to have found favour in the eyes of Venus; the next, that I seemed the greatest prize to you, and that you placed first the honours neither of Pallas [Athena] nor of Juno [Hera] when you had heard of Helen's parts. So, then, I mean valour to you, I mean a far-famed throne!'[17]

The story of Helen, however, is more ambiguous than Ovid describes. Homer and others describe Helen as more 'shameless'[18] and guilty for being seduced and causing a war. In other works still, such as Euripides' *Helen* and Gorgias' *Encomium of Helen*, Helen is absolved of any guilt or shame because she was simply the victim of a system of interrelated forces beyond her control: the *moenera militiai* of Greece and Sparta; the *moenera religio* between the gods; *moenera publica* of Greek property; and the *moenera amoris* of Greek marriage, as Lucretius might describe them. On the one hand (for Ovid and Homer), Helen is an active agent who causes the war for the sake of love. On the other hand (for Euripides and Gorgias), she is the passive victim of powers beyond her control.[19]

Given the tension between activity and passivity, individual and structure, Helen provides an absolutely perfect figure for demonstrating the novelty of Lucretius' theory of the event. In one interpretation of the cause of the Trojan War we are the active agents who create events; in another we are the passive products of the event determined by certain naturalised social institutions. However, Lucretius rejects both of these accounts because both reduce events to pre-conjoined things or persons who claim to be the cause of them in a clear chronological or causal way. Lucretius now gives us a third option.

The raptam. The Latin word *raptam* that Lucretius uses to describe Helen's state perfectly expresses the ambiguity of coexistence between activity and passivity. *Raptam* means 'to be carried away' in both active and passive senses. In the passive sense, Helen comes under the *rapture* of love and is *carried away* by forces beyond her control. In the active sense, however,

Helen's *raptam* is a form of active resistance against her capture by the *moenera* of gods, state, military power, and the patriarchy of her arranged marriage. Venus gives Paris the paradoxical gift of that which cannot be given but must emerge on its own: love. Venus, according to Ovid and others, does not force Helen to fall in love. Thus, Paris, by choosing the gift of love, rejects the structure of the gift as such. Helen, honoured by the highest compliments of Venus, and Paris' rejection of the *moenera* of the credit/debt structure of the gift, in her own way fulfils it by falling in love. She therefore fulfils the paradoxical gift of love which cannot be given.

From the perspective of the Greeks, however, Helen's departure can only be interpreted as a theft of valuable property, the breaking of multiple social *moenera*, and the duty to recover that property. The Greeks cannot let the wound remain open, but must seal it up and complete the circle of credit and debt. The two must become one. Love must be destroyed in total unity. The circle is the complete, closed-off junction; it is the junction made into the iron yoke (from the same Proto-Indo-European root *-yeug*) of necessity. Agamemnon, Odysseus, and the others obey and 'bend to', τροπαῖος, *tropaian*, as Aeschylus writes, the 'yoke of necessity' [ἐπεὶ δ' ἀνάγκας ἔδυ λέπαδνον].[20] The *moenera* is the yoke of necessity that brings death and evil, as we saw in the case of Agamemnon's sacrifice of his daughter.

In another sense, however, Helen is not the sole active agent of the event, which, for Lucretius, always requires at least two flows to intersect. Paris must also be in love. It is only in the intersection of a mutual *voluptas* that two corporeal flows, as distinct flows can touch each other and produce an event. Love here is not simply intersubjective, because the corporeal flows are themselves not subjects or persons. Paris and Helen are themselves already products of a more primary process of corporeal *voluptas*, which has taken their persons over and carried them away in the rapture [*raptam*] of love.

In other words, both Paris and Helen are caught up and carried away in the flows of Venus. Love is that third person or even impersonal collective process which we are carried away by, but which is nonetheless nothing other than ourselves. This makes Venus the most immanent of all the gods, but also makes Helen, who is described as Venus on Earth,[21] the most immanent expression of desire on Earth.[22] As such, how could we possibly expect Helen to be reduced to the binary opposition between desire and desired, subject and object, activity and passivity. Venus is all of these together and Helen expresses collective agency on Earth.

Future Anterior. The event of the Trojan War happened in the past, but not independently of the material conditions of the corporeal flows which intersected to produce the event and which were sustained in a massive network of consequences which we still see today. Just because they cannot be reproduced again [*cogant*] (1.466) does not mean that they did not at one point require corporeal bodies for their occurrence.

In other words, the event can only be said of that which *will have been capable* [*poterit*] of setting being into motion [*eventum dici poterit quod cumque erit actum*] (1.470). Lucretius' use of the third person future anterior of *possum*, '*poterit*', is crucial to understanding the structure of the event. The event takes place not as first or second person (active or passive agent or intersubjective agent), but as an impersonal, generic, third person 'it' or 'one'. The third person is both active and passive in the same sense in which Helen is. She is both the subject of love and subject to love at the same time: *raptam*. The third person is still an agency but it is a collective agency which one finds oneself already swept up in, as the movements of which you are already a part of sweep you up, but also provide the very conditions of first and second person agency as such. It is the multiplicity of corporeal flows within which events occur and persons emerge.

The event also produces a very specific temporal structure which is not at all strictly chronological, but occurs as a simultaneous convergence of futurity and historicity at the point of intersection. For example, by the time we discover that an important event has occurred, we find it in the form of something which has *already happened* and which was only made discoverable because of the consequences that it produced. Thus, it is not by accident but by necessity that we find the event as already having laid the conditions for our discovery of it. The event is not only retroactive, it is also futural. The event is also such that, when we discover it, it is so powerful [*possum*] that its consequences [*actum*] are infinite in breadth and depth (1.470). There is no conceivable time in the future when the consequences [*actum*] or conjunctions [*coiunctum*] of flows cannot fold back and return to this event.

Finally, the present of the event brings the past and future together into the future anterior. In the present, when we find ourselves caught up in this great event, we discover the event as that which *will have been* capable of happening. In other words, the event can be seen to stretch back to its innumerable precursors leading up to the present and presenting innumerable vectors into a potential future. The event is therefore not only a point of intersection [*conflux*] between two or more corporeal flows, it also includes the trajectories of those flows as they appear to stretch into the past and future. The structure of events therefore has a paradoxical structure: the corporeal flows themselves are stochastic, but once they intersect, the point of intersection can be sustained and repeated by folding the flows back on themselves again and again retroactively, and potentially into the future.

To return to the final line of Lucretius' theory of the event: he emphasises that both time and events themselves are not ontologically fundamental. Events are products of intersecting material flows and time is the product of events, specifically in the future anterior. The Trojan War *will have been* one of the greatest events in history in the sense in which we can see all things leading up to this event and all things following from it. In the *Iliad*, Homer paints just such a picture. In other words, the event is not just a mystical point that occurs out of nowhere, but emerges from a collective and confluent materiality.

Carrying the Event

Events, Lucretius says, are always carried [*gestas*] (1.478) by material flows, but events in turn carry or support the multiplicity of things [*rerum*] which are sustained by the folds, which return to the evental point of intersection (1.469–72).

> *denique materies si rerum nulla fuisset*
> *nec locus ac spatium, res in quo quaeque geruntur,*
> *numquam Tyndaridis forma conflatus amore*
> *ignis Alexandri Phrygio sub pectore gliscens*

> Indeed if there had been no material for things, nor place
> and space, in which all things are carried out,
> never would the fire, fanned by love for the beautiful shape
> of Tyndareus' daughter, glistening in the Phrygian heart of Alexander

If there were no material conditions [*materies*] (1.469) for things [*rerum*] (1.469), or place [*locus* (1.470), or space [*spatium*] (1.470), or confluxing love [*conflatus amore*] (1.471) of Helen and Paris, then there could be no event. If the two flows of *voluptas* in Helen and Paris never intersected there could been no event *ex nihilo*. However, once this small event occurs, the entire world and heavens are transformed. Flows can begin to fold back to this point and repeat it, extend it and so on, which in turn produces things as consequences of this folding (1.481–2).

eventa vocare corporis
atque loci, res in quo quaeque gerantur.

you can rightly call them events
of *corporis* and place, in which all things are carried on.

Events are thus the intersection of corporeal flows [*corporis*] (1.482) and places [*loci*] (1.482) that support or carry [*gerantur*] all things [*res*] (1.482). Events never occur in isolation; they only occur when corporeal flows intersect and they only become visible things [*res*] once the corporeal flows flow back around and produce a place [*loci*], which then defines and delimits the visible things of the world (1.483–4).

Corpora sunt porro partim primordia rerum,
partim concilio quae constant principiorum.

Bodies, moreover, are partly the first beginnings of things,
partly the things that are formed by the assemblage of first beginnings.

Accordingly, all things [*rerum*] are composed of corporeal flows [*corpora*] which are constantly and continually brought together [*concilio*] (1.484) in such a way that they produce the ordered relation of things [*primordia rerum*] (1.483).

Conclusion

Lucretius' five theses on materialism lay the first technical groundwork for the larger theory of matter, space, and the universe, which we will develop in the next chapter through a close reading of his theory of the fold.

Notes

1. For a long list of Cicero's usages of the term as such, see Charlton Lewis and Charles Short, *Harpers' Latin Dictionary: A New Latin Dictionary Founded on the Translation of Freund's Latin-German Lexicon*, ed. E. A. Andrews (New York: Harper & Bros, 1879).
2. See Plato's 'Philebus' in *The Dialogues of Plato*, trans. Benjamin Jowett (New York: Random House, 1937), and Plato, *Meno*, 74d, 72c: 'Tell me then, since you call them by a common name and say that they are all [shapes] . . . what is that common nature which you designate as [shape]? What is the quality in which they do not differ, but are all

alike . . .?' *The Works of Plato*, trans. Benjamin Jowett (New York: Tudor Publishing Co., 1936).

3. See Aristotle's 'Categories', in *The Basic Works of Aristotle*, trans. Richard McKeon (New York: Random House, 1941), l. 254.

4. Gilles Deleuze, *Bergsonism*, trans. Hugh Tomlinson and Barbara Habberjam (New York: Zone Books, 1988), 87–8: 'Qualities belong to matter as much as to ourselves. They belong to matter; they are in matter by virtue of the vibrations and numbers that punctuate them internally.'

5. This problem is also formalised in set theory. See Alain Badiou, *Being and Event*, trans. Oliver Feltham (London: Continuum, 2007), 267–8.

6. Friedrich Nietzsche, *The Will to Power*, trans. Walter A. Kaufmann (New York: Random House, 1967), 565.

7. Deleuze, *Bergsonism*, 74.

8. See Richard Liboff, *Kinetic Theory: Classical, Quantum, and Relativistic Descriptions* (New York: Springer, 2003). See also Sean Carroll, *The Big Picture: On the Origins of Life, Meaning, and the Universe Itself* (New York: Penguin, 2016), 172–3: 'Modern physics says that the particles and the forces that make up atoms all arise out of fields. That viewpoint is called *quantum field theory*.'

9. For a full development of the theory of quantity, see Thomas Nail, *Theory of the Object*, in progress.

10. For a philosophical theory of diffraction, see Karen Barad, *Meeting the Universe Halfway: Quantum Physics and the Entanglement of Matter and Meaning* (Durham, NC: Duke University Press, 2007).

11. Carlo Rovelli, *Reality Is Not What It Seems: The Journey to Quantum Gravity*, trans. Simon Carnell and Erica Segre (New York: Penguin Random House, 2017), 145.

12. See Anatoliĭ Burshteĭn, *Introduction to Thermodynamics and Kinetic Theory of Matter* (New York: Wiley, 1996).

13. In Hesiod, *Works and Days*, ll. 11–24, two different goddesses named Eris are distinguished:

> So, after all, there was not one kind of Strife alone, but all over the earth there are two. As for the one, a man would praise her when he came to understand her; but the other is blameworthy: and they are wholly different in nature. For one fosters evil war and battle, being cruel: her no man loves; but perforce, through the will of the deathless gods, men pay harsh Strife her honour due.
>
> But the other is the elder daughter of dark Night (Nyx), and the son of

Cronus who sits above and dwells in the aether, set her in the roots of the earth: and she is far kinder to men. She stirs up even the shiftless to toil; for a man grows eager to work when he considers his neighbour, a rich man who hastens to plough and plant and put his house in good order; and neighbour vies with his neighbour as he hurries after wealth. This Strife is wholesome for men. And potter is angry with potter, and craftsman with craftsman, and beggar is jealous of beggar, and minstrel of minstrel.

Hesiod, *The Homeric Hymns and Homerica with an English Translation by Hugh G. Evelyn-White. Works and Days* (Cambridge, MA/London: Harvard University Press/William Heinemann, 1914).

14. Pseudo-Hyginus, *Fabulae*, 92, in *The Myths of Hyginus*, trans. and ed. Mary Grant (Lawrence: University of Kansas Press, 1960).
15. Ovid, *Heroides*, XVI.51, in Ovid, *Heroides. Amores*, trans. Grant Showerman, rev. G. P. Goold (Cambridge, MA: Harvard University Press, 1914).
16. Ovid, *Heroides*, XVI.163.
17. Ovid, *Heroides*, XVII.115, 131.
18. Homer, *Iliad*, III.138–46.
19. On Helen's ambiguity in the *Iliad* and the *Odyssey*, see Mihoko Suzuki, *Metamorphoses of Helen: Authority, Difference, and the Epic* (Ithaca: Cornell University Press, 1989), 18–19, 34–38, 66–73. Diana Shaffer argues that Gorgias's *Encomium of Helen* 'is double-edged . . . [it] proves her innocence but only by transforming her from a subject who wills her own actions into a passive object'. Diana Shaffer, 'The Shadow of Helen: The Status of the Visual Image in Gorgias's Encomium to Helen', *Rhetorica*, 16.3 (1998): 243–57 (250). On Helen's problematic agency (defined as her oscillation between subject and object positions) in ancient Greek texts, see in particular Nancy Worman, 'The Body as Argument: Helen in Four Greek Texts', *Classical Antiquity*, 16 (1997): 151–203. For a Derridean reading of Helen's indeterminacy, see Matthew Gumpert, *Grafting Helen: The Abduction of the Classical Past* (Madison: University of Wisconsin Press, 2001).
20. Aeschylus, *Agamemnon*, ll. 217–18.
21. Ovid, *Heroides*, XVI.51–163. Even Venus herself describes her, according to Ovid, as the most beautiful woman on earth, and in that way similar to Venus herself.
22. Homer, *Iliad*, IV.158. Paris describes her as looking like Venus, Homer describes her as 'like one of the immortal goddesses'.

7. The Folds of Matter

Matter flows and folds. These are the core tenets of Lucretius' kinetic materialism. If matter does not flow it cannot fold; if it folds it must also flow. This is what this chapter would like to clearly demonstrate. However, if we wrongly interpret Lucretius' concept of *corpora* as 'discrete particles' or 'atoms' instead of flows, his whole conceptual edifice of folding [*plex*] (*simplex, duplex, complex, amplex*) completely unravels. Atoms cannot fold. If Lucretius is an atomist, then we are left with a truly confounding problem of explaining this crucial aspect of his thought. Discrete particles or things [*res*] cannot, *by definition*, fold themselves because the two sides of a thing cannot touch without reunifying the thing with itself. This is because discreteness implies that the thing [*res*] is already bound and limited, with a single and absolute interior and exterior. There is nothing here to fold.

Folds occur only in that which is continuous. This is because a fold is defined by the curving or bending of something back over itself. The intersection or junction of a flow with another flow is not a fold, but an encounter or event. The first is capable of producing recurring cycles [*iuncta*] and periods [*nexus*], while the second is fleeting and singular [*eventa*]. If being were not continuous there could be no folds or even events, only isolated, vacuum-sealed fragments. Folding presupposes continuity, and continuity makes possible the fold of being. Discreteness is thus only the product of a more primary process of flows which have folded into seemingly discrete things.

In lines 1.485–622, Lucretius introduces one of the most important concepts of the whole book, but one which makes absolutely no sense following the atomist interpretation: the fold [*plex*]. Therefore the aim of this chapter is to show the importance of this concept for Lucretius' kinetic materialism and to contrast it with that of the atomist perspective as well as that of the early Greek philosophers.

Continuum

The folds of matter occur only in that which is continuous (1.485–6).

sed quae sunt rerum primordia, nulla potest vis
stinguere; nam solido vincunt ea corpore demum.

But those that are the *rerum primordia*, no force is strong
enough to destroy. For with continuous *corpore* they are victorious in the
   end.

The first matters [*rerum primordia*] are undivided, solid, and continuous
[*solida*] (1.486). Matter is in continuous movement. However, if being
were *merely continuous*, it would be a homogeneous totality. Being would
be One, a finite or infinite unity, without the possibility of change or
motion outside of itself, since there would be no outside to it. In this
case, all movement, as Zeno and Parmenides once argued, would be an
illusion.

However, if being was One total being which contained all of being,
the being that contained all of being would have to be different than the
being that was contained by it. Being would thus be separate from itself,
that is, non-total. We thus reach the paradox of the One that Gödel and
others discovered long ago:[1] that the One cannot be included in that
which it contains. Ontological continuum without motion thus results
in a paradoxical conception of totality which cannot include itself in its
own totality, which Lucretius discusses later on.

On the other hand, if being were *only movement* without continuity
there could, paradoxically, be no motion at all. A discontinuous movement is, strictly speaking, not a movement. For example, without continuity the movement of translation between point A and point B could
not be said to be the *same* movement. Without continuity, point A and
point B would remain completely different points divided by an infinity
of intermediate points, themselves divided by an infinity of intermediate
points, and so on ad infinitum. We can say there is a 'change' that occurs
as an entity is now at point A, now at point B. It *changes* from point A
to B. But if there is no continuity between A and B then these points
are not different aspects of the same movement, but radically different
points without any movement between them at all. Movement without
continuity is thus not movement at all but merely discontinuous, formal,
or logical *change*.[2]

The problem with 'discontinuous movement', according to the Greek philosopher Zeno, is that if space is infinitely discontinuous or divisible we would have to traverse an infinite distance of intervals in order to arrive anywhere else. Movement would, therefore, be impossible. The same result occurs, according to Zeno, when we understand movement as a series of temporal now-points or instants. If every unit of time is infinitely divisible, it will take an infinite amount of time to move from one point to any other. In both cases the problem remains the same: movement cannot be divided without destroying it. By thinking that we can divide movement into fixed, immobile stages, we spatialise, temporise, and thus immobilise it. 'Discontinuous movement' is just the *difference* between divisible points of space-time and has nothing to do with movement at all. Therefore, if we want to say that being actually moves, then such movement cannot emerge from ontological discontinuity but must emerge from the twin conditions of continuity [*solida*] and motion [*flux*].

But, if all of nature is made of solid continuous flows, why, Lucretius writes, do so many things appear to be porous? Lighting flows [*transit*] (1.489) through the walls of houses. Rocks are vaporised [*vapore*] (1.491) into flows by heat. Metals are dissolved [*solvitur*] (1.492) and liquefied [*liquescit*] (1.493). Cold penetrates our cups and produces a flow of water on the outside. If all the *corpora* are continuous and solid [*solida*], how then do flows pass through things (Lucretius asks at 1.489–500)?

Folds

The answer to this question is twofold. The twofold or *duplex* is what allows all things [*rerum*] to have the appearance of relative solidity while also allowing other flows to pass through (1.503–6).

> *Principio quoniam duplex natura duarum*
> *dissimilis rerum longe constare repertast,*
> *corporis atque loci, res in quo quaeque geruntur,*
> *esse utramque sibi per se puramque necessest.*

First, since the twofold nature of the two
things has been found to exist far different,
that is of *corporis* and of *loci*, in which all things occur,
each must be in and for itself, and unmixed.

Duplex. The *duplex natura* (1.503) of matter is the alternating but unmixed relation between the corporeal flows [*corporis*] (1.505) that fold over themselves and the pore [*foramina*] (2.386) or space [*loci*] (1.505) that is created in the hollow of their fold. All things [*rerum*], as argued in the previous chapter, are nothing other than the alternation of larger and smaller folds and the spaces or pores in those folds. Things are duplex.

When a continuous flow folds over itself it produces the discrete inside and outside that defines the thing. Things are thus folds in continuous flows. *Corpora* and *loci* are two sides of the same duplex fold, not two onto-logically separate 'types' of substance: being and non-being. Lucretius is not a dualist, as will become evident in his critique of monism, dualism, and pluralism, discussed towards the end of this chapter. There is only matter in motion, but when it folds it produces an inside and outside that defines the discreteness of the thing. We should thus never confuse the distinctness of the two [*corpora/loci*] or all of nature would cease to flow.

Lucretius is quite clear on this point (1.510–12):

sunt igitur solida ac sine inani corpora prima.
Praeterea quoniam genitis in rebus inanest,
materiem circum solidam constare necessest;

Therefore the *corpora prima* are solid and without void.
Moreover, since void is present in created things,
it must be that solid matter exists around it.

Corpora are continuous and solid [*solida*] (1.510) without any void [*inani*] (1.510). Void is what is present *in all things* only by virtue of the *duplex* or fold of the solid flows [*genitis in rebus inanest*] (1.511). The continuous flows of matter are thus literally wrapped around the void, but it is the very wrapping or encircling [*circum*] (1.512) that produces the void in the first place. The circular folding back around of the continuous material flows with themselves [*duplex*] is what produces the void. The void therefore emerges through the fold, but is nothing other than the fold itself. Flow and pore are two sides of the same *duplex*. Together they produce the thing [*rerum*].

Therefore, the true material conditions of things [*vera ratione probari*] (1.513) are that the void is concealed by the continuous [*solida*] fold [*duplex*] of the flow [*corpora*] that encircles and embraces [*cohibet*] (1.515) the void through its motion (1.513–15).

nec res ulla potest vera ratione probari
corpore inane suo celare atque intus habere,
si non, quod cohibet, solidum constare relinquas.

And there is nothing that can be the true material condition of things
that conceals void with its *corpore* and to have it within,
unless you admit that what holds it in is solid and continuous.

Space therefore is a product of the folded flows of matter that also lets
other flows move through it. This is why matter appears visually solid,
but also seems to allow for other smaller flows to move through it. The
flows of matter hold [*cohibet*] (1.515) the void in their fold. A thing,
Lucretius says, is therefore nothing more than an assemblage [*materiai
concilium*] (1.516–17) of these duplex folds of matter containing [*cohibere*]
(1.517) void. Matter thus exists as corporeal flows that can be folded and
unfolded without themselves ever being divided, destroyed, or broken.
When they fold up they make things; when they unfold those things are
destroyed, but the flows themselves remain undivided, solid, and continuous, even if they are not folded into things, as Lucretius describes in
lines 1.516–19.

This alternating duplex structure of folds is crucial for the movement
of being (1.520–3).

Tum porro si nil esset quod inane vocaret,
omne foret solidum; nisi contra corpora certa
essent quae loca complerent quae cumque tenerent
omne quod est spatium, vacuum constaret inane.

Then further, if there were nothing which was empty void,
all would be solid. In contrast, unless there were definite *corpora*
which fill up whatever places they hold,
all that is would exist as vacant and empty space.

If everything were simply continuous *corpora* then all would be solid,
static, and unmoved. On the other hand, if everything were void then
again there would be no movement and all would be empty space.
The movement of being is therefore only possible on the condition
that matter flows and that these flows fold into increasingly larger and
smaller loops, each producing or holding [*tenerent*] (1.522) their own
regional hollow, pore, or space [*loca*] [1.522].

The fold [*duplex*] is the only way this alternating [*alternis*] (1.524) structure is possible (1.524–6). Since discrete particles cannot fold, there can be no movement, only the dead stasis of the one and the many: monism or pluralism. Only the multiplicity of the fold can save us from the disaster of plenum or paucity.

If folds are what produce multiplicity, and folds must be made of flows, and folds cannot be divided, it follows that the corporeal flows cannot be destroyed. If there is nothing other than continuous material flows then there is nothing within them capable of division and nothing outside of them capable of dividing them (1.528–30). In other words, the flow of matter is indestructible [*aeterna*] (1.528–30). When a thing [*rerum*] is broken [*frangi*] (1.533) or divided [*findi*] (1.533), this is only because it is nothing other than a fold [*duplex*] which holds [*tenerent*] (1.523) a void [*inane*] and has become unfolded into a flow or refolded into two or more folds, each containing part of the same void.

Therefore the more void a thing has, the more it can be divided or penetrated by other flows and folds, transforming it from within and from without (1.536–7). Soft [*mollia*] (1.567) things such as air, water, earth, and fire, for example, are able to flux and flow more than more rigid things, not because they are not solid continuous matter [*solidissima materiai corpora*] (1.565–6), but because they are elemental flows that are already mixed with void [*admixtum quoniam semel est in rebus inane*] (1.565–9). Everything flows, but for Lucretius there are at least two kinds of flows: flows of matter [*corpora*] and flows of matter folded up into things [*rerum*]. The second is mixed with duplex folds that create void and allow the things to move and bend, but the first remains unmixed with void and is solid and continuous [*solido*] without duplex folds.

Simplex

The flows of matter themselves are not *duplex*, but *simplex*. As Lucretius writes:

sunt igitur solida primordia simplicitate

Therefore primary bodies exist in their solid continuous simplex, (1.548)

sunt igitur solida pollentia simplicitate,

Therefore the primary bodies are solid, powerful in their simplex. (1.574)

Corporeal flows are solid and continuous [*solida*] (1.548, 1.574) only insofar as they are themselves already single-sided continuous fluxes [*simplicitate*] (1.548, 1.574), whose topological distribution and curvature is capable of stretching, bending, and modulating itself into n-dimensional manifolds without breaking. The common English translation of *simplicitate* as 'singleness' misses entirely the topological significance of the Latin word *pli*, meaning fold, in the word *simplicitate*. The corpora are not defined by a *duplication* of the fold back over itself, which would produce a void or space between the flow and itself, but rather by a *simplication* or *wave formation* that bends and curves without completely folding.

Waves are simplex, or one-folds. They bend, curve, and undulate, but they do not yet loop over themselves in a duplex. Because all motion is pedetic, flows are not straight or static lines, but bent, curved, or wavy. What appears to be a straight line at one level is made of innumerable undulations and curves at lower levels, like a fractal coastline or a Koch snowflake. From a continuous sequence of curved or bent lines (waves), a one-dimensional simplex is capable of producing an n-dimensional manifold.

For example, in mathematical topology a simplex is a purely continuous, one-dimensional, single-sided flow that is capable, by bending and morphing, of producing multiple higher-dimensional simplexes or what topologists call 'simplicial complexes'. In other words, all higher dimensionality is *simply* the product of the folding and morphing of a single n-dimensional simplex. On the other hand, a 0-simplex or non-simplex is a point – an unfolded and unfoldable discrete particle. A 1-simplex is a line segment; a 2-simplex is a triangle; a 3-simplex is a tetrahedron, and so on into higher-dimensional topological figures (Fig. 7.1).

However, the difference between the mathematical definition and the materialist definition given by Lucretius of the simplex is that there is no such thing as a 'line segment' in nature. For Lucretius, such a figure already problematically presupposes that it is dealing with discontinu-

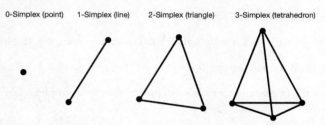

0-Simplex (point)   1-Simplex (line)   2-Simplex (triangle)   3-Simplex (tetrahedron)

Figure 7.1 Simplicial complex. Wikimedia Commons.

ous, discrete quantities, when in fact no such things exist. The simplex must be understood as a single-sided *flow*. Nothing is ontologically discrete; all of nature flows. Therefore the materialist simplex of the *corpora* must be understood as continual flows of matter capable of folding and bending into all the higher dimensions. The simplex flow is simply the most basic topological dimension from which all higher dimensions are derived.

Minima. Every simplex corporeal flow is itself composed of different curvatures and topological regions. We should therefore not think of the simplication of flows as straight or static lines. Corporeal flows are in constant stochastic motion and are therefore morphogenetic, bending, swerving, twisting, and so on. Therefore each corporeal simplex also has its own kinotopological regions: in some places the flow is more curved, in others less; in some places it is twisted, in others not; some regions of the flow are closer to other regions of the flow by virtue of their morphology (what topologists call neighbourhoods); and so on.[3] These topological morphisms in the simplex are what Lucretius calls the *minima* – the waves, bends, and curves in the simplex, capable of producing the vertices discussed above that produce n-dimensionality (1.599–604).

> *Tum porro quoniam est extremum quodque cacumen*
> *corporis illius, quod nostri cernere sensus*
> *iam nequeunt, id ni mirum sine partibus extat*
> *et minima constat natura nec fuit umquam*
> *per se secretum neque post hac esse valebit,*
> *alterius quoniamst ipsum pars primaque et una,*

> Then further, since there is an extreme point in each case
> on that *corporis* our senses are no longer able to discern,
> each point is undoubtedly without parts
> and is endowed with the smallest nature possible, nor did it ever exist
> separately by itself, nor will it ever have the power to do
> so afterwards, since it is itself a primary and single part of another.

The corporeal flow [*corporis*] (1.600) is the extreme [*extremum*] (1.599) limit [*cacumen*] (1.599) at which the senses can no longer discern anything smaller. At this limit there is only the pure continuum of the flow. The corporeal flows are in no way composed of parts [*ni mirum sine partibus*] (1.601) but rather are composed of *minima* of the smallest continuous nature [*constat natura*] (1.602). These *minima* are not parts of a whole since they have no existence independent of the flow, nor will they ever have the power to separate themselves from the flow. They are nothing other, beyond, or above the flow itself.

The *minima* are the kinotopological modulations, waves, or morphisms in the flow and thus constitute the primary features of the flow itself. Just as waves are not separate parts of the ocean, so the *minima* are not separate parts of the *corpora*. The Latin word *pars* here does not necessarily mean 'discrete part', but can also refer to a 'continuous' aspect or dimension of something, as in English we might describe the different parts of a wave (crest and trough) without supposing a discontinuity in the waveform. The crest cannot be separated from the trough without destroying the whole wave. Since Lucretius is quite clear in this passage and elsewhere that *corpora* are continuous, solid, fluid, and indivisible, we should clearly follow this latter meaning of the word *pars*, as an aspect or dimension.

The *minima* are thus ordered together in a single continuous current or stream [*agmine*] of motion (1.605–6).

> *inde aliae atque aliae similes ex ordine partes*
> *agmine condenso naturam corporis explent;*

Thence more and more similar *partes* in their order
flow into and compose the nature of the *corporis* in a tight mass.

Again, we cannot read *partes* as being discrete *partes* since they are ordered [*ordine*] (1.605) in a single continuous train, stream, current, or course [*agmine*] (1.606) which is completely condensed [*condenso*] (1.606) and fills out [*explent*] (1.606) the flow [*corporis*] entirely in plenum. Since there is no void in the corporeal flows there can be no spaces, gaps, or discrete differences between the *minima* in the flow. In other words, the *minima partes* are not discrete *partes* but continuous dimensions, regions, or modulations in the topology of the simplex. The same corporeal flow can thus have different coexisting vectors, oscillations, and regions, which are all part of the same continuous simplex movement (1.607–10).

> *quae quoniam per se nequeunt constare, necessest*
> *haerere unde queant nulla ratione revelli.*
> *sunt igitur solida primordia simplicitate,*
> *quae minimis stipata partibus arte.*

Since these points are unable to exist by themselves, they must
be fixed fast so that they can under no condition be pulled away.

Therefore *corpora* exist in their continuous simplex
closely packed and tightly bound in their minimal parts.

Thus, all the *minima* hold together [*haerere*] (1.608) and cannot be separated [*revelli*] (1.608) from their continuum without being destroyed,
since it is their very condition [*ratione*] (1.608) for existence. To separate
the *minima* would be like trying to separate a ripple from a pond. This
flow and modulation of the *minima* is what defines the simplex continuum of the corporeal flows [*solida primordia simplicitate*] (1.609).

Lucretius is extremely clear on this point: the corporeal flows are
not assembled from a collection of minimal parts [*non ex illorum conventu
conciliata*] (1.611). The corporeal flows are not the product of some more
primary process; they are the primary process itself [*primordia*]. The
important point here is that the primary productive process itself is
radically differential and self-differentiated *quae minimis* (1.610). The corporeal flows have always been different to themselves, self-modulating,
creative, kinotopologically differentiating, that is, simplex [*sed magis
aeterna pollentia simplicitate*] (1.612). The *minima* were not brought together.
They always were together because they are identical with the topo-
kinetic modulation of the *corpora* themselves.

Against Zeno. If *corpora* were composed of divisible discrete parts, the
whole of being would be dead and immobile, just as Zeno argued.
Furthermore, Lucretius argues, there would be no difference between
the minimum and the sum of things (1.615–22).

> *Praeterea nisi erit minimum, parvissima quaeque*
> *corpora constabunt ex partibus infinitis,*
> *quippe ubi dimidiae partis pars semper habebit*
> *dimidiam partem nec res praefiniet ulla.*
> *ergo rerum inter summam minimamque quod escit,*
> *nil erit ut distet; nam quamvis funditus omnis*
> *summa sit infinita, tamen, parvissima quae sunt,*
> *ex infinitis constabunt partibus aeque.*

Moreover, unless a minimum exists, all the tiniest
corpora will be made up of an infinite number of parts,
since in that case the half of a half will always have
a half, nor will there be anything to set a limit.
Therefore what difference will there be between the sum of things
and the least of things? There will be none.

Lucretius does not mean that there is no relative or ordinal difference between smaller and larger infinities. He clearly acknowledges the existence of this difference in the case of larger and smaller duplex folds which have more or less void. Every fold contains and is contained by at least one other fold in an infinity of larger and smaller infinities. Even the flows of matter are composed of an infinite multiplicity of larger and smaller *minima*, which form the infinite ripples and waves on the contoured surface of the flows. This is why the universe is infinite in *all directions*, as we will see in later chapters. But this is not what is at issue in this passage.

What is at issue is whether the corporeal flows that produce these folds are themselves composed of discrete parts, which are in turn composed of parts, and so on to infinity, pace Zeno. Lucretius' answer to this question is central to the rejection of the modern atomist interpretation. *Corpora* do not and cannot have parts or they would be identical with *rerum* and we would have explained nothing of the *nature* of things, but only assumed that all of nature is made of things. We will have simply assumed what we hoped to explain. The world of discrete parts is the world of mechanism [*partes extra partes*]. This is the opposite of what Lucretius is arguing here. The concept of the simplex *minima* make this abundantly clear.

For Lucretius, all *rerum* are composed of indivisible, continuous, simplex flows of *corpora* whose folds [*duplex*] produce *loci* or pores [*foramina*] which in turn make possible a relative difference between interiority and exteriority. In other words, *corpora* produce things by folding; continuous *corpora* are the condition for the solidity [*solida*] and discreteness of things [*rerum*] in the first place. If things are defined by a limit around them, this distinguishes them from what they contain and what contains them. This limit itself is already presupposed to be a continuous limit around the thing that distinguishes it from others. Therefore, the very notion of discreteness already presupposes the continuity of the limit that provides a continuous and unbroken division or flow around the thing in the form of a fold [*duplex*]. If there is nothing that provides a continuous border around the thing, the thing cannot be what it is.

To interpret *De Rerum Natura* as a theory of discrete particles, atoms or things could not be more explicitly rejected by Lucretius throughout the text. The fact that the modern atomist interpretation was capable of remaining blind to so much of the text should stand as a testament to the dogmatism and violence of mechanistic materialism. Modern science

owes its debt therefore not to Lucretius, but to the brutal misinterpretation and mistranslation of his work, whose mechanistic reading essentially sent science in the wrong direction for hundreds of years until the
rediscovery of corporeal flows as 'quantum fields' in the mid-twentieth
century. Quantum fields have much more in common with Lucretius'
corpora than any atom or subatomic particle ever did. Fields and *corpora*
are both continuous, in constant motion or flux, indestructible, indivisible, topologically simplex, duplex and complex, and are responsible
(through waves and folding) for the production of all discrete things or
particles.[4]

Lucretius is concerned not primarily with things but with the relation
of things to their ground or condition [*ratione*]. Again, we should never
confuse *corpora* with *rerum*. *Rerum* are relatively discrete and divisible,
while *corpora* are continuous and indivisible. We have already covered
at length Lucretius' argument for this distinction, but it is important
to keep in mind when it comes to interpreting the status of the *minima*.
Minima cannot be discrete or they would just be small things, and this
would mean that Lucretius would be arguing that *corpora* are composed
of things, which is the opposite of what he says numerous times in Book
I – as we have shown. Things have conditions [*ratione*] and those conditions [*corpora*] must be different than that which they condition [*rerum*] or
we are espousing tautology and not philosophy.

Furthermore, the *minima* cannot be discrete parts because if nature
had been accustomed [*consuesset*] (1.629) to dissolve things into their
minimal parts, the parts would not be able to create anything else after
this because the parts only work on and in relation to other parts they
contain or are contained by. But if there were parts that had no other
kinotopic motion or dimensionality to them, they could not do or make
anything, and the universe would be dead and immobile. Additionally,
purely discrete particles are not sufficiently differentiated without the
limits of the fold around them that contains them. Without anything to
hold them they cannot, by definition, be discrete. Again, total discreteness entails total stasis.

Against the Philosophers

Only the folds of matter can account for the emergence of a true multiplicity of natural things. Nature cannot be made of one, two, or even
multiple kinds of substance. If it were, we would only find finite kinds of

things and not as we do, according to Lucretius, different kinds of things containing and contained by yet still more kinds of things in an indefinite multiplicity. Lucretius therefore rejects the monism, dualism, and pluralism of previous philosophers in the next lines of the poem.

Monism

If everything were composed of fire, as Heraclitus argues, then everything would be fire and appear as fire, which is clearly not the case. According to Lucretius, as long as all the parts of fire were also made of fire, they could only add up to fire and not to the varied appearance of our sensation (1.647–9). Furthermore, if there were only fire and no void at all, then there could be no motion [*possit mittere*] and no light or heat could even emerge [*raptim vaporem*] from the fire (1.647–9). If all of being were only one kind of thing and thus without void it could only be a solid, immobile block of homogeneous substance. Accordingly, one would have to explain the change of the substance from what it is into what it is not (fire into milk, for instance) by positing an *ex nihilo* creation of something from nothing. Furthermore, the emergence of such a different substance, even heat itself, would destroy its previous type, fire, as it was transformed into what it was not and therefore destroyed.

Corpora, according to Lucretius, are not monistic because they are not a kind of substance or element. Since they do not throw off or expel anything that can touch our touch [*adiectu tangere tactus*] (1.686–9), they themselves have no sensation. They are the conditions that produce sensation through the kinotopology of their folds. In other words, the conditions of sensation are themselves nothing sensible. Monism violates the basic law of conditionality [*ratioque*] and insists that something conditions itself, which is pure tautology. Monism, as Lucretius says, fights back against the senses with the senses [*contra sensus ab sensibus*] and thereby undermines the source or condition on which all knowledge of sensation itself is attained [*unde omnia credita pendent*] (1.693–6).

Dualism

Adding another kind of substance only doubles the problem. By joining air to fire or earth to water, according to Lucretius, the same problems of monism remain in failing to explain the vast diversity of things. Furthermore, by not including void, being grinds to a halt, frozen in a twofold state (1.712–13).

Pluralism

The pluralism of Empedocles gets closest to the truth because of the primacy of motion in his philosophy and its direct relationship to the material and geophilosophical conditions of his thought on the island of Acragas. Just as Empedocles was born from an island, so all of being, he says, begins in Love and isolation, perfect, total, and complete. But just as the Ionian sea flows around [*fluitans circum*] (1.718) the island of Acragas, spraying and assaulting [*aspargit*] (1.719) it with its harsh, briny waves [*virus*] (1.719) and dividing it [*mare dividit*] (1.720) from Aeolia [southern Italy], so Strife and chaos, in Empedocles' philosophy, emerge at the periphery of being and begin to swirl and attack the loving unity of the island. Just as the destructive whirlpool Charybdis introduces turbulence at the periphery of the island, so for Empedocles does Strife work its way inward into love, like a spiral, until it concentrates itself in the centre. Then just as Mt Etna centripetally 'gathers the anger of its flames' together and spews forth flames back outwards again, so the Strife that has accumulated in the centre of being begins to move back outwards centrifugally again to the periphery, and so on, forever.

For Empedocles, being may have begun as a perfect homogeneous and isolated spherical unity, but the constant vortical motions of Love and Strife are the real material kinetic conditions by which all of being and the elements are topologically distributed. Empedocles is the first Greek philosopher of the primacy of vortical motion. The work of Democritus and Epicurus is simply a further development of the idea of the ontological δινε or vortex that distributes and redistributes being. Love and Strife are not kinds of things, but continuous flows of motion that give order to things. Motion is the condition of things and not just another thing. That which conditions (motion) is thus different from that which is conditioned (the elements). Love and Strife are distinct but also two sides of the same vortical spiral folded and folding over itself. Empedocles is therefore also the first philosopher of the fold.

Lucretius thus admires the 'divine affection' [*divini pectoris*] (1.731) of Empedocles in a paradoxical way. However, what is apparently so 'divine' about Empedocles is not that he best describes the perfection of the gods, but actually that he completely undermines all divinity and perfection by reducing them to the purely vortical movement of matter. Divinity, for Empedocles, is nothing other than the material kinetic conditions that distribute, order, and disorder elemental matter. Divinity becomes material at the same time that matter becomes divine: the *corpore sancto* (1.38). Matter becomes creative through motion. The gods (Love and Strife) become identical with the fluid dynamics of nature.

Furthermore, what is so 'divine' about Empedocles, according to Lucretius, is that his philosophy is the one most explicitly modelled on his own material conditions in Acragas, and not on some abstract idea which bears no resemblance at all to the natural world he knows. Empedocles becomes, for Lucretius, the first precursor of transcendental materialism insofar as he describes precisely the regional (not universal) and material (not idealist) conditions for things; not how being is as such, but what being must at least be like in order for that which appears on Acragas to be.

Summary of Critique

Lucretius thus synthesises the four main points of his critique of early so-called materialist philosophies with respect to his own theory of the fold.

1. *No Void.* The philosophers say that the elements are porous and have motion but do not allow for the folding that would produce void that would allow for motion and pores. Thus, without the fold, they end up positing a complete motionless plenum (1.740–5).

2. *No Minima.* The philosophers posit elemental division by rarefaction and expansion of more and less parts, but in doing so, they fail to set an absolute limit or minima that would be undivided. Thus they set no limits on things, and therefore, as we have seen, cannot produce any discreteness or limitation at all. Again, since the fold is what creates the loop that defines discreteness, without the fold there is no discreteness; and if elements are made of parts and not flows, then there can be no fold (1.745–53).

3. *No Conditions.* The philosophers make all things soft and perishable and therefore do not distinguish between the conditions of things and the things themselves. This method fails to provide an account of the emergence of things and simply presupposes what needs to be explained.

4. *No Variation.* The philosophers insist that all things are made of a finite number of kinds of elements, which means that in order to explain the variation of appearance they have to appeal to *ex nihilo* creation. Alternatively, if the finite elements change into something they are not, then the element is destroyed *ex nihilo*.

In contrast to the abstractions of the early Greek philosophers, Lucretius puts forward his own materialist theory of poetic and philosophical method, as we will see in the next chapter.

Notes

1. See Kurt Gödel, *On Formally Undecidable Propositions of Principia Mathematica and Related Systems* (New York: Basic Books, 1962).
2. Geach used this phrase to describe Russell and McTaggart's theories of formal change. P. T. Geach, *God and the Soul* (New York: Schocken Books, 1969), 71–2. See also Alfred North Whitehead's theory of change in his *Concept of Nature* (Cambridge: Cambridge University Press, 1978), 73, 59. According to Whitehead, change is only 'the difference between actual occasions comprised in some determined event' and thus it is 'impossible to attribute "change" to any actual entity'. Change and motion thus relate to a succession of actual entities, and are constituted only by the differences among them. Every entity is simply 'what it is' and it becomes with its whole set of relations to other entities inherent therein; thus it *cannot change or move*. See also Leonard J. Eslick, 'Substance, Change, and Causality in Whitehead', *Philosophy and Phenomenological Research*, 18.4 (1958): 503–13. Whitehead's transition 'is not a real transition, not a flow or flux, and change so understood is merely a fact consequent upon the successive existence of a series of different unchangeable actual entities. *The very notion of change has been made incurably static*' (p. 510).
3. In contemporary physics this is called 'topological quantum field theory', the study of the folds, curves, bends and knots in quantum fields.
4. For an introduction and survey of quantum field theories and their possible unification with general relativity, see Lee Smolin, *The Trouble with Physics: The Rise of String Theory, the Fall of a Science, and What Comes Next* (Boston: Houghton Mifflin, 2006), and Lee Smolin, *Three Roads to Quantum Gravity* (New York: Basic Books, 2001).

8. The Emancipation of the Senses

Lucretius differs dramatically from previous philosophers in another important way: he grounds his philosophical method in material sensation and not in the pure intellection of the mind. This point becomes expressly clear in his comparison of previous philosophers with himself and the Delphic Oracle, beginning at lines 1.734–41.

> *Hic tamen et supra quos diximus inferiores*
> *partibus egregie multis multoque minores,*
> *quamquam multa bene ac divinitus invenientes*
> *ex adyto tam quam cordis responsa dedere*
> *sanctius et multo certa ratione magis quam*
> *Pythia quae tripodi a Phoebi lauroque profatur,*
> *principiis tamen in rerum fecere ruinas*
> *et graviter magni magno cecidere ibi casu.*

Nevertheless he and those I mentioned above, ranked
far below him in many ways and lesser by far,
although they made many [*multa*] fine and divine discoveries,
and issued responses from, so to speak, the shrine of their holy hearts
and with much more [*multo*] certain reasoning than
the Pythia who speaks from the tripod and laurel of Phoebi,
nevertheless about the first beginnings of things, they have come
crashing down, and though great, with a great fall they fell there mightily.

Empedocles was by far the greatest of the earliest philosophers because, as we have seen, his philosophy was the most grounded in the materiality of his natural geographical sensations on the island of Acragas. From this sensuous ground came the first real philosophy of vortical motion which undermined the peace, unity, and totality presupposed by the other philosophers.

According to Lucretius, the other philosophers produced inferior philosophies because they discovered their many [*multa*] (1.736) ideas in the divinity of the inner sanctuaries of their own minds [*divinitus invenientes ex adyto tam quam cordis responsa dedere sanctius*] (1.736–7). As such, their ideas were defined by the finite and fixed conditions [*certa ratione*] (1.738) of the minds from which they were taken. This is quite different than looking for one's philosophical conditions in the vastly more infinite natural or material conditions of the earth itself as Empedocles had done and as the Pythian priestess does on her tripod as she eats the laurels of the goddess Phoebi and speaks prophetically [*profatur*] (1.739) under the influence of the earth's volcanic fumes and her herbal beverages.

Just as Apollo the god of light tried to cover over the original watery spring [*fontes*] (1.230) of the Delphic Oracle, so the early philosophers tried to build their beginnings from their own inner temple on top of the natural flows of nature. Both came crashing down because both failed to start from nature and her wild springs [*fontes*], and began instead by trying to create their own temples on top of her, blocking her flows and damming them up into perfect and immobile totalities. The key to understanding Lucretius' critique of the early philosophers, and by contrast his own philosophical method, lies in their different relations to the Delphic Oracle.

Note on the English Translation

Before we go into detail on the significance of the Delphic Oracle for philosophical method, we need to make a small note on the English translation of these lines, which often make it sound as though Lucretius is condemning the Oracle when he is in fact praising it. Specifically, we should not translate Lucretius as saying that the early philosophers made discoveries with 'more holiness' than the Oracle. First of all, the Oracle at Delphi was widely accepted to be the most holy place on Earth; it was the *omphalos*, or navel of the earth, from which the earth spoke and gave birth. For Lucretius to say that the inner mind of some Greek philosopher is more holy than this makes no sense. But more importantly, the phrase 'more holy' is not even in the Latin text.

Englert's translation has run together two different aspects of the same sentence. Two separate points are made: 1) The early philosophers made *many* [*multa*] good and divine discoveries from the inner temples of their minds [*multa bene ac divinitus invenientes ex adyto*] (1.736);

and 2) in addition to these discoveries they also discovered *more* fixed or determinate conditions than Pythia [*multo certa ratione magis quam Pythia*] (1.738–9). The Latin word *multa/multo* can mean both many and more, but since the word is used *twice* in these lines with respect to two different parts of speech, a quantity of the noun 'discoveries' [*invenientes*] and a quality of the adjective 'certain or fixed' [*certa*], it makes much more sense that they would refer to two different types of things and to say, '*many good* and divine' things and '*more certain* conditions than Pythia'.

The difference between quantity and quality is not a trifle. Englert even follows the Latin accurately by translating 'many fine and divine discoveries', in line 1.736, but then goes on to add that they are also 'more holy', in line 1.738, where such a phrase is not present in the Latin text. In the lines above I have thus modified his translation to reflect this. In short, this is an important distinction because it more faithfully matches Lucretius' critique of the lesser philosophers and his admiration for nature and its material flows. Why would Lucretius say that the lesser philosophers discovered 'more holy' ideas than the Oracle, the most divine place on Earth, if ultimately he thinks that their temples completely failed and their philosophies led to a dead and immobile universe?

Another related but more ambiguous translation issue is the substitution of the goddess Phoebi by the god Apollo. Apollo is often called Phoebus Apollo, and sometimes just Phoebus, because he is the grandson of Phoebi, the goddess of light, purity, and prophecy, and because he eventually took over the Oracle. Lucretius, however, does not lack a Latin word for Apollo, but has chosen specifically to name the more primary titan goddess of the Oracle from which Apollo gets his name: Phoebus. It will soon become clear why it is important to remember that the goddess Phoebi is the more primary source and origin of Apollo's prophetic powers.

The Goddesses of Delphi

In order to understand how Lucretius' materialist philosophical method differs from the older philosophers, one must first understand something about the political, historical, and philosophical significance of the Oracle itself described in the poem. For Lucretius, the fact that the lesser philosophers failed to successfully build [*rerum fecere*] (1.740) their temples and that their great, heavy [*graviter*] (1.741) stones came falling back down [*ruinas*] (1.740) to earth, while Empedocles and the Oracle succeed, should be understood as indicative of Lucretius' own philosophical method. The oracular truth of Delphi is based on a materialist theory of knowledge or 'hylo-noetics' that inspires Lucretius' own philosophy. The structure of this truth emerges from the interrelation of four goddesses.

Gaia. First and foremost the Oracle is the endless source of the material flows of the earth goddess Gaia. The Oracle has always been the navel of the earth, the source [*fontes*] of an infinite flow of matter at the same time as it is an infinite source of knowledge. Delphi is therefore both the origin of truth and the origin of the endless source of material flows. It is the mouth-orifice through which Mother Earth speaks, the vulva through which she creates, and the navel or scar that connects her to that which made her (Chaos, according to Hesiod; Oceanus and Tethys, according to Homer). At Delphi, *the flows of matter and the flows of knowledge are one and the same sensuous flow.*

Telphusa. Before Apollo, the Delphic site was a freshwater spring presided over by the water nymph Telphusa. This was an archaic shrine and sacred oracle responsible for the production of prophetic knowledge.[1] Before the wellspring of the mind there was the wellspring of the earth from which the body and mind both emerged. Gaia therefore first presents her creative knowledge in the form of an endless spring or flow of water. The babbling of the spring is the speaking of nature. As Bachelard writes, 'These laughs, these babblings are, it seems, the childhood language of Nature. In the stream the child Nature speaks . . . Springs found in groves, these forest springs, so often hidden, are heard before being seen.'[2] The fresh spring of water speaks and then pools. The cold and still pool forms a mirror, not the mirror of subjective narcissism, but the cosmic mirror of nature itself, the eye through which nature sees itself by projecting itself to itself. This is the material kinetic origin of the emergence of oracular knowledge at Delphi.

Python. According to the Homeric *Hymn to Apollo*, Hera gave birth to a female dragon (*drakaina*) named Delphyne to guard the Oracle of Delphi. She was often also called Python or equated with Echidna, a dragon with the torso of a woman and the lower part of a snake, and was the consort of Typhon. Python is thus connected directly to the long pre-Greek history of the snake goddesses, whose spiral formations resisted the perfect circle exchange and other social and divine *moenera* invented by the Greeks.[3]

Kinetically, the spiral structure of knowledge is in distinct contrast to the circular rotations and spherical cosmologies of the Greek philosophers, where the circle or sphere, according to the philosophers, is the perfect motion because it allows the centre to remain unmoved and eternal. The spiral or fountain of Delphi is continuous, non-repeating, but also folded, and changing in a constant process of creation, destruction, and recreation. In short, the spiral nature of Python expresses the spiral nature of Delphic (and Lucretian) truth as open and non-total. Being is not a closed sphere, totality or 'one'. Therefore knowledge itself is open and incomplete. There is no direct inner or idealist knowledge of being in itself. Instead one thinks and knows only insofar as one rides the material flows of the spiral dragon. One knows only the transcendental material conditions of being and not being as such, as totality.

Phoebe. The titan goddess Phoebe, another early child of Gaia, is the goddess of light, intellect, and purity, from the Greek words *phoibos*, 'bright' or 'radiant', *phoibaô*, 'to purify', and *phoibazô*, 'to give prophecy'. According to Aeschylus, Delphi was originally held by Gaia, the first prophet, but then managed by Themis (Tradition), and then 'in the third allotment, with Themis' consent and not by force, another Titan, child of Khthon (Earth), Phoibe, took her seat here'.[4] Phoebe is thus the direct and consensual priestess of the Oracle. She is the purity of the clear spring waters; she is the prophetic truth of their babbling and the radiant light that illuminates them and allows them to see and reflect the world back to themselves. It is important to clarify here that the light does not come from beyond nor by force, nor is light sufficient on its own for oracular truth. Phoebe is herself a product of Gaia and only one of the important conditions, along with Themis, by which truth is generated, retained, and passed on to future generations in the light of the wooded clearing where the pure waters speak and are seen.

Apollo of Delphi

According to the Homeric *Hymn to Pythian Apollo*, Apollo, the grandson of Phoebe, searched all over the earth looking for a place to build a temple for his oracle, and could not find one. Finally, he went to Telphusa's spring and said, 'Telphusa, here I am minded [φρονέω] to make a glorious temple, an oracle for men, and hither they will always bring perfect hecatombs.'[5] He begins to lay the stone foundations for his temple and Telphusa becomes angry. She then tries to convince him that her loca-tion is just a noisy watering hole for nearby cattle and that he should go elsewhere. In particular, she says that it is his mind [φρονέω] that has convinced him to build here and that he is physically stronger than her. In contrast to mind and strength, she asks that he let her words into his heart and that they move him. 'But if you will be moved by me, for you, lord, are stronger and mightier than I, and your strength is very great; build at Crisa below the glades of Parnassus.'[6]

In contrast to his temple made of stone and the interiority within it modelled on the temple of his own mind, Telphusa's oracular shrine comes from the dark depths of the earth and comes through the infinite flows of matter into the light of the forest clearing. Just as Apollo is in contrast with Delphi, so Lucretius rejects the work of the lesser philosophers because they have built from the inner temples of their minds and not from the inner material conditions of the earth and its flows, as Empedocles and Delphi do.

Apollo is convinced by Telphusa and abandons his half-built temple at Delphi and moves a little further along. However, after building another temple, Apollo realises that near the spring and his new temple resides a she-dragon protectress, Typhaon, the consort of Typhon, or Python. Apollo now realises that Telphusa's spring is sacred, oracular, and valued enough to be protected by one of the greatest monsters on earth.[7] Apollo then kills the she-dragon.

> But nearby was a sweet flowing spring, and there with his strong bow the lord, the son of Zeus, killed the bloated, great she-dragon, a fierce monster wont to do great mischief to men upon earth, to men themselves and to their thin-shanked sheep; for she was a very bloody plague.[8]

The death of Python, like the life of Python, is turbulent, spiral, stochastic, and unleashes material flows of blood.

> Then, heavily, she lay there, racked with bitter pain, gasping for breath and rolling about on the ground. An unspeakable scream came into being, a more than mortal sound. All over the wood she writhed incessantly, now here, now there, and then life left her, breathing out blood.[9]

After slaying Python, Apollo returns to Telphusa, confronts her, buries her waters under a mountain, and takes over her oracular shrine.

> 'Telphusa, you were not, after all, to keep to yourself this lovely place by deceiving my mind, and pour forth your clear flowing water: here my renown shall also be and not yours alone?'

> Thus spoke the lord, far-working Apollo, and pushed over upon her a crag with a shower of rocks, hiding her streams: and he made himself an altar in a wooded grove very near the clear-flowing stream. In that place all men pray to the great one by the name Telphusian, because he humbled the stream of holy Telphusa.[10]

Not only are the clear flowing streams buried by the mountain, but so is Python's rotting body, from the Greek word *pythein*, πύθειν, after which Apollo and the place are named. Apollo thus becomes Pythian Apollo and Telphusian Apollo, and the Oracle becomes the Delphic Oracle after Delphyne, its spiralled she-dragon protectress. Although Aeschylus tries to smooth things over by saying that Phoebe gave Apollo the shrine for his birthday, the much older Homeric Hymns make clear the non-consensual history of patriarchal violence and idealism that historically took over the Oracle of the goddesses.

Apollo's conquest is only partial. Like many colonialists, Apollo still relied on the pre-existing oracular structure before him, with some modifications. The Delphic Oracle was still the same opening in the earth, the same voice of Gaia, the same clear, flowing, refreshing, and oracular waters. But in addition, the waters became encased inside the mountain itself: the noxious flows of Python's rotting body rose up into a chamber in the mountain, and the waters grew a special herb or laurel that gave oracular powers.

The Pythian priestess sat on a tripod, each leg of which was dedicated to a goddess: Hera, mother of Python, facing forward east; Pasiphae, the bull/moon goddess, facing right; and Ino, the goddess of pools and streams, facing left. The tripod was positioned over the chasm left by Python and the priestess would inhale the fumes emanating from Python's rotting body. The fumes would induce a theoleptic state, causing the priestess to channel the sacred words of the earth into oracular prophecy. In addition to these serpent-knowledge flows, Pythian priestesses would also drink a bowl of spring water mixed with the wild herbs or 'laurels' that grew around the Oracle. These oracular laurels induced a state of divine hallucination which facilitated the emergence of oracular truth, just as Telphusa's springs had done before.

This time, however, the male priests of Apollo would interpret the priestess's speech outside the enclosed oracle in the daylight of Apollo's revelation. Apollo could not reveal the truth on his own, but required the goddesses and priestess of the earth and their sensuous knowledge as a basis for interpretation. Apollonian truth is thus secondary to the hylo- and kino-noetic truth of matter itself. Just as Apollo's first temple, built from his own mind, crumbled, so philosophy crumbles when it fails to begin with nature.

In other words, the temple of Apollo is dead; long live the Oracle of Delphi. Apollo destroys Python, but Python remains the material condition under which oracular knowledge is possible. Even in her death the Pythonic spiral serpent continues to move, flux, and flow, generating the material conditions by which nature and truth are thought. Without these sensuous flows there is no thought, no truth, no knowledge, no Apollonian oracle at all. In short, thought remains fundamentally structured by sensation and not by some idealist inner temple. By valorising Delphic knowledge over the crumbling idealism of the lesser philosophers, Lucretius is valorising a materialist philosophy of knowledge based on the flows, fumes, and springs of nature itself.

Lucretius at Delphi

The similarities between Lucretius' philosophy and the Delphic Oracle are absolutely striking. Just as the flows of Python's fumes and the mountain springs [*fontes*] remain fundamentally infinite, indestructible, and hidden, so too do the corporeal flows of *De Rerum Natura* (1.778–81).

> *at primordia gignundis in rebus oportet*
> *naturam clandestinam caecamque adhibere,*
> *emineat ne quid, quod contra pugnet et obstet*
> *quo minus esse queat proprie quodcumque creatur.*

> But the first beginnings in creating things must
> of necessity possess a nature that is secret and invisible,
> so that nothing can show forth which would fight against and hinder
> whatever is created from being able to exist with its own character.

The corporeal flows of nature that create things must by nature remain hidden [*oportet naturam clandestinam*] (1.778–9). If corporeal flows had any essential qualities they would be no different than the monism, dualism, or pluralism of the lesser philosophers. Quality-less flows are the only way to ensure that an infinity of qualities can be produced through their infinite folding and assembly. Just as the Pythonic flows of sensuous knowledge do not repeat the same oracular message again and again, but are capable of responding to the singularity of the situations, sensations, bodies and questions they are embodied in, so the corporeal flows are not limited by finite kinds of connections.

Accordingly, qualities [*quali*] (1.818) are produced not by the mixing together of other pre-given qualities. Rather, the production of qualities is determined, like the flows of vapour and water at Delphi, by the exact and singular relations produced in the movements and folds of matter itself. Lucretius is very explicit about the production of quality through folding (1.817–22).

> atque eadem magni refert primordia saepe
> cum quibus et quali positura contineantur
> et quos inter se dent motus accipiantque;
> namque eadem caelum mare terras flumina solem
> constituunt, eadem fruges arbusta animantis,
> verum aliis alioque modo commixta moventur.

And it often makes a great difference with these same
first beginnings with what and in what position they are held,
and what motions they impart and receive among themselves.
For sky, sea, earth, rivers, and sun are composed
of the same things, and so too crops, trees, and animals,
but they are mixed with different things and are moved in different ways.

Qualities are produced by the distribution or placing [*positura*] (1.818) of *corpora* into specific relations of folded enclosure, binding, limitation, and holding [*contineantur*] (1.818). These material folds then produce different qualities depending on the relation between [*inter*] them as motion is transferred [*dent*] back, forth, and around the folds [*motus accipiantque*] (1.819). Each folded flow produces a unique quality depending on the size, speed, and motion of the flow that composed it, and what relations it enters into with other folds in motion [*commixta*] (1.822).

Therefore, by folding, the corporeal flow produces qualities according to two distinct, but interrelated, operations: 1) first, by folding, the corporeal flow produces a place [*positura or loci*] by holding or surrounding [*contineantur*] itself; 2) secondly, by transferring or circulating its motion back and forth [*motus accipiantque*] between the folds in a determinate kinetic mixture [*commixta*], it produces things with more or less affective capacities or qualities.

Therefore, Lucretius says, the idea that *corpora* already have qualities before the qualities are made is so ridiculous that the *corpora* will laugh so hard that they begin to cry (1.919–20).

fiet uti risu tremulo concussa cachinnent
et lacrimis salsis umectent ora genasque.

The first beginnings will rock with rolling laughter, howl aloud, and with salty tears drench their faces and cheeks.

This poetic locution is not a joke, although it is funny. The *corpora* are being explicitly contrasted with the fixed, static, and pre-determined qualities of elements and things. Instead of being qualitatively determined in advance, the *corpora* move with joyful [*fiet uti*], sensuous laughing [*risu*] that shakes [*concussa*] and quakes [*tremulo*] them, as they laugh out loud immoderately [*cachinnent*] so hard that they begin to flow [*umectent*] in tears (1.919–20).

Therefore, in contrast to static determinate things with qualities, the *corpora* are unqualified stochastic flows that move and shake with sensuous pleasure. Qualities come from material sensation, joy, pleasure, tears, and motion and not as pre-existing fixed aspects of things [*rerum*]. This immoderate sensuous expression of the *corpora* mirrors Lucretius' own sensuous and poetic response to the problem of philosophy, drawn from Dionysus, Delphi, and the Muses.

Dionysus at Delphi

After Apollo takes over Delphi, he later ends up sharing it with Dionysus. Dionysian cults eventually took up residence during the winter months at Delphi, while Apollo was away. Dionysus, as the bull god at Delphi, thus becomes connected to the goddess Pasiphae, the bull goddess, and to oracular truth revealed in the sacrifice of the bull during the rising of the star Sirius and the New Year. After the Dionysian sacrifice of the bull, its head is filled with bees which swarm from its skull like the living souls of the dead, producing life from death. The humming of the bees is heard as the 'voice' of the goddess, and the 'sound' of creation. Virgil describes the sound as 'the cymbals of the Great-Mother'.[11] Hence the other description of the Pythian maidens as 'Delphic bees'.[12]

Lucretius imagines himself as a philosophical poet participating directly in this tradition of materialist epistemology: the truth of the sensuous, and the emancipation of the sensuous in the name of truth (1.921–6).

> nec me animi fallit quam sint obscura; sed acri
> percussit thyrso laudis spes magna meum cor
> et simul incussit suavem mi in pectus amorem
> Musarum, quo nunc instinctus mente vigenti
> avia Pieridum peragro loca nullius ante
> trita solo.

> I am very aware how obscure these things are.
> But great hope for praise strikes my heart with a sharp thyrsus
> and at the same time strikes into my breast sweet love
> for the Muses. Now roused by this in my lively mind
> I am traversing the remote places of the Pierides, untrodden by the
> sole of anyone before.

The *corpora*, like the hidden material flows of vapours and water that move under the earth at Delphi, are obscure [*obscura*] (1.921) and invisible; but they are no less corporeal and material truths that can be attained through sensation. The great laudable discovery of the flows of matter penetrates [*acri*] Lucretius' heart [*cor*] and strikes [*percussit*] him like a sharp thyrsus [*thyrso*] that brings a love [*amorem*] for the Muses that will give him the power to discover these hidden matters (1.921–3).

The *thyrso* is the wand of Dionysus, a symbol of fertility, pleasure, and sensation. The wand was made of fennel, shaped like the shaft of the penis, and had a pine cone full of seeds on the end of it. As Euripides writes, 'Make the violent fennel-wands holy all round! Immediately the whole land will dance . . .'[13] The *thyrso* was then dipped in honey, connecting it both to the tradition of the oracular bees of Dionysus and to the alcoholic mead made from honey, and to the tradition of truth-telling through intoxication and thus to Delphi, where the Bacchic revels were held and connected to oracular revelation.

Lucretius' philosophical poem and materialism fit perfectly into this combination of truth through sensation and contrasts with the mental divination of the lesser philosophers. Lucretius allows his body to be penetrated by the *thyrso* and impregnated by its seeds. Through the introduction of matter into the body in the form of intoxicating or altering substances, mead, herbs, fumes, and so on, Lucretius' mind blooms [*mente vigenti*] (1.925) and comes to life. The mind is no longer its own little divine inner temple from which all things come forth, but itself becomes invaginated, unfolded to the exterior of the material world, through the sensation of the flows of Dionysus' seed laden honey-wine. The seeds are planted in Lucretius and they begin to grow, blossom, flourish like plants in his love-intoxicated mind.

With his living blooming mind Lucretius begins to wander [*peragro*] (1.926), just as Epicurus did through the universe, through the remote, obscure, wild, mountainous regions of the Muses, where no one has gone before: *Pieridum* (1.926). Sensuous love for the Muses, through Dionysus, is going to transport him to regions of nature yet untravelled. The Muses, the goddesses of song, dance, poetry, and drama,[14] live in the Pierides, but Lucretius is going to wander in the most wild and obscure parts of these mountains to bring back something new. This kind of invocation is in direct contrast to the Platonic idea that philosophy should only make use of the Muses through the intellect and not through sensation. As Plato writes in the *Timaeus*:

> And attunement, which has coursings akin to the circuits in our soul, has been given by the Muses to him who makes use of the Muses with his intellect, not for the purpose of irrational pleasure (which is what it's now thought to be useful for), but as an ally to the circuit of the soul within us once it's become untuned, for the purpose of bringing the soul into arrangement and concord with herself.[15]

Plato rejects the use of the Muses for pleasure and sensation, as they are most often invoked and as Lucretius invokes them. Instead, Plato believes that what is true about the arts is not their sensations, but the pure ideal forms that they express. Lucretius thus differs starkly both from Plato and from the typical use of the Muses. On the one hand, he does not subject the Muses and arts to a purely formal intellection from his own mind; on the other, he does not simply remain at the level of so-called irrational sensation either.

Instead, Lucretius wants to get at the material conditions by which sensation is itself produced. But these conditions can only be discovered through the material process which we are. Even though the most obscure regions of the Pierides are invisible, this does not mean they are immaterial. Lucretius thus discovers the material conditions of sensibility itself through sensation, and not as a rejection of it or a naive acceptance of it. In other words, he puts forward neither an anthropic constructivism nor a metaphysics, but a transcendental materialism; the minimal conditions that nature must at least be like such that our sensations are possible.

The Muses

In the Pierides, Lucretius drinks from the obscure flowing source of all things [*fontes*] and by revealing the material conditions of things also reveals the possibility of the emancipation of the senses from the *moeneric* knots of *religio* (1.927–34).

> *iuvat integros accedere fontis*
> *atque haurire iuvatque novos decerpere flores*
> *insignemque meo capiti petere inde coronam,*
> *unde prius nulli velarint tempora Musae;*
> *primum quod magnis doceo de rebus et artis*
> *religionum animum nodis exsolvere pergo,*
> *deinde quod obscura de re tam lucida pango*
> *carmina musaeo contingens cuncta lepore.*

> It is a joy to approach pure springs
> and to drink from them, and it is a joy to pick new flowers
> and to seek a pre-eminent crown for my head from that place
> whence the Muses had wreathed the temples of no one before;
> first because I am teaching about great things and proceeding
> to free the mind from the narrow bonds of religion,
> next because I am writing so clear a poem about so obscure
> a subject, touching everything with the charm of the Muses.

Lucretius receives pleasure [*iuvat*] from the undivided [*integros*] flows of mountain water sources [*fontes*] in the Pierides (1.927). Their dark, forested, mountain regions are nourishing and unbroken by social or political divisions or borders; they remain wild and undivided. Lucretius drinks or draws up [*haurire*] (1.928) the hidden waters from the pure [*integros*] (1.927) mountain springs, like those who drank from Telphusa's oracular Delphi in its hidden forest, just as others now drink from those same hidden waters inside the craggy Apollonian Delphi. Materialist knowledge has its kinetic source in the babbling and speaking of matter, which is internalised through the body.

Lucretius then receives pleasure by picking the young mountain flowers [*iuvatque novos decerpere flores*] (1.928) and forming them into a laurel wreath around his head, just as the Dionysians and Apollonians do at Delphi. But the laurels at Delphi are also oracular hallucinogens which make the mind come alive like a plant. The mind is freed not through the destruction of an external obstacle, but through the transformation of its inner material conditions: the body itself. The knots [*nodos*] (1.950) of *religio* are loosened or untied [*exsolvere*] (1.932). *Religio* is not something separate from nature, but rather a knot in nature itself. Topologically, a knot occurs when two or more corporeal flows have become stuck and are bound together in a seemingly fixed pattern. Unknotting does not mean the destruction of the flows, but rather their redistribution and open circulation into other formations.

Again the conditions of transformation are not ideological, but material. 'Changing' one's mind is literal and material for Lucretius. Or, as Marx writes, 'The philosophers have only interpreted the world, in various ways; the point is to change it.'[16] The emancipation of the senses quite literally means *moving* differently [*religionum animum nodis exsolvere pergo*] (1.932); to stop moving in the same knotted pattern and loosen up the bonds so that one can wander and move more freely [*pergo*]. The emancipation of the senses is thus a kinetic and material process.

The Honeyed Cup

Lucretius concludes this section on his poetic method with his famous description of his poetry as a cup of bitter medicine with honey around the lip. This description operates on several different levels at once (1.936–9).

sed vel uti pueris absinthia taetra medentes
cum dare conantur, prius oras pocula circum
contingunt mellis dulci flavoque liquore

just as when physicians try to give loathsome wormwood
to children, they first touch the rim of the cup
all around with the sweet, golden liquid of honey

Metaphorical. On the first most straightforward and uninteresting level, Lucretius is giving his Roman audience a revolutionary critique of all previously existing philosophy, which they do not want to hear, but he is giving it to them in 'sweet Pierian song', or poetic hexameter (1.947).

Methodological. On another level, however, this implies a certain philosophical methodology. It implies a rejection of at least three kinds of philosophical method. First, it is opposed to a purely idealist method of simply consulting one's 'inner temple of the mind', and deriving first principles exclusively from the mind itself or its supposed logical connection (analogical or otherwise) to being qua being. If this were the case no liquid or medicine of any kind would be needed, since the problem of knowledge is not related to the body at all. It is not a question of medicine but of pure thought.

Secondly, it is opposed to an abstract philosophical materialism, which, despite its claim to materialism, proceeds entirely without reference to any sensuous existence, history, or actual matter and merely through the bitter juice of logic and reason.

Thirdly, it is opposed to a naive empiricist account where all of nature is reduced to our sensuous experience of it. If nature is merely the sum total of our experiences of it, we have failed to explain the *nature* of things. The conditions by which things themselves appear are themselves not things. In other words, it is not enough to drink a cup of honey and simply indulge the senses. One needs the hidden bitter herbs as well.

The philosophical method implied by the honeyed cup of bitter herbs is distinct from all three methods above. For Lucretius, the knowledge of nature originates not in the mind, but in the nature of nature itself, of which our bodies and minds are folds. Thought is a product of this more primary ontogenetic process. Nature is the material condition under which thought occurs as such. Therefore, knowledge is material and kinetic and emerges first and foremost from the earth in fresh liquid flows, which the body draws up and invaginates into itself like a thyrsus penetrating one's heart. It emerges in places like the oracular freshwater spring of Telphusa and the volcanic gases at Delphi, anywhere where nature enters into the body and transforms it, giving it speech and thought – knowledge is not merely an interpretation of nature.

Thus, for Lucretius, knowledge of nature comes not through contemplation or interpretation but through material transformation. The honeyed cup of bitter herbs is not just a metaphor; the knowledge of nature comes through our enfolding of nature into our own body in different and transformative ways; in other words, through medicinal [*medentes*] (1.936) matter that makes us stronger and transforms our ways of thinking and being. Philosophical knowledge comes through the pleasure of the senses in the honey, but in combination with the transformative herbs the conditions of sensation themselves are altered, allowing us see that the senses themselves function only on the material condition of the body and the body only on the condition of nature itself, which must have a specific kind of structure to make this possible. From the difference introduced by this material transformation of medicine we are able to see that nature must be *at least* structured in certain ways to make such a change in sensation itself possible.

Nature is pleasurable to our senses in the honey, but also corporeally transformative in the bitter herbs. By ingesting the *pharmakon* of herbs, the body and mind are exposed and vulnerable to the externality of nature, which through nourishment and digestion becomes the enfolded and internal conditions of corporeal sensation itself. Through the vulnerability of the wound or orifice [*vulnere*] (1.34) of the body, the inside is exposed to the outside and revealed as nature folded, complicated in the body and explicated by the mind.

Philosophy, for Lucretius, is not reflection, contemplation, or communication, but material transformation. Knowledge never comes from the closed-up rotting *moenera* of a mind closed off from the world, but from the earth whose flows we are folds in, from whose pure externality our internality is produced. Material knowledge comes from our vulnerability to the flows of nature and capacity to affect and be affected by them. The honeyed cup of herbs is a corporeal flow that springs up from the earth and offers us the two basic conditions of philosophical thought: the pleasure of the senses in the honey and the transformative possibility of the herbs which expose to us the material conditions of sensation itself in nature.

Mythological. A third level of meaning in these lines is mythological. It is not a coincidence that the honeyed cup example comes directly after the valorisation of oracular truth and the inspiration of the Muses. The honeyed cup integrates three major material aspects of oracular or kinetic knowledge: 1) the honey made in the Dionysian bull's skull by the Delphic bees, whose humming is the oracular speech of life itself coming from dead matter; 2) the bitter herbs or laurels ingested by the Pythian priestess at Delphi to produce oracular speech by psycho-physical transformation; and 3) the fresh spring water of the Telphusan, Delphic, and wild mountain Pierian springs of the Muses that makes oracular and poetic speech possible.

The honeyed cup is therefore a poetic synthesis of all the oracular materials directly referenced in the previous lines of the poem. In addition, it is also a reference to the drinking cup of Dionysus. The *thyrso* wand and the honeyed cup are core materials at Dionysian festivals, related both to fertility, pleasure, and oracular speech. The fennel wand is the shaft of the penis, the pine cone at the end contains the seeds dipped in the sweet honey of desire. The wand is then dipped into the cup or vulva filled with bitter-sweet honey wine. The process brings pleasure, fertility, intoxication, and oracular speech.

The honeyed cup image operates at all three of these levels at once. The general implication that all three share is that the knowledge of nature comes not through contemplation, reflection, or communication, but through the emancipation of the senses by the material transformation of nature.

Matter flows and folds: these are the twin theses of Lucretian materialism. What remains to be revealed, however, is what consequences such flowing and folding have at the largest level of nature: the cosmos. In the final section of Book I, Lucretius proposes four of the most revolutionary and daring theses in the history of philosophy. He puts forward here an immanent theory of infinity, matter, and continuum without totality that reconciles his theory of the fold with his theory of multiplicity. This will be the topic of our next chapter.

Notes

1. Joseph Fontenrose, 'The Spring Telphusa', *Transactions and Proceedings of the American Philological Association*, 100 (1969): 119–31.
2. Gaston Bachelard, *Water and Dreams: An Essay on the Imagination of Matter* (Dallas: Pegasus Foundation, 1983), 32.
3. See Thomas Nail, *Being and Motion* (Oxford: Oxford University Press, under review), ch. 19.
4. Aeschylus, *Eumenides*, 1ff., trans. Herbert W. Smyth and Hugh Lloyd-Jones (Cambridge, MA: Harvard University Press, 1996). 'The Pythia [prophetic priestess of the oracle at Delphoi, speaks]: "First, in this prayer of mine, I give the place of highest honor among the gods to the first prophet, Gaia (Earth); and after her to Themis (Tradition), for she was the second to take this oracular seat of her mother, as legend tells. And in the third allotment, with Themis' consent and not by force, another Titanis, child of Khthon (Earth), Phoibe, took her seat here. She gave it as a birthday gift to Phoibos [Apollon]."'
5. *Hymn to Pythian Apollo*, 245–50, in Susan Shelmerdine, *The Homeric Hymns* (Newburyport: Focus Information Group, 1995).

6. *Hymn to Pythian Apollo*, 270.

7. Fontenrose, 'The Spring Telphusa'.

8. *Hymn to Pythian Apollo*, 300–10.

9. *Hymn to Pythian Apollo*, 360.

10. *Hymn to Pythian Apollo*, 375–85.

11. 'This intense drama of epiphany suggests that, as well as these connotations, the humming of the bee was actually heard as the "voice" of the goddess, the "sound" of creation. Virgil, for instance, describing the noise of howling and clashing made to attract swarming bees, says: "They clash the cymbals of the Great-Mother." Virgil, *Georgics*, IV, 63.' Anne Baring and Jules Cashford, *The Myth of the Goddess: Evolution of an Image* (London: Viking Arkana, 1991), 119.

12. Baring and Cashford, *The Myth of the Goddess*, 119. The tombs at Mycenae were shaped as beehives, as was the *omphalos* at Delphi in classical Greece, where Apollo ruled with his chief oracular priestess, the Pythia, who was called the Delphic Bee. In the Greek Homeric *Hymn to Hermes*, written down in the eighth century BC, the god Apollo speaks of three female seers as three bees or bee-maidens, who, like himself, practised divination.

13. Euripides, *Bacchae*, ll. 113–14, trans. Stephen J. Esposito (Newburyport: Focus Publishing, 1998), 28.

14. Calliope (epic poetry), Clio (history), Euterpe (flutes and lyric poetry), Thalia (comedy and pastoral poetry), Melpomene (tragedy), Terpsichore (dance), Erato (love poetry), Polyhymnia (sacred poetry), Urania (astronomy).

15. Plato, *The Timaeus*, 47e, in Plato, *Timaeus: Translation, Glossary, Appendices and Introductory Essay*, trans. Peter Kalkavage (Newburyport: Focus Publishing/R. Pullins, 2001).

16. Karl Marx, 'Theses on Feuerbach', in *Early Writings*, ed. Lucio Colletti and Rodney Livingstone (Harmondsworth: Penguin in association with New Left Review, 1992), 423, Thesis XI.

9. The Infinity of Matter

If nature is nothing but flows and folds of matter in motion, it follows that it must be infinite. This is the radical thesis put forward by Lucretius in the final lines of Book I. He makes this argument following four distinct theses on infinity: 1) all of nature is infinite; 2) space is infinite; 3) matter is infinite; and 4) the universe has no centre or origin. Put synthetically, each thesis forms a part of the following single definition of infinity: Nature is infinite because space and material flows alternate infinitely without beginning or end.

In order to further demonstrate the primacy of motion in Lucretius' poem, this chapter examines each of these theses and compares them in turn with some of the most recent findings in contemporary physics and cosmology. Although written almost two thousand years ago, Lucretius' ontological and cosmological theses remain surprisingly contemporary, cutting edge, and generally consistent with today's understanding of these matters.

First Thesis: Nature is Infinite

Lucretius' first thesis of infinity is that nature is infinite. This is the case not because nature is an infinite totality or unity, but because nature is an open infinity in all directions without final limit (1.960–4).

> *extremum porro nullius posse videtur*
> *esse, nisi ultra sit quod finiat, ut videatur*
> *quo non longius haec sensus natura sequatur.*
> *nunc extra summam quoniam nihil esse fatendum,*
> *non habet extremum, caret ergo fine modoque.*

And, moreover, it seems that there cannot be an end point for anything, unless there is something beyond it which limits it, so that there is seen

to be a place beyond which this nature of our senses cannot follow.
Now since it must be confessed that there is nothing outside the universe,
it does not have an endpoint, and therefore lacks boundary and limit.

This thesis is possible because of the paradox of the limit. The limit
is produced by active processes of limiting or bordering which, in the
very act of demarcation, produce an extension beyond the limit. Every
limit thus presupposes a division on either side. On one side of the limit,
for example, things are included, on the other they are excluded. Each
limitation therefore presupposes both *that which is limited* and that *which it
is limited by*. If things were only limited but not limited by anything else
they would not be limited. Therefore, all limitation presupposes that
which does the limiting. However, that which does the limiting is itself
not contained in the limits, which it produces. If it were, it would be no
different than that which is limited and thus there would be no limit.
Therefore, since every limit presupposes that which is limited and that
which it is limited by, nature cannot, by definition of limitation, be a
totality, a unity, or 'one'.

The second part of this paradox is that our senses can never follow
[*sequatur*] (1.962) beyond the limit. Although any given limitation can
be overcome by yet another larger limitation, it is only the process of
limitation itself, in the form of the fold of the corporeal flows, that provides the conditions of sensation, as was shown in Chapter 1. Therefore,
sensation cannot follow beyond the limit, but this does not mean that
the logic of the limit itself does not presuppose by its very nature such a
beyond which, in principle, could be sensed. Sensation thus follows the
process of limitation up to but never beyond the limit, though there is no
absolute or final limit of nature [*caret ergo fine modoque*] (1.964). Therefore,
just because there is no absolute or final limit does not mean that there
is not an infinite multiplicity of limitations alternating in turn like *corpora*
and *inane*.

Nature is Infinite in all Directions

Nature is therefore infinite not only in a single direction of limitation,
but in all its dimensions (1.965–7).

> *nec refert quibus adsistas regionibus eius;*
> *usque adeo, quem quisque locum possedit, in omnis*
> *tantundem partis infinitum omne relinquit.*

> It does not matter in what region of the universe you place yourself;
> so true is it that whatever place anyone occupies, he leaves
> the universe infinite in all directions to the same extent.

In whatever place [*locum*] (1.966) one occupies, the all of nature [*omnis*] (1.966) can be infinitely limited in all directions and dimensions without final limit [*omnis tantundem partis infinitum*] (1.966–7). Nature is therefore both infinitely large and infinitely small at the same time.

This is the second paradox of the limit. The same logic applied to the infinitely large is also applied to the infinitely small. Therefore, the universe is not only expanding and surpassing its own limits outward but also inward at the same time. In other words, because matter is nothing but corporeal flows in motion that make larger and smaller folds or limitations, and limitations are fundamentally unlimited, there can be no smallest fold.

This, of course, does not mean that there are no *minima* – as we have shown. There is no kind of matter smaller than the purely continuous assembly of *minima* in the corporeal flows. The *minima*, or kinotopological waves, in the corporeal flows are not divisible or made of anything smaller. But this does not mean that these purely continuous flows are not capable of producing increasingly smaller folds without limit.

As discussed previously, for Lucretius, there are larger and smaller infinities, but there is no 'smallest' infinity. This is the case because the *corpora/minima* are infinitely continuous and at no level divided. Accordingly, they are capable of an infinity of smaller folds within folds – like fractals. Their folding has no absolute limit because they are absolutely continuous. There is no point at which the corporeal flows can no longer fold, or else they would no longer be continuous, but in fact discrete, which is explicitly not the case for Lucretius.

Cosmological Infinity. Although Lucretius comes to the conclusion of infinite infinities or (unlimited limitation) through purely sensory and logical deductions without the aid of contemporary mathematics and experimental data, his conclusions are surprisingly consistent with cutting-edge physics on two points.

First, Lucretius' rejection of a so-called smallest infinity is mirrored by the rejection of 'singularities' in loop quantum gravity (LQG) theory. The idea that black holes and the big bang are effects of singularities, where matter has been contracted to a single infinitely smallest point, than which there is nothing smaller, not only contradicts general relativity and quantum theory, but also contradicts all our other mathematical formalisations of the universe. Loop quantum gravity physicists argue that there are no such things as singularities, but rather continuous quantum fields folded up very tightly. With respect to black holes, the first experimental evidence has been released giving support for this thesis.[1] With respect to the big bang, LQG cosmologists argue that our universe as we know it was not the first, but rather the effect of a previous contracting universe which had condensed to a very small but not absolutely singular region and then exploded back outwards, without passing through any kind of singularity. Instead of the 'big bang' they call it the 'big bounce'. The consequences of loop quantum cosmology are consistent with Lucretius' position that the universe is infinitely large insofar as nature has neither a beginning (singularity) nor an end, since it is continuously expanding in every direction.[2] All current observations suggest that our current universe is infinite within a margin of error of only 0.4 per cent.[3] In other words, the universe shows no sign of curvature, which would indicate that our flat space is ultimately part of a very large topological shape such as a sphere or torus. To the best of our knowledge, it is flat and infinite.

Secondly, Lucretius' rejection of an absolute limit of the small is mirrored both by quantum field theory and LQG in their discovery that quantum fields are both infinitely continuous and topologically differentiated. Just like Lucretius' *minima*-corporeal flows, quantum fields are infinitely continuous flows of moving matter whose vibrations, waves, and folds have no theoretically absolute smallest limit (since they are infinitely continuous). However, below a certain threshold such quantum modulations are paradoxically termed 'vacuum fluctuations', since 'nothing' seems to be generated from the movements. Vacuum assumes nothing, fluctuation assumes matter in motion; vacuum fluctuations are thus the active and creative capacity of matter to produce at increasingly smaller levels on an infinitely continuous surface. LQG goes the farthest by showing that even space is a product of quantum folding or loops.[4] Contemporary physics is therefore not moving farther away from Lucretian materialism, but only just now approaching it.

Entropy
According to Lucretius, nature flows infinitely. This means that the folds that it produces can be continuously sustained but also that these

folds continuously leak. Nature is always fleeing [*fugae*] from the things it makes, as Lucretius writes (1.982–3).

effugiumque fugae prolatet copia semper.

an opportunity for flight always extends the flight.

Nature is not the absence of limitation but the infinite *multiplication of limitation*, since it is by limitation that the limit itself is surpassed. Nature pushes itself to its limits and then goes beyond its own limits by making the limit. It makes itself, but in doing so surpasses itself. There are no folds or things which do not leak. The energy of the sun grows plants on the earth, which in turn release energy in the form of oxygen, which is in turn used as energy by animals to breathe, which is excreted as waste, and so on. What Lucretius is describing in these passages is entirely consistent with the second law of thermodynamics: natural entropy has a strong tendency to increase. By continually fleeing itself, nature is increasing the total disorder in the universe.

Regional entropy in closed systems still moves energy from hot to cold, from dense to less dense and so on, unless supplemented from outside. Thus, nature always escapes the things it makes and releases from them new flows to make something go further along, without destruction or *ex nihilo* creation. But nature must flee itself entropically, because if it did not, all matter would have, given infinite time, already flowed together into a single immobile block (1.992–4).

at nunc ni mirum requies data principiorum
corporibus nullast, quia nil est funditus imum,
quo quasi confluere et sedes ubi ponere possint.

But as things are, of course, no rest has been given to the *corporibus*
of the first beginnings, since there is absolutely no bottom
where they could flow together, so to speak, and take their places.

Nature is in constant motion without any rest. If the movement of the corporeal flows eventually ran out or stopped, it would have already flowed together [*confluere*] (1.994) into a single fixed point [*ponere*] (1.994). But since this is not the case, nature must be in constant motion, without rest, and it must flee from itself infinitely.

Nature keeps flowing and escaping because it is infinitely supplied with constant motion on all sides [*semper in adsiduo motu res quaeque geruntur partibus in cunctis*] (1.995–6). Motion is infinitely supplied by *corpora* from elsewhere [*infernaque suppeditantur ex infinito cita corpora materiai*] (1.996–7). Nature is entropic, but it is an infinite and open entropy, which is constantly resupplied by itself since there is no beginning and no end, but only an oscillation or bounce between universes. Things [*res*] are thus literally carried along by the *corpora* [*semper in adsiduo motu res quaeque geruntur*] (1.995), since things themselves are nothing other than the corporeal flows. The appearances of discreteness and rest are just that: relative appearances of the constant motion of corporeal flows. Matter in motion is the subterranean support [*infernaque suppeditantur*] (1.996) for things.

There is no lack of borders here, but rather an infinite proliferation of them. The air limits the hills, the mountains the air. Land bounds the sea, which is in turn bound by the land. Nothing comes from nothing and nothing is bounded by nothing. Everything is bounded by something else without any absolute limitation from outside [*nil est quod finiat extra*] (1.1001). Nature is not a boundless unity, but an infinitely limited multiplicity of limits without a fixed absolute limit. In other words, everything in nature moves, even its limits.

Second Thesis: Space is Infinite

Lucretius' second thesis on infinity is that space is infinite. This is the case because space is the product or pore of the folded flows, which are themselves infinite. Nature has no absolute limits because it is nothing other than the *process of delimitation itself*. The process of infinite delimitation has two infinite sides: space [*loci*] and *corpora* (1.1001–6).

> *est igitur natura loci spatiumque profundi,*
> *quod neque clara suo percurrere fulmina cursu*
> *perpetuo possint aevi labentia tractu*
> *nec prorsum facere ut restet minus ire meando;*
> *usque adeo passim patet ingens copia rebus*
> *finibus exemptis in cunctas undique partis.*

Therefore the nature of place and the space of the abyss
is such that neither could shining thunderbolts traverse it on their
endless journey, gliding on through an eternal tract of time,
nor, further, by their traveling make it so that there remained any less
to go, such an immense supply of space extends everywhere for things,
with no limits anywhere in any direction.

Space is what occurs on either side of the corporeal flow. When the corporeal flow folds back over itself, it produces an interior space that it contains but also an exterior space within which it is contained by an even larger fold, and so on, infinitely.

Space is not emptiness or lack; it is poured out like the other side of the fluid *corpora*. This is why Lucretius uses the word *profundi* (1.1001), meaning to pour out or forth, to shed copiously, to cause to flow, from *prō-fundo, fūdi, fūsum*, to describe it. Space flows and moves because *corpora* flow and move as two dimensions or facets of the same process. Flows produce space like bubbles or foam as they flow. This is precisely why a bolt or flow of lightning or light could never traverse [*percurrere*] (1.1002) space, because as it moves it is also the producer of the space which it traverses.

Here Lucretius uses the same Latin word from earlier to describe the continuous flow of light as it glides [*labentia*] (1.2) along forever. By flowing, light actually draws, drags, or pulls, [*tractu*] space along with it, leaving behind a trail [*tractu*] of space (1.1003). Again, this is precisely why its movement does not reduce the amount of space left to traverse [*nec prorsum facere ut restet minus ire meando*] (1.1005): because it makes the space by moving. Space and limits are therefore both produced by movement, which is precisely why there can be no absolute limit; because nature is always continually delimiting itself.

Another way of putting the point is that space is the result of an infinite delimitation. Delimitation is not the absence of limits but rather the multiplication of limits without absolute limit. Delimitation is at once both a marking out of a limit and the removal of that same limit with the line of the limit itself, since, as we said before, the line of the limit-flow itself is not inside that which it limits and is thus 'de-'limited.

For Lucretius, nature is not just infinite, it is an infinity of larger and smaller infinities. This is the case because space itself is infinite. Every time a flow folds and delimits an interior and exterior, it produces a space; but every interior and exterior space is itself capable of holding together an infinity of sub-folds within it. Therefore, space is not just infinitely large, it is also infinitely small insofar as it has no inner or outer limit to how many flows can fold within it. Every given fold makes possible an infinity of smaller folds within it. This infinity is possible, as we said before, due to the infinite continuity of the flow itself, but also because this infinite continuity, through folding, opens up an infinity of delimited larger and smaller spaces. Each delimited space is therefore its own *actual infinity* insofar as it contains an infinity of smaller spaces. Each space is actually and not just potentially infinite. Space is not therefore 'unlimited' but rather 'infinitely delimited'. Just as there is an infinity of larger and smaller folds, so there is an infinity of larger and smaller spaces produced by these folds.

Third Thesis: Matter is Infinite

The third thesis of infinity is that matter is infinite. Nature is the infinity of actual infinities produced by delimitation or folding. Lucretius says that nature 'forces *corpora* to be bounded by void, and what is void to be bounded by *corpora*, so that it thus renders the universe infinite by their alternation' (1.1012–13). Clearly, nature is not strictly unlimited but rather multi-limited or delimited such that it always exceeds its own limits. Nature is therefore fundamentally excessive, unrestrained [*inmoderatum*] (1.1013) with respect to itself, without final measure or numerical totality. Nature is, Lucretius says, '*simplice natura pateat*' (1.1013), openly simplex, or a one-fold-multiple-fold which continuously keeps on folding and unfolding without end.

In a brilliant move of micro/macro symmetry, Lucretius takes the smallest dimension of nature, the *minima* whose simplex continuity composes the kinotopological dimensionality of the *corpora*, and describes the 'whole' of nature in the same way. Nature itself is one open, non-whole simplex, whose continuous dimensions, modulations, waves, and bifurcations are indivisible, yet kinotopologically diverse and distinct qua corpora. Since nature itself is made up of nothing other than *simplex corpora*, it too, as an open and expanding 'whole', is nothing other than a much larger simplex. There are larger and smaller simplexes (complexes); nature is just the largest simplex, whose kinetic modulations and folds are nothing other the corporeal simplicated complexes themselves. Therefore if nature is infinite, then matter must also be infinite, since nature is nothing other than simplex of matter itself. The simplex of nature is that it is an infinity [*sim*] of actual infinities [*plex*].

Neither Contemplation or Communication

As such, there is no prearranged order which precedes nature's plication or folding. Nature orders itself ontogenetically without contemplation or communication (1.1021–3).

nam certe neque consilio primordia rerum
ordine se suo quaeque sagaci mente locarunt
nec quos quaeque darent motus pepigere profecto

For certainly not by design did the first beginnings of things
arrange themselves in their order with keen intent, nor surely
did they reach an agreement about what motions each would take.

The *corpora* or *primordia rerum* do not order or distribute [*locarunt*] (1.1022)
themselves according to the design [*consilio*] of a keen mental [*sagaci
mente*] order [*ordine*] which is given in advance of their material distribution (1.1021–2). Order does not pre-exist the process that produces
order in the first place. Order is the product of a more primary ordering process [*primordia*], which itself is not already pre-contained in some
idealist mental state, form, or blueprint, simply waiting to be expressed
in matter. The corporal flows are not like little minds; they have no
trace of anything mental or spiritual. Neither is order produced through
communication [*darent*] (1.1023). Corporeal flows are not fundamentally
linguistic entities ordered in and through the structure of language. In
short, the order [*primordia*] of nature is irreducible to the twin idealist and
anthropocentric categories of mind and language. Lucretius rejects the
Platonic legacy of both mental and linguistic eternal forms which would
provide a predetermined order or structure to nature.

Morphogenesis

Instead, Lucretius insists that order emerges from matter itself ontogenetically. Form emerges from matter morphogenetically (1.1024–8).

sed quia multa modis multis mutata per omne
ex infinito vexantur percita plagis,
omne genus motus et coetus experiundo
tandem deveniunt in talis disposituras,
qualibus haec rerum consistit summa creata,

But since many of them are moved in many ways throughout the
universe and from endless time are stirred up and excited by collisions,
by trying motions and unions of every kind
they finally arrive at arrangements like those
which produce and maintain this sum of things.

Through a series of infinite collisions and unordered shakings [*infinito
vexantur*] (1.1025), matter itself strikes and folds against itself [*plagis*]

(1.1025), exciting itself [*percita*] (1.1025) into experimental [*experiundo*] (1.1026) kinetic connections [*motus et coetus*] (1.1026) until finally coming into a self-ordered arrangement [*disposituras*] (1.1027).

A *dispositura* is thus a process of ordering which is immanent to the order which it produces. The emergence of order is nothing other than, beyond, or in excess of the process by which that same order is produced. Matter, for Lucretius, is capable of ordering itself without the aid of transcendent deities, idealist forms, or *ex nihilo* creation. This thesis is entirely compatible with most contemporary cosmologies insofar as they accept that all order in the universe came from the disordered movement of matter as it exploded outwards after the big bang or bounce. Lucretius' thesis about the self-ordering of matter is also echoed by a number of other contemporary phenomena in physics such as turbulence and weather systems, which describe the emergence of ordered patterns and metastable states from unordered or chaotic ones.[5]

Fourth Thesis: The Universe has no Centre

From Anaximander to Aristotle and the Stoics, practically all ancient philosophers argued that the universe is a perfect rotating sphere.[6] The rotating sphere provides the perfect image of being because it allows it to be both one single continuous unity, but also to distinguish between two fundamentally different parts of the same sphere: the centre point that remains static and unchanged no matter which way the sphere rotates, and the peripheral region that moves and changes around the centre: being and becoming. The same sphere is thus both eternal and mortal, unmoved and moved.

De Rerum Natura is the culmination of a minor tradition, beginning with Empedocles, Democritus, and Epicurus, which rejects the ontological fantasy of this perfect eternal rotating sphere (1.1053–7).

> *in medium summae quod dicunt omnia niti*
> *atque ideo mundi naturam stare sine ullis*
> *ictibus externis neque quoquam posse resolvi*
> *summa atque ima, quod in medium sint omnia nixa,*
> *ipsum si quicquam posse in se sistere credis,*

> that everything tends to the center of the universe,
> and that thus the nature of the world stands firm without any
> external blows, and that top and bottom cannot be undone

in any direction, because all things tend toward the center
(if you can believe that anything is able to stand on itself!)

For Lucretius, spherical being encounters several contradictions. First, as we have shown, the very notion of a limited sphere already presupposes that the sphere itself is bordered by something else outside it.

Secondly, as we have shown, the notion that all of being came from a single central point and caused the periphery to move, as in Anaximander, Aristotle, and others, contradicts Lucretius' rejection of *ex nihilo* creation. For Lucretius, motion comes from motion and not immobility.

Thirdly, the centre cannot be unmoved because all of matter is in motion and is subject to external collisions [*ictibus externis*] (1.1055). If some bit of matter were exempt from collisions, this could not have arisen as a consequence of moving matter itself. Absolute stasis could not have emerged from absolute motion just as motion could not have emerged from stasis; in both cases we must posit *ex nihilo* intervention.

Fourthly, and finally, if all of being stands or rests on the foundation of the unmoved centre, what does the centre itself stand upon? Spherology claims the contradictory position that the centre stands on itself [*posse in se sistere*] (1.1057). For Lucretius, this is another version of an *ex nihilo* tautology: the centre supports itself. However, every foundation, for Lucretius, in turn requires another foundation in an infinite multiplicity of mutually supportive foundations. There is no foundation which supports its own foundation *out of nothing*. In other words, the notion of the cosmic sphere encounters the same paradox at its internal limits as it does at its external limits (1.1068–9).

*sed vanus stolidis haec * * ***
*amplexi quod habent perv * * ***

But empty <error has commended> these false things to fools,
because they have tackled <the problem with circular reasoning.>

These philosophers of spherology and their followers have fallen into this false belief based on circular reasoning [*amplexi*] (1.1069) or tautology: the centre is its own foundation because it is; because they have held [*habent*] (1.1069) thought in a similarly encircled, encompassed, circular way [*amplexi*]. The projection of the cosmos as a sphere is nothing other than a projection of the kinetic structure of circular thought itself, which simply thinks itself alone in its inner temple, wrapped and folded over itself: *amplexi*. The sphere is the image of mental circular reflection and idealism. Philosophy based on reflection projects reflection on to the world in the form of the sphere: the perfect image of a mental or philosophical *moenera*. The problem is that they have modelled nature on the *amplex* of the fold, as if it had already been pre-folded, but they have failed to account for the flows that produce the *amplex* of the circle in the first place.

Janus: God of Motion

For Lucretius, the very logic of the cosmic sphere destroys itself. Einstein's self-proclaimed 'biggest mistake', of thinking of the universe as a sphere, is here already logically debunked by Lucretius (1.1011–13).[7]

> *nam qua cumque prius de parti corpora desse*
> *constitues, haec rebus erit pars ianua leti,*
> *hac se turba foras dabit omnis materiai.*

> For from whatever part you will first decide *corpora* are missing,
> this part will be the door of death for things,
> and by it the whole throng of matter will make its exit.

The idea that the sphere of nature is delimited without being delimited *by anything* is a contradiction. However, even if it were true that beyond the sphere was 'nothing', then once matter, in its turbulent [*turba*] (1.1013) motion, deviated slightly from its rotational course, it would exit the sphere and be destroyed. Following Lucretius' second thesis of materialism, nothing can be destroyed into nothing; such an exit would quickly result in the destruction of all matter, which, since it already would have happened after an infinity of time, is impossible.

Implicit in Lucretius' rebuttal of spherology is a certain (physically correct) assumption about the nature of motion: that it is turbulent. If the movement of matter was fundamentally laminar and regular, it is theoretically possible that it could rotate infinitely without deviation from its course. All matter would remain in a perfectly periodic sphere. Lucretius' argument is incisive here: movement is actually both the condition for the possibility and the impossibility of the spherical cosmos itself. Without motion the sphere remains a mere solid dead block of immobile and eternal matter. It is only when the sphere rotates that a distinction emerges between the unmoved centre and the changing periphery. The very conditions of the ontological distinction between being and becoming are therefore the movement of matter itself. However, once movement is allowed into nature, for Lucretius, it also becomes the condition for the impossibility of the sphere itself, because motion is fundamentally stochastic or turbulent. The greatest error of ancient philosophy was to have ignored the most important unsolved problem of classical physics: turbulence. If there is turbulence there can be no spherical cosmos.

The Latin word Lucretius uses here to describe the process by which the turbulent flow of matter would leave the sphere is *ianua* (1.1012), meaning passage or door, named after the Roman God Janus, the god of motion, passage, beginnings/endings, bridges, and doors, from the Proto-Indo-European root *ei-*, to go. Janus is different from all other gods because he has two faces that see both in front and behind at the same time. Even Mercury is limited in his motion by a single face. Janus, unlike Mercury, expresses perfectly the paradox of delimitation: that every delimitation is both an ending and a beginning at the same time. Every movement produces a limitation or space, while at the same time opening up that same limit through delimitation further along.

Movement is therefore never absolutely limited, but is itself the process of delimitation that opens itself up to the outside. Janus, unlike other gods, is not reducible to the division between internal and external, since one and the same god is both at once qua motion. Janus is the god of the fold. He is the god who has been folded over himself such that his inside is only the inside of his outside and his outside only the outside of his inside. If Venus is the goddess of desire and creation, Janus is her perfect complement because his destruction is at the same time a creation in another form. He is therein complemented by Diana, the goddess of birth and midwifery, but also the hunt, who brings new life, yet also takes it away.

Concluding Remark on Photonoetics

Lucretius concludes Book I with a short remark on photonoetics or the epistemology of natural light that echoes earlier remarks about the shores of light [*luminis oras*] (1.22) and the material conditions [*ratioque*] (1.148) for the appearance [*species*] of nature [*naturae*] (1.1114–17).

Haec sic pernosces parva perductus opella;
namque alid ex alio clarescet nec tibi caeca

nox iter eripiet, quin ultima naturai
pervideas: ita res accendent lumina rebus.

Thus you will learn these things, led with little effort.
For one thing will be clarified by another, nor will dark night
deprive you of your way, until you see deeply into the ultimate
principles of nature: so things will illuminate other things.

De Rerum Natura does not aim to reveal some metaphysical truth by the transcendent light of god or reason, or some other abstract Platonic principle like the 'rays of the sun and the clear shafts of the day' [*radii solis neque lucida tela diei*] (1.147). In contrast, Lucretius proposes to develop an entirely immanent philosophy in and through the senses which will nonetheless allow us to understand the transcendental structure [*naturae species ratioque*] (1.148) of the things of sensation.

In other words, *De Rerum Natura* is not simply reducible to an empirical description of *rerum*, leaving the *natura de rerum* untouched. Rather, it is a description of things insofar as they illuminate a path or *perductus* (1.1114) between them, which is not reducible to them, but which expresses and describes their very conditions. The luminous relations between things are themselves *not merely things* [*rerum*]. Things are nothing other than *corpora* in *relations* of folding [*nexum*] or weaving [*contextum*] (1.243), which produce the things.

What will cast light, what will be sensible, are things, but the distribution of the light itself, that is, the arrangement of things, the *primordia*, will be the transcendental condition for the things. In other words, a regime of light which is immanent to the things but which is itself not simply a thing constitutes the *corpora* or material kinetic conditions by which things illuminate one another in a given structure. The path of the *corpora* is the path of knowledge – the regime of light.

Just as the flows of light are the condition of visibility, so the flows of the *corpora* are the conditions by which things allow other things to appear. *Corpora* are the luminous flows of motion that connect things together with each other and allow them to illuminate one another. Just as we can learn more about the structure of light by examining the things which light illuminates (mirrors, paintings, windows, etc.), so we can learn more about the *corpora* through the folds or things which they create for sensation.

In this way, Lucretius rejects both the metaphysics of nature in itself (a light above things) and the empiricism of nature as it is simply to our senses (the light on things) by discovering the transcendental conditions or immanent structure of relations within which the things that appear come to appear (the light within and between things). The photonoetics of Lucretius' transcendental materialism is neither the light of god nor the light of the mind, but the real immanent light of things themselves in relation.

Conclusion

This chapter concludes our exposition of Book I of *De Rerum Natura* and the theories of the flow, fold, and infinity of matter. While Book I focused largely on methodological and ontological issues pertaining to the nature of philosophy, matter, and infinity, Book II, by contrast, focuses on more technical issues of the physics of matter and motion. These issues are of primary importance for the recovery of Lucretius' philosophical materialism and for overcoming his misinterpretation by modern atomists. We proceed now to a closer description of the motion of matter in Book II.

Notes

1. Davide Castelvecchi, 'Hawking's Latest Black Hole Paper Splits Physicists', *Nature*, 27 January 2016, http://www.scientificameri-can.com/article/hawking-s-latest-black-hole-paper-splits-physicists/ (accessed 29 July 2017).
2. See Carlo Rovelli, *Reality Is Not What It Seems: The Elementary Structure of Things*, trans. Simon Carnell and Erica Segre (New York: Penguin Random House, 2017); Sean Carroll, *The Big Picture: On the Origins of Life, Meaning, and the Universe Itself* (New York: Dutton, 2017).
3. 'Will the Universe Expand Forever?', NASA, http://map.gsfc.nasa.gov/universe/uni_shape.html (accessed 29 July 2017).
4. See Carlo Rovelli, 'Loop Quantum Gravity', *Physics World*, 16.11 (2003); Carlo Rovelli and Lee Smolin, 'Loop Space Representation of Quantum General Relativity', *Nuclear Physics*, B 331.1 (1990): 80; and Lee Smolin, *Three Roads to Quantum Gravity* (Oxford: Oxford University Press, 2000). See also Rovelli, *Reality Is Not What It Seems*.
5. See Manuel De Landa, *Intensive Science and Virtual Philosophy* (London: Continuum, 2002).

6. See Thomas Nail, *Being and Motion* (Oxford: Oxford University Press, under review), ch. 19.

7. Donald Goldsmith, *Einstein's Greatest Blunder? The Cosmological Constant and Other Fudge Factors in the Physics of the Universe* (Cambridge, MA: Harvard University Press, 1995).

Book II

10. The Motion of Matter

Lucretius begins Book II of *De Rerum Natura* with a detailed description of the movement of matter. In these often-cited lines, Lucretius defends, among other things, the pedetic motion of matter, and his materialist theory of will [*voluntas*].

Through a close reading of lines 1–332, this chapter and the next aim to overturn three prevailing interpretations of some of the most important lines in the entire poem: 1) that Lucretius believed that atoms fall through the void; 2) that one of those atoms randomly swerves; and 3) that this swerve grants freedom to the human mind in contrast to the mechanistic necessity of non-mental matter.[1]

Theory of the Eye

The proem of Book II opens with a poetic description of the pleasure of sensation grounded in the material conditions of turbulent motion. Perhaps counter-intuitively, Lucretius argues that the conditions of pleasure are nothing other than the pedesis of matter itself (2.1–4).

Suave, mari magno turbantibus aequora ventis
e terra magnum alterius spectare laborem;
non quia vexari quemquamst iucunda voluptas,
sed quibus ipse malis careas quia cernere suavest.

Sweet it is, when the wind whips the water on the great sea,
to gaze from the land upon the great struggles of another,
not because it is a delightful pleasure for anyone to be distressed,
but because it is sweet to observe those evils which you lack yourself.

How pleasurable [*suave*] (2.1) it is to gaze [*spectare*] (2.2) upon the turbulent movements [*turbantibus*] (2.1) and labour [*laborem*] (2.2) of the winds

upon the ocean waves from the calm of the shore [*terra*] (2.2). Or as the
French poet Paul Valéry writes:

> *Quel pur travail de fins éclairs consume*
> *Maint diamant d'imperceptible écume,*
> *Et quelle paix semble se concevoir!*

> What grace of light, what pure toil goes to form
> The manifold diamond of the elusive foam!
> What peace I feel begotten at that source![2]

Contrary to most of the history of philosophy, including Epicurus, pleasure, for Lucretius, is not the calm or peace which lacks all motion or
turbulence. Peace and calm are not the lack of activity but the process
of a purely excessive creation [*laborem*] (2.2) or 'conception' [*concevoir*], as
Valéry writes. Pleasure is not the eternal stasis of the unmoved mover,
God, or other such metaphysical absolutes. Pleasure [*voluptas*] (2.3) is the
sensation of an excess turbulent motion which inclines or desires along a
metastable curvature or fold that brings pleasure to itself. The sensation
of the curved eye captures the turbulence of light from the ocean scene
and gathers it together in a metastable state where it can fold over itself
in the eye and produce visual sensation or ocular pleasure. The transition from the turbulent sea to land is the same as the turbulent flows of
light gathered into the calm of the eye, which is again repeated in the
philosophical method of inquiring into the turbulent motion of matter
through the metastable state of the philosopher who holds things before
herself.

Things [*rerum*] appear stable and peaceful, but this brings no pleasure
or knowledge regarding the material conditions for the emergence of
these things. What brings pleasure and knowledge is *to see that the conditions of stability and peace are fundamentally turbulent and pedetic*. Through their
pedesis, things are formed and ordered into discrete objects. Order and
pedesis are not opposed and so neither are pleasure and pain. There is
no rejection of life and motion in Lucretius but rather an affirmation of
it.

The Eye of the Storm
The philosophical question is therefore also an aesthetic question:
pleasure/knowledge is not gleaned just by knowing that everything is
turbulence, but by *seeing* how such turbulence itself is the material kinetic

condition for the emergence of stability itself: morphogensis and meta-stability. Aesthetic and philosophical pleasure is achieved by the mental and visual sensation of the constitutive process of turbulent materialisation. The 'eye' is not just the *oculus*, but the fold itself. Every fold is an eye produced by the curvature of a turbulent flow. The fold harnesses a flow and by folding, senses or affects itself, extracting a bit of enjoyment or pleasure from the process without mastering it (2.4–7).

> *suave etiam belli certamina magna tueri*
> *per campos instructa tua sine parte pericli;*
> *sed nihil dulcius est, bene quam munita tenere*
> *edita doctrina sapientum templa serena,*

> Sweet, too, to gaze upon the great contests of war
> staged on the plains, when you are free from all danger.
> But nothing is more delightful than to possess sanctuaries
> which are lofty, peaceful, and well fortified by the teachings of the wise.

How sweet it is also to gaze with the eyes [*tueri*] (2.4) upon the experimental struggles [*pericli*] (2.5) of the military from a distance, knowing that one holds up a kind of wall [*munita tenere*] (2.6) around one's self made from the teachings of wisdom [*doctrina sapientum*] (2.7) that marks out a peaceful opening, broad space, or circuit [*templa*] (2.7) around one's self.

How pleasurable it is to take in through the eyes [*tueri*] these battles, as it is pleasurable to take in through the sensation of the mind the invisible and stochastic flows of the *corpora* that compose things. We watch and think not as separate from this process, but from a calm *within it*, like the metastable 'eye of the storm'. The eye is the calm which is not removed from the process, but rather that which is the stabilised product of the process by which one looks to the constitutive conditions of production. What pleasure there is to watch the storm from the eye, to be at once the product of such turbulence and to see the material conditions of this formation at the same time. The eye is the serene clearing or fold which is not separate from the flows, but which provides a stable vantage point from which to view the conditions of the fold itself.

The eye itself already expresses this process in the unique coloured turbulent patterns of the iris, which moves and shifts its aperture around the peaceful inner circle of the pupil. The eye is already a dynamic process of struggle back and forth between larger and smaller dilations which produce the serenity of the solid pupil, which lets light in from the outside and enjoys it. The 'eye of the storm' or the 'eye wall' [*munita*] (2.6) is the serene inner circle which is itself the product of the storm.

Eye and Mind

From the metastable position of the fold, or eye, which extracts an enjoyment and pleasure from that which flows through it, one can then look down upon the struggles of those who try to master this constitutive turbulence through thought, power, or prestige (2.9–14).

> *despicere unde queas alios passimque videre*
> *errare atque viam palantis quaerere vitae,*
> *certare ingenio, contendere nobilitate,*
> *noctes atque dies niti praestante labore*
> *ad summas emergere opes rerumque potiri.*
> *o miseras hominum mentes, o pectora caeca!*

> From there you can look down upon others and see them lose
> their way here and there and wander, seeking a road through life,
> struggling with their wits, striving with their high birth,
> exerting themselves night and day with outstanding effort
> to rise to the level of the greatest wealth and to have mastery over things.
> O wretched minds of men, O blind hearts!

The eye of pleasure looks down upon and despises [*despicere*] (2.9) those it sees [*videre*] (2.9) fighting [*certare*] (2.11) their way through life by their own ingenuity or wits [*ingenio*] (2.11), prestige [*nobilitate*] (2.11), or power [*labore*] (2.12) in order to accumulate more power, prestige, or property [*summas emergere opes*] (2.13). For Lucretius, the struggle for the ultimate domination of nature's pedetic flows [*rerumque potiri*] (2.13) is doomed to failure. While the eye simply enjoys the plication and sensation produced by the metastable motion of nature and extracts an enjoyment from its surplus in the form of the mountain spring [*fontes*] (2.590) or young flower [*flores*] (2.74), the mind [*mentes*] (2.14) or heart [*pectora*] (2.14) that tries to enslave the flows for its own accumulation and gain [*opes*] (2.13) and not for pleasure [*voluptas*] (2.3) is blind [*caeca*] (2.14), miserable, and lost. By trying to forge their own path they are lost. By trying to use their mind and heart alone to 'see', they are blind. The eye enjoys the flows, but when the mind and heart fail to 'see' and enjoy, like the eye, they become miserable in their impossible attempt to enslave nature.

Ocular Surplus

Nature produces pleasure through sensuous folding but also ensures that the folds will not become stuck in a pernicious cycle of crushing *moeneric* weight, by *unfolding them* as well (2.15–19).

> *qualibus in tenebris vitae quantisque periclis*
> *degitur hoc aevi quod cumquest! nonne videre*
> *nihil aliud sibi naturam latrare, nisi ut qui*
> *corpore seiunctus dolor absit, mente fruatur*
> *iucundo sensu cura semota metuque?*

> In what darkness of life and in what great dangers
> this little span of time is spent! Don't you see
> that nature cries out for nothing except that somehow
> pain be separated and absent from the *corpore*, and that she enjoy in the
> mind pleasant feelings, and be far from care and fear?

Many people spend their lives trying to control the corporeal flows of nature and trap them into fixed *moeneric* cycles of military, amorous, social, religious, or philosophical contracts and limits. Such attempts to enclose and enslave nature into *moeneric* circles produce rot, darkness [*tenebris*] (2.15), and blindness in the eye. The eye becomes shut and closed up. The circulation of the flows become sealed off and enclosed.

However, for Lucretius, we must see with our eyes [*videre*] (2.16) that nature desires nothing more than to open up [*latrare*] (2.17) these enclosures to the fresh air of the outside world. Nature unfolds the corporeal flows from the pernicious folds [*corpore seiunctus*] (2.18) of *moeneric* pain and striving [*cura*] (2.19). Much of contemporary philosophy has locked us up in the dark and rotting *moenera* of social and epistemological constructivism without access to the nature of things. Lucretius brings us back to the pleasure of a sensuous realism. He brings us back to the receptive pleasure of the eye or fold, opening and closing, folding and unfolding in sensation.

Nature asks for nothing in return for this (2.20–5). In nature there is no *moeneric* cycle of exchange. Everything flows. Nature unfolds only in order to scatter [*substernere*] (2.22) new seeds of desire for our enjoyment [*delicias* (2.22), *gratius* (2.23)]. Nature requires no fixed statues [*simulacra*] (2.24) to be erected or sacrifices to be made. There is only waste, excess, surplus, and the enjoyment of reordering or folding that waste, only to waste it or unfold it again.

Nature is not like states. It is an open system and not a closed one of debt-credit and servitude; it is an open system that simply redistributes. Pleasure comes from the redistribution of motion without compensation or exchange. Nature brings pleasure because it brings disjunction [*seiunctus*] (2.18) and redistribution [*coniunctum*] (1.451).

Bodies and Pleasure

The corporeal flows need nothing other than themselves to produce the auto-affective pleasure of the fold. The fold of matter is the self-affection or corporeal subjectivity of matter itself. Lucretius' poetics of the fold are strikingly beautiful on this point (2.29–33).

> *cum tamen inter se prostrati in gramine molli*
> *propter aquae rivum sub ramis arboris altae*
> *non magnis opibus iucunde corpora curant,*
> *praesertim cum tempestas adridet et anni*
> *tempora conspergunt viridantis floribus herbas.*

> when nevertheless people lie in groups on the soft grass
> beside a stream of water beneath the branches of a tall tree
> and at little expense delightfully tend to their bodies,
> especially when the weather smiles and the seasons of the year
> sprinkle the green-growing grass with flowers.

When bodies [*corpora*] (2.31) lay strewn like seeds [*prostrati*] (2.29) folded up in self-affection [*corpora curant*] (2.31) alongside the continuous flow of the river [*aquae rivum*] (2.30), they bring pleasure to themselves without any struggle or difficulty [*opibus*] (2.31). Especially when the season smiles and laughs [*tempestas adridet*] (2.32) it moves and shakes pedetically, but in a pleasant way that opens its mouth for enjoyment and sprinkles a flow of spittle [*conspergunt*] (2.33) down that strews the soft grass with flowering plants, like the seed of Ouranos, whose flows of seeds and shoots open and unfold into the air like the coitus of Flores and Favonus.

The 'strewing' or distributive flow of matter here is dramatic: nature strews delights [*substernere*] (2.22) for the strewn bodies [*prostrati*] (2.29) among the strewn flowers [*conspergunt*] (2.33). Matter does not need the stamp of form from God or the causality of an unmoved mover for its pleasure; it strews and pleasures itself alongside the river. The natural erotics of this image are later rendered explicit by the French poet Georges Bataille.

La mer se branle continuellement

The sea continuously jerks off.

La terre se branle parfois avec frénésie et tout s'écroule à sa surface.

The earth sometimes jerks off in a frenzy, and everything collapses on its
surface.[3]

The movements of nature are reciprocal and self-transformative and it is
precisely their fold or auto-affection that gives them erotic pleasure and
defines their material coitus. The movement of the ocean, as Bataille
writes, is therefore the coitus and pleasure of the earth and moon. But
the sea also pleasures itself when its waves fold over and touch each
other. The earth too has geological waves of strata that bend and fold
over themselves underground, whose tectonic movements give rise to a
volcanic ejaculation of spittle on to the surface.

Once we open our eyes and allow the material flows of light to
penetrate us with bodily pleasure, we see [*videmus*] (2.20) that the
whole struggle to enslave nature into fixed *moeneric* forms is laughable
(2.47–50).

quod si ridicula haec ludibriaque esse videmus,
re veraque metus hominum curaeque sequaces
nec metuunt sonitus armorum nec fera tela
audacterque inter reges rerumque potentis

But if we see that these things are ridiculous and frivolous,
and in truth the fears of men and the cares that follow them
neither fear the clash of arms nor fierce weapons,
and boldly walk among kings and those who have power over things

The quest of mastery makes us laugh [*ridicula*] (2.47) in mockery [*ludibriaque*] (2.47) of its impossibility. Just as nature smiles and laughs
[*adridet*] (2.32) in spring, creating pleasurable and creative motions of
self-affection, so we shake stochastically with joy as well by laughing in
response to the fear, darkness, and labours [*laboret*] (2.54) that plague
humanity in its self-created darkness [*tenebris*] (2.15). Just as children fear
the dark, so humanity has locked itself up in the darkness of the enclosed
moenera and now fears itself. For Lucretius, this *moenera* will not be broken
by the external light of a transcendent illumination beyond nature, but
by the material conditions of nature itself [*naturae species ratioque*]. As

Nietzsche writes, 'Perhaps laughter will then have formed an alliance with wisdom, perhaps only "gay science" will then be left.'[4]

The Motion of Matter

After this beautiful proem, Lucretius moves on to describe in detail the desirous and pedetic motions of the corporeal flows [*motu genitalia materiai corpora*] (2.62–3) that produce the folds of pleasure and their unfolding [*resolvant*] (2.63) found in sensuous things [*res*] (2.63).

Everything flows. If it did not, as we have seen, it would be a solid, inert block and nothing would exist, which is clearly not the case. Everything flows. If it did not the totality of matter would be One and limited, which is a contradiction of the process of delimitation itself. Matter is continuous flow without beginning or end. Things are simply relay points within a larger continuous movement (2.78–9).

> *inque brevi spatio mutantur saecla animantum*
> *et quasi cursores vitai lampada tradunt.*

> generations of living creatures change
> and like runners pass on the torch of life.

Matter has no fixed essences or forms but only regional topological folds sustained by an infinite flow of movement which courses through them like relays. Creation is never *ex nihilo*, but is transmitted [*tradunt*] (2.79) like torches [*lampada*] (2.79) between runners. Matter is never created or destroyed but simply transmitted through motion into another distribution (2.80–2).

> *Si cessare putas rerum primordia posse*
> *cessandoque novos rerum progignere motus,*
> *avius a vera longe ratione vagaris.*

> If you think that the first beginnings of things can stop
> and by stopping produce new motions among things,
> you are wandering astray, far from the true conditions.

Things are less like crystallisations than like intervallic habits or eddies in a river. They repeat but only on the condition that what is repeated is the movement of repetition itself, and not a fixed thing that exists independently or that can cut itself off from the flows that sustain it.[5]

Intervallis

The structure or pattern of corporeal folds, according to Lucretius, are thus defined by their intervals [*intervallis*] of motion (2.97–9).

> *sed magis adsiduo varioque exercita motu*
> *partim intervallis magnis confulta resultant,*
> *pars etiam brevibus spatiis vexantur ab ictu.*

> Rather, driven on in continuous and varied motion,
> some are pressed together and then leap apart at great intervals,
> others move violently at small distances after the blow.

Matter flows in unbroken [*constat*] (2.95) continuous [*adsiduo*] (2.97) variation [*varioque*] (2.97), coming together [*confulta*] (2.98) and returning back to itself [*reddita*] (2.96) in folds, but also moving apart in certain intervals of motion [*motu partim intervallis*] (2.97–8), creating short spaces [*brevibus spatiis*] (2.99) between their pedetic or 'shaking' motions [*vexantur*] (2.99).

Matter does not simply fold once and for all or in one single shape or pattern, but continuously folds again and again in various ways and various intervals that define the kind of thing [*res*] that it is. Matter flows and folds over itself; but once it returns and connects to itself again it creates an interval. An interval is the movement between the departure of a flow from a bifurcation point and its return or arrival to that same point. This point is a point of periodicity or what we should, more kinetically, call an interval. While the concept of identity has been historically conceptualised as a purely logical or formal concept, often relating to essences, the term *intervallis* more accurately reflects the primacy of motion of things which cycle and return within the kinetic limits of their identity. Identity is thus a product or an effect of a more primary process of intervallic motion. The interval is the area of a flow where the flow habitually intersects with itself and appears to be identical with itself (Fig. 10.1).

An interval is the kinetic repetition of the self-intersection of a flow, but this does not mean that the flow has been arrested or rendered completely discrete. The interval is simply a slice or selection from the continuous process of joined motion. When we mistake the interval for a static being, we lose the flow entirely; we see only the product without the motion that composed it. It is as if we looked at a Jackson Pollock painting and wondered how he was able to paint such wonderfully

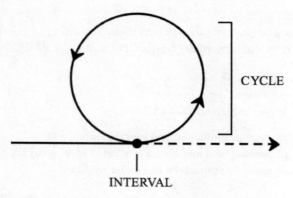

Figure 10.1 Interval.

detailed replicas of paint splatter; we have misunderstood everything about the kinaesthetics of painting.

Intervals produce identity through motion. Since a flow is a continuous movement, the junction is not only continually receiving a constant source of new motion from outside, but also losing some motion that passes through the junction. Thus, a junction is only a regional capture of motion in a certain interval. When it intersects itself it is actually intersecting itself at a different point in the flow each time. Since a flow is also a continually moving and self-differentiating process, it is impossible that it should ever be the same as itself. But insofar as it is redirected into a repeating pattern of motion, the pattern of motion repeats and we say it is 'identical'.

Thus, we can say, against Heraclitus, that we *can* step in the same river twice, but only on the condition that the river also turns over itself in local eddies and whirlpools.[6] Each interval of the eddy is composed of entirely different water molecules, but the interval of the whirlpool persists; the interval remains 'the same'. Each period in the eddy of the river is composed of entirely different water molecules, but the cycle of the whirlpool persists; the cycle remains 'the same', like Valéry's depiction of Narcissus' reflective pool.

Admire dans Narcisse un éternel retour
Vers Gonde où son image offerte à son amour
Propose à sa beauté toute sa connaissance:
Tout mon sort n'est qu'obéissance
A la force de mon amour.

Admire in Narcissus the eternal return
towards the mirror of the water which offers his image to his love,
and to his beauty all his knowledge:
the tranquil water awaits where I extend my arms:
I do not resist this pure madness.[7]

As the continuous flows of being slow and pool into cyclical folds, they make possible a smooth and stable surface in which sensible forms can emerge. As Gide writes:

> Alas, when will Time cease its flight and allow this flow to rest? Forms, divine and perennial forms which only wait for rest in order to reappear! O when, in what night, will you crystallize again?
>
> Paradise must always be re-created. It is not in some remote Thule; it lingers under the appearance. Everything holds within itself, as potentiality, the intimate harmony of its being, just as every salt holds within itself the archetype of its crystal. And a time of silent night will come when the waters will descend, more dense; then, in the unperturbed abysses, the secret crystals will bloom . . .[8]

The complete process of movement from point to point is the interval of the junction. The interval of the junction can be defined as the unity of the junction, but only in a strictly kinetic way. Since the junction is only a fold in a continual flow that constantly enters and exits the junction, renewing it each time, its unity or interval cannot be said to be the unity of ideal identity, but of a practical or kinetic *intervallis*. It is the unity of a process of differentiation: an interval. Just like a whirlpool in a river, its interval is only a unity of a differential process refreshed each time with new water: 'paradise re-created in appearance', as Gide writes. Lucretius thus replaces the concepts of identity and unity with the concepts of interval and fold.

Perplexis
For Lucretius, there are thus larger and smaller intervals and more or less densely packed intervals. The differences in size and density of the intervals define the characteristics of the composite thing produced (2.100–4).

et quae cumque magis condenso conciliatu
exiguis intervallis convecta resultant,
indupedita suis perplexis ipsa figuris,

haec validas saxi radices et fera ferri
corpora constituunt et cetera de genere horum.

And whichever ones in their more tightly condensed union
meet and leap back at tiny intervals,
and are themselves tangled together in their intricate shapes,
these make up the strong roots of rock
and the constitutive matters of iron, and others of this type.

The frequency, size, and density of the kinetic intervals determine how matter is brought back to itself and collected [*convecta*] (2.101) into a specific folded [*perplexis*] (2.102) form or shape [*figuris*] (2.102). For example, rocks and other hard things are made of very small and tightly folded intervals, making it difficult for them to move very far apart or be easily separated. Other material movements habitually return or recur [*recursant*] (2.106) at larger intervals [*magnis intervallis*] (2.107) that produce air [*aera*] (2.107) and light [*lumina solis*] (2.108).

Others move so far that they do not return and are therefore rejected [*reiecta*] (2.110) entirely and never form a self-receptive unity of their motion [*consociare etiam motus potuere recepta*] (2.111). Lucretius' kinetic theory of *intervallis* and *perplexis* is physically consistent with Einstein's kinetic theory of matter: all of matter is moving; solids move in small and dense intervals, liquids move in larger and less dense patterns, and gases move in the largest and least dense intervals.

Turbulence

Again, prefiguring Einstein's theory that the kinetic motion of the molecules inside solids, liquids, and gases was stochastic, Lucretius put forward a theory consistent with this almost two thousand years earlier: that the movement of matter is fundamentally pedetic. More generally, Lucretius was the first to discover and name turbulent motion. This discovery is most often credited to the Scottish botanist Robert Brown in 1827. Thus, stochastic or pedetic motion was first called 'Brownian motion'. But in the next lines of Book II of *De Rerum Natura*, and arguably earlier in Book I's description of turbulent air and water flows (1.1–20), Lucretius was clearly the first to describe this motion in his account of the movement of dust motes in sunlight. Brownian or pedetic motion should therefore more accurately be called 'Lucretian motion' (2.112–13).

Cuius, uti memoro, rei simulacrum et imago
ante oculos semper nobis versatur et instat.

Of this process, as I recall, a model and image
always exists and is present before our eyes.

According to Lucretius, an example of the type of motion which defines
the movement of the *corpora*, its turbulence, intervals, and *perplexis*, is
always before our eyes [*ante oculos*] (2.113). There is a double meaning
of the Latin word *ante* here, meaning both 'present' and 'before', that
we should draw attention to. The movement of the corporeal flows of
matter, for Lucretius, is in one sense completely present [*ante*] to our eyes
insofar as things are nothing other than the folds of the *corpora* themselves. However, the *corpora* are also before [*ante*] our eyes in the sense
that they are the material conditions for both the things we see and the
eye itself as a thing. They are thus 'before' in both a chronological and
conditional sense, and as such are themselves not sensible. Just like the
example of the dust motes, the movement of the *corpora* is both present to
our eyes in the movement of the motes, but also before our eyes insofar
as the pedetic air patterns remains invisible to our eyes. Again, the eye
[*oculos*] already describes the intervallic flow of light through the ocular
fold and thus the noetic/aesthetic pleasure gained from the image [*simulacrum et imago*] of the motes in the sunlight (2.114–20).

contemplator enim, cum solis lumina cumque
inserti fundunt radii per opaca domorum:
multa minuta modis multis per inane videbis
corpora misceri radiorum lumine in ipso
et vel ut aeterno certamine proelia pugnas
edere turmatim certantia nec dare pausam,
conciliis et discidiis exercita crebris;

For gaze closely, whenever the rays of the sun enter
and pour their light through the dark places of houses.
You will see many minute *corpora* mixed in many ways
through empty space in the very light of the rays,
and, as if in an unending struggle, giving rise to battles
and fights, struggling in squadrons and never taking a rest,
driven on by their frequent meetings and partings.

When the rays [*radii*] (2.115) of light pour [*fundunt*] (2.115) in through
the dark places of an enclosed house [*opaca domorum*] (2.115), like *corpora*

flowing through space and like the light pouring into the eye itself, we see [*videbis*] (2.116) minute bodies [*corpora*] (2.117) mixing [*misceri*] (2.116) and engaging in an infinite turbulent struggle [*aeterno certamine proelia*] (2.118) without rest [*pausam*] (2.119). This is a sensuous image for the eye of how the *primordia rerum* are scattered [*iactari*] (2.122) about pedetically. It is also a sensuous image for the mind [*notitiai*] (2.124) or a concept that renders [*dare*] (2.124) a trace [*vestigia*] (2.124) of how the corporeal flows move in nature. The dust motes that we can see with the eye are like the *rerum* that are driven by the invisible corporeal flows of air that swirl turbulently. We watch them enter into battle as things enter into battle with other things. We watch them with our eye from the calm of the fold just as we watch the war games from the safety of the circular opening, a safe place of vision (2.125–8).

> *Hoc etiam magis haec animum te advertere par est*
> *corpora quae in solis radiis turbare videntur,*
> *quod tales turbae motus quoque materiai*
> *significant clandestinos caecosque subesse.*

> It is even more important that you turn your attention to these bodies
> that are seen to create disturbances in the rays of the sun,
> because such disturbances indicate that there are also motions
> of matter lurking below, hidden and unseen.

The motes, for Lucretius, do not refer to the battle of discrete atoms floating through the void. Rather, what is most important to see [*videntur*] (2.126) in this example is that the motes are only the sensible indication of the more primary, subterranean, and invisible [*materiai significant clandestinos caecosque subesse*] (2.125–6) turbulent movements [*turbae motus*] (2.127) of air whose corporeal flows [*corpora*] (2.126) are the true material conditions for the sensible motes. In other words, *corpora* are not discrete; only *rerum* are discrete. The turbulent flows of air are the *corpora* and the motes are the sensible *rerum* or things constituted and directed by the turbulent motions of air.

The motes are struck, just like the *rerum*, by more primary invisible collisions that produce a collective change [*commutare*] (2.130) in the whole distribution of motion as it folds back over itself [*viam retroque repulsa*] (2.130) into metastable patterns of spirals, circles, and other *contextum* or circulations. One should never confuse *corpora* with *rerum*. The example of the dust motes is no exception. The invisible *corpora* [*primordia rerum*] are the primary or first movers [*prima moventur enim*] (2.133) of all wandering things [*omnibus error*] (2.132).

To synthesise these points: first, the corporeal flows move themselves. Then, these flows come together with themselves [*parvo sunt corpora conciliatu*] (2.134) and compose the smallest composites or folds [*iuncta, coniuncta*]. These in turn move and stir up [*inpulsa cientur*] (2.136) increasingly larger composites. Eventually, these composites become large enough to appear to our senses in the light of the sun [*nostros ad sensus . . . solis quae lumine*] (2.139–40). We call them 'things'.

The Speed of Matter

The speed of matter, for Lucretius, is related directly to the density and size of the corporeal folds that are moving. He gives the beautiful example of the sun's light (2.147–8).

> *quam subito soleat sol ortus tempore tali*
> *convestire sua perfundens omnia luce,*

> how suddenly the sun, rising at this time, is accustomed
> to pour forth and clothe everything with its light,

The speed of corporeal flows [*mobilitas sit reddita materiai corporibus*] (2.142–3) can be understood easily when we consider the way in which the sun scatters [*spargit*] (2.144) its light over the earth [*lumine terras*] (2.144), pouring [*perfundens*] (2.148) forth its flows of light over all [*omnia luce*] (2.148). The sun's flows of warm light [*vaporis*] (2.153), however, are not instantaneous. This is because they are not travelling through an empty space, but are held back not only through waves of air [*aerias quasi dum diverberat undas*] (2.152), but also by themselves, just as in the case of the dust motes. The small bodies [*corpuscula*] (2.153) of warm heat [*vaporis*] do not move in a pure flow like unfolded *corpora* but rather travel in small groupings of folded-up sensible qualities [*complexa meant inter se conque globata*] (2.154). The motion of the corporeal flows is hindered by the folded structure [*complexa*] (2.154) of the *vaporis*, since the motion of the fold requires the corporeal flows to turn back [*retrahuntur*] (2.155) on themselves as they move forward and different folds come in the way of the others [*officiuntur*] (2.156), causing their collective motion to proceed more slowly [*cogantur tardius ire*] (2.156).

In contrast to this, unfolded corporeal flows move without any thing [*res*] delaying their motion (2.157–64).

at quae sunt solida primordia simplicitate,
cum per inane meant vacuum nec res remoratur
ulla foris atque ipsa suis e partibus unum,
unum, in quem coepere, locum conixa feruntur,
debent ni mirum praecellere mobilitate
et multo citius ferri quam lumina solis
multiplexque loci spatium transcurrere eodem
tempore quo solis pervolgant fulgura caelum.

But the primary *corpora* which exist in their solid simplex,
when they travel through the empty void, and nothing delays them
from without and they, themselves forming a unity from their own parts,
are carried along in haste in the one direction in which
they began to move, ought of course to surpass in speed
and be carried along much more quickly than the light of the sun,
and cover many times the extent of space in the same
time in which the flashing light of the sun spreads across the sky.

The continuous and simplex corporeal flows [*solida primordia simplicitate*] (2.157), unlike the sensible folds [*complex*] (2.155) of the sun's heat and light [*vaporis*] (2.153), move, not through the waves of air, but through the void [*inane*] (2.158), because things [*res*] (2.158) do not block their movement from outside [*remoratur ulla foris*] (2.158-9). Since the *corpora* are the material conditions that compose and change things, they are not slowed down and blocked by things, unless they themselves begin to fold, and thereby produce an internal delay in themselves and collide with other folds.

However, insofar as the *corpora* remain unfolded they remain *prima moventur* (2.133) and therefore cannot be delayed by that which they cause to move. The *corpora*, insofar as they form a continuous and simplex unity of their 'parts' [*partibus*], or *minima*, cannot be divided from what they are, and therefore cannot be delayed with respect to themselves. However, insofar as the folds they produce are considered, they can move more or less quickly with respect to other folds. In fact, the speed of the corporeal flows is faster even than the light of the sun travelling through the multi-folded space, faster than a flash of light across the sky.

Corporeal flows are faster than the speed of light precisely because they are continuous [*solida*] (2.157) and infinite. This bold statement should not surprise us. The concept of speed as 'movement through space in time' only makes sense for things [*rerum*] which have folded extension in space [*loci*] and time [*tempore*]. Lucretius has been quite clear that the movement and modulation of the *corpora* does not occur in time and space [*nec tempore/loci certo*] (2.259–60). *Corpora* are not spatial or temporal; they are the material conditions of space and time itself. Therefore, we cannot say that there is a point of space-time which the *corpora* have not yet reached and then measure how long it takes them to get there. Their movement produces space and time as it goes, just as loop quantum gravity describes. We thus reach the radical and yet paradoxical sounding conclusion that the speed of matter is infinite or simultaneous, only on the condition that we understand matter to be productive of space itself.

Quantum Speeds

The thesis that matter in motion produces space through folding – what is today called 'spin foam theory' – has only recently been mathematically demonstrated in physics, with experimental confirmation already in progress.[9] One of the many correlates of this thesis is that, as we have seen, matter moves instantaneously. The truth of this thesis has only now been discovered by contemporary quantum field theory. For example, in quantum entanglement experiments in which two electrons are entangled and then physically separated, the two electron spins change simultaneously. This is possible because, when one spin is changed, it does not 'cause' the other to change by communicating information to the other. The electrons are two topological regions of the same quantum field. There is no transfer of information across the quantum field in the case of entanglement. The field simply changes what it is as a whole. Once a quantum field produces an electron, the speed of the electron can be measured from one point to another more classically, but speed does not work like that at the quantum level. Quantum movement is intensive, not extensive.[10] There is no third electron between the two entangled ones. In short, Lucretius' description of the speed of *corpora* versus the speed of their folds or things [*res*] remains entirely consistent with the insights of quantum entanglement.

Appropriately, Lucretius concludes his discussion of speed with the injunction not to pursue *corpora* as single and moving one by one [*singula*] (2.165), but to pursue the conditions [*ratione*] (2.156) by which matter is carried along in its continuous, simplex, and undivided motion (2.166–7).

nec persectari primordia singula quaeque,
ut videant qua quicque geratur cum ratione.

nor to pursue the first beginnings of things one by one,
to see in what way each is borne along.

Against Divine Control

Following from the above thesis about the instantaneous speed of matter
is the additional correlate that the gods are not in any way needed to
create, sustain, or change the world. If one understands that matter can
move itself and change itself instantaneously and on a very large scale,
it becomes immediately obvious that all the changes we perceive in the
world are possible by matter alone.

The Weight of Matter

Corporeal flows, and therefore all things made of them [*corpoream*], have
weight [*pondera*]. Matter is moved by its own weight because, in itself
[*quantum est in se*], it is the creation of weight. Just as the *corpora* create
space and time through motion, so they also create weight by their
motion (2.184–6; 2.201–2).

Nunc locus est, ut opinor, in his illud quoque rebus
confirmare tibi, nullam rem posse sua vi
corpoream sursum ferri sursumque meare.

Now is the place, I think, in these matters to prove
to you this, too: that nothing corporeal is able
by its own force to be borne upwards and move upwards.

nec tamen haec, quantum est in se, dubitamus, opinor,
quin vacuum per inane deorsum cuncta ferantur.

Nor yet do we doubt, I think, that all these, in so far
as in them lies, are borne downward through the empty void.

Just as Lucretius says that *corpora* move through or by space [*per inane*]
(2.202) as they produce it, so *corpora* move by or through [*per*] their own
weight as they produce it. The *corpora* move downwards [*deorsum*] (2.202)
by their own weight and not upwards [*sursum*] (2.186), in the sense that
'down' refers simply to the direction in which motion is tending to
create more of the weight and space which it has left behind and which

'weighs' on it from behind. *Ponderas* (2.189) is the trail left behind by the movement of the corporeal flow. The flow weighs on itself when it folds over itself and makes a thing, hence the danger of getting crushed by the weight of the *moenera* and bind of *religio*.

By weight [*pondera*], Lucretius cannot possibly mean here how much a *corpora* weighs on a scale. *Corpora* cannot be weighed on a scale because they are fundamentally insensible. Their motion yields no sensible quality of weight. Lucretius therefore must mean something similar to what physicists today would call energy and momentum, the basic material conditions for weight. In contemporary quantum physics, for example, weight, space, and gravity are interrelated terms. The three are created simultaneously insofar as weight is reducible to gravity, according to general relativity, where gravity is nothing other than a certain curvature of space-time. Space, in turn, for loop quantum gravity physicists, is made up of nothing other than folded quantum fields which have no mass, but only energy and momentum.

In other words, putting together general relativity and LQG, one could say that quantum fields are driven only, and in themselves [*quantum est in se*] (2.189), by their own 'weight', if what we mean by weight is nothing other than the energy and momentum that produces space and gravity itself. In the pre-spatial world of quantum flows, orientations such as 'down' and 'up' simply mean forwards and backwards with respect to the previous flow of energy and momentum. Down simply means moving forwards along a path with continuous energy and momentum behind you. In this sense, quantum fields only move 'down' or forwards. This is consistent with the fact that quantum fields are for the most part thermodynamically irreversible.[11] Even at the quantum level, matter is still entropic and thus only moves 'forwards' in this sense.

Fire, heat, and all other *rerum* made of corporeal flows follow the same trajectory: downward motion; expenditure and recombination of energy, not energy from nowhere. Matter may appear to move upwards or backwards, negentropy, but only on the condition that another flow of energy has coupled with it externally and not from within. Corporeal flows fold and produce distinct spaces and weights which all weigh upon the others to different degrees, depending on the density of the folds. Even light, according to Lucretius, is bent downwards by the weight of its sensuous folds. Lucretius' explanation of this fact relates to watching lightning hit the ground – this is not a correct example. He is nonetheless correct that photons are subject to gravity and can be bent by the space curvatures of large objects.

But all these – the turbulence, enjoyment, interval, speed, and weight of matter in motion – are aspects of motion for one very important and fundamental reason: matter swerves. This is one of the most important arguments of *De Rerum Natura*, as we will see in the next chapter.

Notes

1. For an excellent articulation of these three theses in Book II, see Don Fowler, *Lucretius on Atomic Motion: A Commentary on De Rerum Natura 2.1–332* (Oxford: Oxford University Press, 2002).
2. Paul Valéry, *The Graveyard by the Sea*, trans. C. Day Lewis, http://unix.cc.wmich.edu/~cooneys/poems/fr/valery.daylewis.html (accessed 29 July 2017).
3. Georges Bataille, 'The Solar Anus', in *Visions of Excess: Selected Writings, 1927–1939*, trans. Allan Stoekl (Minneapolis: University of Minnesota Press, 1985), 8.
4. Friedrich Nietzsche, *The Gay Science: With a Prelude in Rhymes and an Appendix of Songs*, trans. Walter A. Kaufmann (New York: Vintage Books, 1974), 74.
5. Don Fowler is careful to note the difference here between the insensible speed of the corpora and the sensible change of the res. '*[S]ince* many atoms fly continually through the void in many ways with inconceivable speed, the *variae res* of our world are produced and dissolve, change takes place in the world, and the generations of men come and go, but men cannot perceive the causes of these phenomena.' Fowler, *Lucretius on Atomic Motion*, 233.
6. The river rolls itself up like the periodicity of an electron shell.
7. Paul Valéry, *Cantate du Narcisse* (Paris: Gallimard, 1944), Scene II.
8. André Gide, *Le Traité du Narcisse*, in *Romans et récits: Œuvres lyriques et dramatiques*, ed. Pierre Masson (Paris: Gallimard, 2009).
9. See Carlo Rovelli, 'Loop Quantum Gravity', *Physics World*, 16.11 (2003); Carlo Rovelli and Lee Smolin, 'Loop Space Representation of Quantum General Relativity', *Nuclear Physics*, B 331.1 (1990): 80; and Lee Smolin, *Three Roads to Quantum Gravity* (Oxford: Oxford University Press, 2000).
10. Karen Barad, *Meeting the Universe Halfway: Quantum Physics and the Entanglement of Matter and Meaning* (Durham, NC: Duke University Press, 2007), 174.

11. Lisa Zyga, 'Physicists Confirm Thermodynamic Irreversibility in a Quantum System', *physics.org*, 1 December 2015, http://phys.org/news/2015-12-physicists-thermodynamic-irreversibility-quantum.html (accessed 29 July 2017).

11. The Swerve

Matter swerves constantly. This is one of the most important theses of Lucretius' kinetic materialism. Matter is not, *contra* Epicurus, a rain of laminar atoms through a void, until one spontaneously swerves. The aim of this chapter is to develop Lucretius' theory of the swerve through a close reading of lines 2.216–311.

Declination

The corporeal flows in themselves move according to their own weight [*ponderibus propriis*] in a rectilinear [*rectum*] or non-circular motion, which also modulates or changes its motion as it moves (2.216–20).

> *Illud in his quoque te rebus cognoscere avemus,*
> *corpora cum deorsum rectum per inane feruntur*
> *ponderibus propriis, incerto tempore ferme*
> *incertisque locis spatio depellere paulum,*
> *tantum quod momen mutatum dicere possis.*

In this matter there is this, too, that I want you to understand,
that when the first bodies are moving straight downward through the
void by their own weight, at times completely undetermined
and in undetermined places they swerve a little from their course,
but only so much as you could call a change of motion.

Corpora move downwards carried by their own energy and momentum through and by making space [*deorsum rectum per inane feruntur ponderibus propriis*] (2.217–18). At an unassignable space-time before any measurable discrete time or space [*incerto tempore ferme incertisque locis spatio*] (2.218–19), the *corpora* change, modulate, or deviate [*depellere*] (2.219) their motion [*momen mutatum*] (2.220) to the smallest possible degree [*paulum*] (2.119). This is not the cause of any other external or oblique motion, but internal to the motion of the corporeal flow itself. Just like the turbulent currents of air that drive the dust motes, so the movement of the *corpora* themselves is also fundamentally turbulent in that it changes its motion on its own [*momen mutatum*].

Habit

Contrary to the Epicurean and modern interpretations, Lucretius is extremely clear in the following passage that this change of motion, *mutatum*, *depellere*, or *declinare*, does not happen *ex nihilo*. Such a change would contradict the first thesis of materialism: nothing comes from nothing. There is not first a rain of parallel atoms falling through the void, and then out of nowhere one of the atoms swerves. Rather, matter has *always been in the habit of curving*. It has always been pedetic (2.221–4).

> quod nisi declinare solerent, omnia deorsum
> imbris uti guttae caderent per inane profundum
> nec foret offensus natus nec plaga creata
> principiis; ita nihil umquam natura creasset.

Because unless they were accustomed to swerving, all would fall
downwards like drops of rain through the deep void,
nor would a collision occur, nor would a blow be produced
by the first beginnings.

If and only if [*nisi*] (2.221) matter was not already in the habit [*solerent*] (2.221) of curving or bending [*declinare*] (2.221) would it fall downwards without collision like rain [*caderent*] (2.222). The *caderent* is therefore a *counter-factual* and not a speculative point in time which ever existed. The swerve was already before space and time, or at least coexistent with their emergence. There was never a time when there was only the *caderent* without collision [*plaga*] (2.223). Such a time is a total abstraction. If there was such a time, nothing would be, which is obviously not the case.

Matter curves and bends by its own autonomous change of motion. Since void equally gives way everywhere, the corporeal flows, with respect to themselves, are moved equally fast (2.235–9). There is no possibility that the corporeal flows collide with each other from behind because one is heavier or lighter. They all move at the same (infinite) speed through the void.

Nec plus quam minimum

The change in the motion of matter is not caused by any other oblique motion external to the corporeal flow. The swerve of matter is always and necessarily [*necessest*] the autonomous swerve [*inclinare*] of motion itself, but only at the level of its *minima* (2.243–5).

> *quare etiam atque etiam paulum inclinare necessest*
> *corpora; nec plus quam minimum, ne fingere motus*
> *obliquos videamur et id res vera refutet.*

Wherefore again and again it is necessary that *corpora*
swerve a little, but no more than a minimum, lest we seem
to be inventing oblique motions, and the true facts refute it.

The flows of matter, as we have seen, are made of *minima*, which are its topological dimensions, simplex, waves, or aspects. The *minima* are not units or particles. The flows of matter curve the smallest possible amount [*paulum*] (2.219) because their curve is identical to the curved dimensions of the *minima* themselves. The inclination of matter is the inclination of its turbulent *minima*.

No oblique or non-simplex motions are required for the *corpora* to curve at the level of their *minima*. The *minima* curve and bend at the smallest possible level without introducing a division into the *corpora* [*sine partibus extat et minima constat natura*] (2.601–2). The weight of the material flow cannot cause it to swerve on its own, since void gives way in all directions equally. Matter therefore makes itself swerve [*regione viai declinare quis est*] (2.249–50). However, since this declination occurs at the level of the *minima*, it remains insensible. Therefore, although we cannot see the curve, we know that it must be there as the transcendental material condition of sensibility itself. The eye itself already presupposes that *corpora* have collided and produced the complex sensory apparatus of the eye's materiality. Since collision is impossible with weight alone, it requires that matter be autonomous and pedetic.

Voluntas

Lucretius calls the minimal swerve of matter the *voluntas* of matter. From within the infinite chain of interconnected and continuous *minima*, the will [*voluntas*], inclination, or desire [*voluptas*] is the name of the kinetic novelty of matter. The swerve does not break the continuous chain of movement [*motu conectitur*], but responds to what came before in a novel way that is irreducible to any mechanistic laws (2.251–60).

> *Denique si semper motu conectitur omnis*
> *et vetere exoritur motus novus ordine certo*
> *nec declinando faciunt primordia motus*
> *principium quoddam, quod fati foedera rumpat,*
> *ex infinito ne causam causa sequatur,*
> *libera per terras unde haec animantibus exstat,*
> *unde est haec, inquam, fatis avolsa voluntas,*
> *per quam progredimur quo ducit quemque voluptas,*
> *declinamus item motus nec tempore certo*
> *nec regione loci certa, sed ubi ipsa tulit mens?*

And next if every motion is always linked
and a new one always arises from an old one in sure succession,
and if by declining the primary bodies do not make
a certain beginning of motion to burst the laws of fate,
so that cause does not follow cause from infinity,
from where does there arise for living creatures throughout the world,
from where, I say, is this *voluntas*, torn from fate,
by which we go wherever pleasure leads each of us,
and likewise decline our motions at no fixed time
or fixed region of space, but where the mind itself carries us?

Again we should think of the causal necessity of matter-flows as a counter-factual. There was never a time when there were only atoms falling through the void driven by fate and necessity [*fati foedera*] (2.254). If motion is always continuous and joined with what precedes it [*motu conectitur omnis*] (2.251), like the *minima* of the *corpora*, and there are clearly creatures with will [*voluntas*] (2.257), then it is necessary that matter is and always has been creative and novel in its motion. If it were not, then, counter-factually, there would be nothing but motion locked into a contract of fate [*fati foedera*] and necessity. Since this is not the case, it follows that such a time never existed.

Lucretius does not use the term *libre voluntas* or 'free will', as some have translated it, but rather simply *voluntas*. Lucretius makes this word choice because the word *voluntas* is related to the Latin word *voluptas*, which is not simply reducible to freedom or necessity. As we saw in the invocation of Venus and later in the description of the event of the Trojan War, desire is not reducible to simple activity or passivity. *Voluptas* is immanent to matter itself; it is nothing other than a name for matter's stochastic self-movement.[1] Desire is the movement of matter. It is both the activity by which we move [*per quam progredimur*] (2.258) and the passivity by which we are moved [*quo ducit quemque*] (2.258). Venus moves through all, carrying us all away in rapture [*raptam*] (1.464). Since movement or desire is contemporaneous with the active production of space and time it therefore occurs at no assignable time or space. Time and space occur in and through [*per*] the kinotopological regions of matter's motion. Only after matter moves do we go back and divide it into discrete spaces or times.

In addition to the danger of the *moenera* we should add the danger of the *foedera*. If the *moenera* occurs when matter gets stuck in the same habitual fold, as if trapped by something other than its own motion (military service, credit-debt, exchange, etc.), then the *foedera* – treaty, agreement, or contract – is when matter gets stuck in an endless chain of motion [*semper motu conectitur*] (2.251) without being able to introduce curvature. These are the twin dangers of matter: the fold without flow or to flow without fold. On the one hand matter gets stuck in a circle, imagining that it is cut off from the flows. On the other hand it gets stuck in the flow, imagining that it cannot introduce curvature. In the first, matter is crushed from inside in the bind of *religio*; in the second, matter is constrained from outside by a causal series of mechanistic and deterministic laws [*fati*]. The divine contract [*moenera religio*] and the natural contract [*fati foedera*] are two sides of the same danger where *voluptas* and *voluntas* are thought to be absent from matter.

The Will of Things

Voluntas is nothing other than the flow of matter. *Voluntas* streams and flows [*rigantur*] motion through the limbs [*motus per membra*] (2.261–2).

> nam dubio procul his rebus sua cuique voluntas
> principium dat et hinc motus per membra rigantur.

> For doubtless one's own will provides for each a beginning
> of these things, and from it motions stream through the limbs.

Voluntas, as the flow of matter, provides the beginning [*principium*] (2.262) of things [*rebus*] (2.261) because it is movement that curves and produces the fold which results in the thing. All things [*rebus*] have will [*voluntas*] because all things are nothing other than the flow of matter folded back over itself. *Voluntas* streams and flows through the limbs [*membra*] (2.262) just as matter flows and streams through all things.

It follows that, since there are different things, they also have different wills. *Voluntas* streams motion into the limbs, but also streams motion from the limbs to the heart, and to the mind, and vice versa. *Voluntas* is not one-directional, but flows from one thing to another and back again at different speeds and to different degrees. Lucretius gives three examples of *voluntas* in the case of the human body. Since humans are made of many things they also have many wills. We have many wills, not for psychological reasons, as Freud describes in the polymorphous nature of the Id, but for materialist reasons because there are many material processes going on inside us whose *voluntas* or motions do not necessarily match up.

Mente. The first example Lucretius gives is the kinetic difference between the *voluptas* of the mind [*mente*] and the limbs [*membra*]. For example, he says, when horses are released from their gates suddenly [*tempore puncto*], their minds desire to flee faster than their limbs are able to move (2.263–5).

> *nonne vides etiam patefactis tempore puncto*
> *carceribus non posse tamen prorumpere equorum*
> *vim cupidam tam de subito quam mens avet ipsa?*

> For don't you also see that while the starting gates drop in an instant,
> the desirous force of the horses is nevertheless not able
> to burst forth as suddenly as the mind itself desires?

In this example, the *voluntas* of the mind tries to move the body, but since *voluntas* is a material kinetic flow, there is a lag in the transfer of motion from the mind to the limbs. If the mind and will were purely immaterial forces, there would be no material or kinetic delay in the action of the limbs. Since this is clearly not the case, it is obvious that *voluntas* is nothing other than a regional material transfer of motion from one part of the body, the mind, to another, the limbs.

Corde. The second example Lucretius gives is the kinetic difference between the *voluntas* of the heart [*corde*] and the mind [*mente*] (2.269–71).

> *ut videas initum motus a corde creari*
> *ex animique voluntate id procedere primum,*
> *inde dari porro per totum corpus et artus.*

So you can see that a beginning of motion is created in the heart,
and comes forth first from the will of the mind,
and then is conveyed through the whole body and limbs.

Voluntas begins first in the material movement of the heart. In Roman physics the *corde* names the entirety of internal bodily affectation: heartbeat, respiration, blood circulation, and so on. *Voluntas* is thus always already in action in the internal movements of the body, whether or not we are consciously aware of them. *Voluntas*, therefore, is not reducible to conscious or mentalistic volition for Lucretius. The body is already desiring and willing without thought, and according to its manifold internal motions. As Artaud writes,

> The body under the skin is an overhead factory,
> and, outside,
> the patient glistens,
> he shines,
> from all his pores,
> burst open.
> Like a landscape
> by van Gogh
> at noon.
> Only perpetual war explains a peace which is only a passing phase.[2]

Before the mind thinks, the body is already in the process of a thousand fluid processes under the skin, as Artaud writes. The pores on the surface glisten with sweat showing the thermal byproduct of the process. The peace of the stable body and the thinking mind is only there on the condition of a constant battle of corporeal collisions. The *voluntas* of the mind is thus the byproduct of the more primary motion of the body which creates it [*creari*] (2.269). This *voluntas* is then transferred to the limbs through another motion.

Membra. The third example Lucretius gives is the kinetic difference between the *voluntas* of the limbs [*membra*] and the heart [*corde*] (2.277–80).

> *iamne vides igitur, quamquam vis extera multos*
> *pellat et invitos cogat procedere saepe*
> *praecipitesque rapi, tamen esse in pectore nostro*
> *quiddam quod contra pugnare obstareque possit?*

Now you see, don't you, that although an external force pushes many,
and often forces them to move forwards and to be thrown headlong

in rapture, there is nevertheless something in our breast
which is able to offer resistance and fight back?

Through external motions, the *membra* are also capable of being carried
away or caught up in their own motions [*rapi*] (2.279) and moving
the body along without the *voluntas* of the heart or mind. The English
translation of *rapi* as 'against our will' is misleading here, as we have
shown in Chapter 6 with the related word *raptam*, and assumes the complete identity of *voluntas* with 'our mental will'. Since Lucretius believes
that all matter has inclination, *voluptas* and *voluntas*, this assumption is
unfounded. If matter did not have *voluntas* there would be no swerve and
thus no things. It therefore follows that the human body, which is made
up of things, has many wills. This is not a rejection of will or a contradiction of will but a multiplication and entanglement or embattlement of
it. Again, Lucretius is clear that *voluntas* is not one-directional. The heart
[*pectore*] (2.279) can fight back [*contra pugnare*] (2.280) against the *voluntas*
of the limbs.

The mind, heart, and limbs are therefore distinct bodily regions
with their own distinct but related motions or wills [*voluptas*].
Although Lucretius does not give examples of every single permuta-
tion, it is clear from his three examples that he could. The mind can
move the limbs and the heart since we can think about moving our
arm and we can consciously hold our breath. The limbs can move
causing us to think of their pain or pleasure, but the limbs can also
move in such a way that they modify the circulation of blood through
our body. The heart in turn, by lack or excess of oxygen, can affect
our thoughts, but through the nervous system reflexes directly control
certain limb motions (patellar reflex). Not only can each affect the
other, but each can therefore affect the other through the third. *Voluntas*
is therefore materially and kinetically distributed in a kind of triplex
(Fig. 11.1).

Voluntas vs Free Will

The whole philosophical division between freedom and determinism
is undermined by the concept of *voluntas*, as Lucretius uses it. In these
lines of his poem, Lucretius overturns the philosophical assumption that
matter moves according to necessary, mechanistic, and causal laws, in
contrast to the mind, which is free of their constraint. The whole philosophical problem of freedom, for Lucretius, is badly posed. However, by

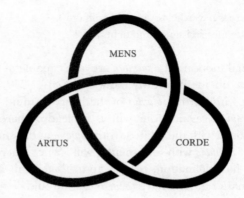

Figure 11.1 *Voluntas.*

making matter itself unconstrained by necessity, as Lucretius does, the distinction between freedom and necessity is no longer tenable – there is only *voluntas*.

By defining freedom in purely mentalistic terms, the philosophy of free will introduces two presuppositions that Lucretius rejects: 1) free will can only be an unconstrained conscious mental activity, and 2) free action must have a necessary and causal effect in the world. First, the restriction of the type of substance which can have freedom (the mind) is arbitrary, if for no other reason than that the mind is an emergent historical product of a long material process to which it is connected. The mind has no meaning independent of the matter which composes and supports it. The idea of an independent mental substance, for example, adds nothing to what we know of the brain. In short, mental activity is material activity and there is no reason to suppose that freedom exists only in one type of matter and not others.

Secondly, for Lucretius, the requirement that freedom have a necessary and causal effect in the world is an un-demonstrable metaphysical condition. Matter moves, but not by necessary, mechanistic, or universal causal laws of nature. Matter moves pedetically, and therefore has no necessity except the paradoxical necessity of its contingency or pedesis. There are very regular patterns, folds, or habits in which matter moves, but they are not necessary causations, only *habituations or kinetic correlations*.

The Brain

Lucretius' account of *voluntas*, in contrast to notions of mental and causal free will, is again surprisingly consistent with recent discoveries in cognitive neuroscience and physiology. For example, a number of neuroscientists have tried to isolate brain activities which could be described as 'pre-reflective intentions' or 'readiness potentials'. In the 1980s, Benjamin Libet tried to show that these occurred in the motor cortex.[3] More recent studies have found that there is no necessary causal link between these or other 'ambient brain states' to a given action.[4] Both the body and the brain are always moving and active, but no necessary causal relation has been found between them. The ongoing series of Libetian-style experiments continue to show, consistent with Lucretius, that conscious mental activity [*mente*], background body and brain activity [*corde*], and muscle activity [*membra*] can all affect and move one another, but not according to any absolute or necessary causal laws. This suggests, as Lucretius describes in *De Rerum Natura*, that although related to one another, the relations between mind, heart, and limbs are non-necessary relations of *voluntas*, and not at all cases of mechanistic laws of necessary causality. The mind, heart, and limbs all have their own 'free' motion [*voluntas*], but they can also interrupt and interact with one another as well.

In short, matter, including human matter, for Lucretius, has within it an inner power [*innata potestas*] of motion [*motibus*], since if it did not, material collisions would have to come about *ex nihilo* (2.280–90). Lucretius is extremely clear on this point: what keeps mind, heart, limbs, and all other matter from having any inner necessity to it [*sed ne res ipsa necessum*] is precisely the fact that all matter has a *clinamen* within it from the beginning [*clinamen principiorum*] (2.285–95).

Omnia inclinare!

Matter has always been swerving. Lucretius formulates this thesis *no less than three times* in this section of the poem. In line 2.221 he writes that matter has always been in the habit of swerving [*declinare solerent*]. In line 2.293 he writes that all matter has the *clinamen* or swerve within it from the beginning [*clinamen principiorum*]. In lines 2.294–307, for those still tempted to think that there was ever the counter-factual state of atoms falling through the void, Lucretius clearly states that the swerving motion of matter has *always been this way and always will be* (2.297–9).

qua propter quo nunc in motu principiorum
corpora sunt, in eodem ante acta aetate fuere
et post haec semper simili ratione ferentur,

Wherefore with whatever motions the first beginnings
now move, they moved with the same motions in ages past,
and in the future they will always be carried along in a similar way.

Corpora have always moved according to the same motions [*motu principiorum corpora*] (2.297–8). There never was a *cataract*. There never was a point in time or space when they started swerving, because it is only their swerving motion that produces time and space in the first place. They were always moved and carried along under the same conditions [*semper simili ratione ferentur*] (2.299), and they always will be. Pedetic motion extends infinitely in all directions and through all time.

Foedera naturai

Against the *fati foedera* or the contract of fate and necessity, the *foedera naturai* is the simple and single law that there are no necessary laws. There are only habits, nothing but habits. There is only pedetic motion which folds itself into regular habits (2.300–2).

et quae consuerint gigni gignentur eadem
condicione et erunt et crescent vique valebunt,
quantum cuique datum est per foedera naturai.

and whatever things usually arise will arise under the same
conditions and will exist and grow and flourish in their strength,
insofar as it is granted to each through the laws of nature.

The only *foedera naturai* is therefore a kind of anti-*foedera* or anti-contract, which is the only assurance we have to keep away all other contracts that would claim universal or absolute status. In other words, it is not by chance that all of matter is pedetic. If it were by chance, then it would be possible that all of matter might not be pedetic, in which case it might be possible for all of matter to be necessarily determined by causal and mechanistic laws. But this cannot be the case; if it were, the flows of matter would never swerve and there would be nothing. Since there is not nothing, but something, contingency itself must be necessary. It is necessary that matter be pedetic or contingent. This does not mean that matter is random. Randomness is only another version of *ex nihilo* crea-

tion. Each motion comes from another, just not in an absolutely necessary or completely determined way.

Everything moves, but nothing is ever created or destroyed. In this
sense the all of nature [*omnia*] appears in the gaze of our eye [*videa-
tur*] inactive [*quiete*]. As an infinite sum [*summa*] there is neither more
nor less motion, but simply a redistribution of corporeal motions
in themselves relative to other motions [*proprio dat corpore motus*]
(2.309–11).

Conclusion

The motion, weight, and speed of matter all determine the kinds of qualities and kinds of things that are in the world. Movement *is* the nature of
things. However, this account still leaves untouched the question of the
shape [*figura*] or patterns of corporeal motion, which are fundamental
for understanding the kinetic nature of things. This is the subject of our
next chapter.

Notes

1. See Walter Englert, *Epicurus on the Swerve and Voluntary Action* (Atlanta:
   Scholars Press 1987), 65: 'The activity that is singled out as the chief
   function of the *voluntas* is movement.' I also follow Englert's argument
   here that the swerve is not about 'free choice' or other strictly mental
   phenomena.
2. Antonin Artaud, *Selected Writings*, trans. Don E. Levine (New York:
   Farrar, Straus and Giroux, 1976), 507.
3. Benjamin Libet, Curtis A. Gleason, Elwood W. Wright and Dennis
   K. Pearl, 'Time of Conscious Intention to Act in Relation to Onset of
   Cerebral Activity (Readiness-Potential)', *Brain*, 106.3 (1983): 623–42.
4. William P. Banks and Eve A. Isham, 'We Infer Rather than Perceive the
   Moment We Decided to Act', *Psychological Science*, 20.1 (2009): 17–21; Judy
   Trevena and Jeff Miller, 'Brain Preparation before a Voluntary Action:
   Evidence against Unconscious Movement Initiation', *Consciousness and
   Cognition*, 19.1 (2010): 447–56.

12. The Form of Matter

The motion of matter produces its form. For Lucretius, form is not something immaterial, immutable, or pre-existent. Forms mix and change because matter itself mixes and changes through motion. Therefore, in addition to the theory of material genesis developed in the previous chapters, that matter is infinitely creative, Lucretius now develops a theory of formal genesis. For Lucretius, material and formal genesis (hylogenesis and morphogenesis) are two names for the same ontogenetic process by which matter infinitely recomposes itself in new ways. Matter continually folds and weaves itself into new and changing material configurations, but it does so in very specific patterns, shapes, or forms. The process of materialisation is thus inseparable from the process of formation. The form of matter is therefore nothing other than the shape produced by the patterned flow of matter itself.

This theory of formal genesis is distinct from Platonic formalism in three ways: 1) form is not immaterial or ideal; 2) form is not a purely active and pre-existing model by which matter is passively stamped as a copy of this model; and 3) form is not immutable. Lucretius rejects the triple cross upon which matter is crucified: idealism, identity, and immutability.[1] Lucretius does not try to separate form from matter by submitting it to these three criteria. Form and matter are united in the same kinetic process of materialisation.

One of the major aims of this chapter is to overcome the atomist interpretation of Lucretian materialism that has reinserted formalism into it by attributing pre-existent forms to it. Just as we debunked the atomist attempt to reinsert idealism into *De Rerum Natura* by redefining the *clinamen* as 'mental or spiritual human freedom' in the previous chapter, so in this chapter we debunk a similar effort to reinsert formalism into *De Rerum Natura* by interpreting the *corpora* as preformed little spheres, hooks, or spikes. Aside from the fact that such an interpretation erroneously presupposes that *corpora* are discrete particles, something we have argued against at length, there is another problem.

If *corpora* are nothing but matter in pedetic motion and matter is defined solely by its weight [*pondera*] or entropic energetic momentum, then form cannot be pre-given; it must be a co-emergent aspect of matter in motion. As matter moves, it draws out its own form, but it is a form that changes as it moves. In this way Lucretius makes matter active at the same time as he makes form passive. In contrast to the pure activity of form and the pure passivity of matter (model vs copy in Plato, pure *energia*, God vs pure *dunamis*, *prote hyle*, in Aristotle), Lucretius makes both matter and form active *and* passive. Matter and form both enter into a mutual and continuous process of self-transformation without pre-existing forms or inert matter.

Marx was the first to overcome this formalist reading of matter in Lucretius.

> The consequence of this [the primacy of the flow of matter] for the monads as well as for the atoms would therefore be – since they are in constant motion – that *neither monads nor atoms exist*, but rather disappear in the straight line: for the solidity of the atom does not even enter into the picture, insofar as it is only considered as something falling in a straight line.[2]

Insofar as matter flows in constant motion it is wrong to understand it as discrete atoms. The so-called discreteness of 'atoms' is an abstraction from the primacy of their continual motion. It follows, similarly, as we will see in this chapter, that it makes no sense to talk about the pre-formed shape of discrete particles. Lucretius has something quite different in mind.

Form and Figure

In contrast to the theory of forms as immaterial, immutable, and identical, Lucretius introduces a theory of *formal figuration* (2.333–7).

Nunc age, iam deinceps cunctarum exordia rerum
qualia sint et quam longe distantia formis,
percipe, multigenis quam sint variata figuris;
non quo multa parum simili sint praedita forma,
sed quia non volgo paria omnibus omnia constant.

> Now let us see the motion from which all things are first woven
> and how far different they are
> in form, how varied they are in their many kinds of *figuris*.
> Not that only a few are endowed with similar *forma*,
> but that they are not everywhere all like all.

Now let us see the motion or movement [*nunc age*] from which all things [*rerum*] are first woven [*exordia*] (2.333). The opening lines of Lucretius' theory of forms here clearly state that he is about to 'lead us' through motion to the motions of the *corpora* from which the *rerum*, not the *corpora* themselves, are going to be first woven [*exordia*]. The Latin word *exordia* means 'first' and 'to weave', fitting perfectly with Lucretius' poetic language of weaving [*textum, contextum, nexum*] throughout the poem. His emphasis on the constitutive power of matter to move and to weave already makes clear that we are not going to receive a theory of pre-existing, ideal and immobile forms, but rather a theory of how *rerum* are the formed products of the weave of corporeal and material flows.

Furthermore, the Latin phrase *qualia sint et quam longe distantia formis* (2.334) indicates that the *qualia* or qualitative constitution of things occurs over a *long distance of formation*. Lucretius does not say that there are simply different pre-existing forms, but rather that there is a long or far distance or difference between the forms. The language of distance is introduced here because form [*forma*] (2.336) is something that emerges through or over the course of motion [*nunc age*] and the length of the weave [*exordia*] (2.333). This important kinotopological sense is lost when *longe distantia* is translated into English as 'different'. Plato's forms, for example, can be 'different', but they cannot be woven over a long distance, since they are immaterial and immobile.

Take hold with the eye [*percipe*] how many kinds of various figurations [*figuris*] there are (2.335). Lucretius introduces the Latin word *figura* here not as a mere synonym for form, but for two related reasons: first, to make it clear that by 'form' he means nothing other than the 'shape' made by matter in weaving motion and not some idealist essence; secondly, to describe how it is that form itself its produced. The Latin word *figura* means not only shape but shape produced by drawing, sketching, or the movement of outlining. A *figura* is a form produced through the motion of a trace, line, or sketch. If matter were already formed, or forms already existed, there would be no need for them to be woven over distances and traced out by figuration.

The Threads of Form

This is further emphasised in his description of the corporeal flows as threads which draw out or weave different figures (2.340–1).

debent ni mirum non omnibus omnia prorsum
esse pari filo similique adfecta figura.

they doubtless all should not be precisely equal
in form to all, nor furnished with a similar *figura*.

All of the corporeal flows [*omnia*] do not follow the same motion (2.340). Earlier in Book II, Lucretius argued clearly against any notion of a *caderant* of homogeneous atoms falling through the void. Corporeal flows are pedetic and have always been pedetic. They move in highly heterogeneous ways. Continuing with this poetics of weaving, Lucretius now writes that the corporeal threads [*filo*] of which the shapes of things are woven strive or draw [*adfecta*] dissimilar shapes [*figura*] (2.341). Again, the Latin words *filo* and *adfecta* clearly indicate that *figura* is a shape that emerges through the motion (weaving of threads, drawing of paths) of matter and not some pre-existing set of ideal forms. The next lines clearly follow this language of kinetic figures in the examples of the different flows of animal life: the flows [*natantes*] (2.342) of fish, the flocks of beasts, the flying flows of birds along the flowing springs [*fontisque*] and rivers (2.345).

Filiation. As an example of material formation Lucretius gives the beautiful poetic image of the mother cow looking for her sacrificed calf. This is particularly striking because it operates at several levels at once. On one level it describes the arbitrary suffering inflicted on the cow by the sacrificing of its baby at the hands of *religio*. On another level it describes the creative power of maternal [*mater*] matter to actively create new life but also to passively hold within it all the *figura* which it creates, both of which will be dramatised later in lines 2.630–65 on the Great Mother.

The most important level of this example, however, is as a description of morphogenesis, of which there are two sides. On the one hand, the mother cow actively draws within her the figure of the calf insofar as she produced the calf and insofar as she is looking for the calf even in its absence. She traces the figure of the hoofprint in her vision. On the other hand, the calf draws its own form in the earth with its cloven hooves for the mother to look for. So not only does the calf have a figure (the hoof) from the mother, but the calf in turn draws its figure on the earth, which is impressed with the trace [*pedibus vestigia pressa*] (2.356). The material condition of form is thus the activity of the foot, *pedibus*, pedesis, that draws [*pressa*] a trace or track [*vestigia*]. Form does not pre-exist, but must be born from the mother and traced by the calf. Once the form is produced it can be continually reproduced by habit or pattern such that the flows of willows, wet grass, or rivers are not able to remove the fixed [*perfixa*] (2.360) figure from the mother's inner senses.

At another level the poetic image of the mother cow demonstrates how figuration is not something that emerges *ex nihilo* or that is impressed like a model from elsewhere. The mother distinguishes the figure of her calf from others because its figure has been habitually drawn in her. The mind is not like a computer that stores data,[3] but more like a path that gets easier to walk each time, and must be walked to work. The matter of the calf comes from the mother, just as figuration comes from something and is based in the patterned and figured motion of matter in the senses of the mother cow.

The same thing occurs in grains, Lucretius writes. No two grains are identical to each other but certain material differences are literally drawn or run [*intercurrat*] between the grains through genetic relay and distance [*distantia formis*] (2.371–3). In other words, form is not stamped on matter from above by God, but kinetically transferred through the movement of matter and its active creation. Matter and form co-emerge in the same kinetic process of ontogenesis. Shells on the beach, for example, are all drawn or painted [*pingere*] (2.375) with a similar figura-tion and differently distributed by the flow of the waves and the flow of sands on the curved beaches. The thread of filiation [*filo*] (2.341) is more like the curved shoreline than the rectilinear line of identity and resemblance in model and copy relation. Form is produced through the moving threads of genetic and material filiation. Nothing comes from nothing, thus form and figure themselves have a history.

Since the *figura* drawn by the *corpora* are necessarily produced under the natural conditions [*ratione necessest natura*] of filiation and movement and not by hand according to a single fixed form [*neque facta manu sunt unius ad certam formam*], the *corpora fly* around in different figurations [*dis-simili inter se quaedam volitare figura*] (2.373–80). Thus some, like lightning, can pass through walls because the figures and folds they draw are smaller, and others, like water, with larger figures cannot. Wine can pass through a colander quickly, while olive oil takes longer. *Corpora* themselves are not fundamentally larger or smaller than each other since they have no sensible size, form, shape, or structure unless they have moved or folded themselves into larger or smaller figures. However, if *corpora* fold, then any fold can be folded up by a larger one, meaning that there are larger and smaller corporeal folds. Larger and smaller, with respect to the *corpora*, are not absolute forms, but only relative forms since they are only larger or smaller than something else.

Lucretius brings up the size of *corpora* in this section for a reason: size is part of shape. Without shape, there is no size. Anything of any size has a shape, *but corporeal flows have no predetermined shape or any quality other than weight so they cannot have a predetermined size either*. Furthermore, since there is nothing smaller than *corpora*, it makes absolutely no sense to say that there are larger and smaller corporeal flows, only larger and smaller *figura* or folds drawn by the *corpora*. Both size and shape are therefore products of the woven [*exordia*] threads [*filo*] of corporeal flows and not pre-given shapes of the *corpora*. Of course, the formal products of the *corpora* are nothing other than the *corpora* themselves in a certain motion.

The Waveform Theory of Matter

In Book I, Lucretius focused his attention on the corporeal conditions of space itself [*inane*] and of discreteness in general [*rerum*]. We learned that the flows and folds of the *corpora* are material conditions of space and discrete things. We saw not only how such an account differed from the atomist interpretation but also how it matched up quite consistently with some of the core theoretical tenets of quantum gravity theory.

In Book II, however, Lucretius shifts his attention to the corporeal structure and material conditions of the differences between things [*rerum*]. In other words, the question is: 'What must be the corporeal conditions such that we perceive so many different kinds and forms of things if they are all products of the same corporeal folding?' The answer requires the development of a materialist theory of forms or morphogenesis that can account for how different sizes, shapes, sensory attributes, and densities of things can be understood by the very minimal apparatus of corporeal flows and folds. Again, this is not only different from the formalism of the atomist interpretation of 'different shaped atoms', but is also consistent with the core ideas of the waveform theory of matter held by contemporary physicists: that all particles constantly move and vibrate in a continuous wave pattern of motion. All of sensible matter, that is, matter above the Planck scale, can be understood according to its kinotopological waveform. Subatomic particles, atoms, and molecules all move continuously and thus have a frequency of some kind.

Within the waveform theory of matter, however, there are both classical and quantum features. In the quantum framework the continuous movement of matter is fundamentally insensible, non-discrete, and exists in superposition and non-locality. Here movement must be understood intensively as a continuous internal self-transformation of the whole. We have shown in previous chapters that Lucretius grants these basic quantum features to the motion of the corporeal flows.

However, if we want to understand the movement of the corporeal folds of things or discrete particles, their differences and relations, forms, figures, and sensations, we must shift to a more classical interpretation of the waveform theory of matter that deals strictly with sensible particles (subatomic, atoms, and molecules) and no longer primarily with the quantum fields that produce them. The two models (quantum and classical) are not opposed because particles are nothing other than folded fields – quantum states that have produced a discrete and sensible thing. The classical waveform theory of matter is just a quantified and spatialised degree or dimension of the quantum fields. Just as there are key differences between classical and quantum physics, so Lucretius stresses the difference between the waves of *corpora* and the waves of *rerum*.

The waveform theory of matter is that all particles move and vibrate and thus have frequencies or waveforms, even though they appear as particles because particles are nothing other than the emergent properties of corporeal flows in the first place. If all matter moves, all matter also has a frequency or figuration of its movement that defines its formal features.

Lucretius' theory of sensation is yet another example of a thesis in his work that was thought to be correct according to the atomic interpretation for hundreds of years, but now appears hopelessly archaic and mistaken. What I would like to show in the following section, however, is that Lucretius' theory of sensation is actually much closer to our contemporary understanding of sensation than to the atomic one of modern science. In short, Lucretius is much more contemporary than he is given credit for. In order to defend such a claim, we turn now to a consideration, following a close reading of the text, of Lucretius' waveform theory sensation and its consistency with contemporary physics and chemistry.

Taste

Foods taste different or more pleasant than others because the *corpora* are drawn or shaped into different forms (2.402–7).

ut facile agnoscas e levibus atque rutundis
esse ea quae sensus iucunde tangere possunt,
at contra quae amara atque aspera cumque videntur,
haec magis hamatis inter se nexa teneri
proptereaque solere vias rescindere nostris
sensibus introituque suo perrumpere corpus.

Thus you may easily recognize that those things which can touch
the senses pleasantly are made up of smooth and round figures,
but in contrast whatever things seem bitter and harsh are held
entangled with one another by figures which are more rough,
and consequently they are accustomed to tear open paths
into our senses and burst through the body by their entrance.

Pleasant sensations such as sweet honey, for example, move more smoothly [*levibus*] (2.402) and roundly [*rutundis*] (2.402), in contrast to bitter wormwood, which moves roughly or crookedly [*hamatis*] (2.405) and unevenly on the tongue. Although Lucretius lacked the experimental evidence to support his claims about the nature of taste, it turns out that he was nonetheless generally correct in his theory.

All atoms and molecules vibrate at different frequencies that can be mapped by spectroscopy, which graphs the frequency and waveform of radiation on the electromagnetic spectrum. Molecules not only have different shapes depending on the atoms conjoined in them, but also vibrate in different shapes depending on the collective vibrations of atoms in the molecule. Molecules thus draw or make their shape by moving.

According to contemporary biochemistry, there are two competing models of taste: the standard lock-and-key model and the more recent vibratory olfactory theory. According to the first model, the reason different foods taste different is because we have taste receptors on our tongues which are literally shaped in such a way to receive certain shaped molecules. According to the second model, the exceptions to this lock-and-key model can be accounted for by the theory of quantum tunnelling, allowing us to smell and taste the difference between different vibrations, even though they have the same molecular shape.

Since Lucretius' claim about taste sensations is quite general, stating that pleasant and unpleasant tastes depend on the shape of material flows, he is, by contemporary standards, correct in his theory. Furthermore, his thesis that the shapes of the material flows of taste are made by motion, what we would call today subatomic motion, is equally compatible with both the lock-and-key theory and the vibrational theory. Both theories demonstrate significant overlap in their evidence and differ only on a number of exceptional cases.

Lucretius is therefore correct to say that the sensation of taste is a question of the shape, figure, and waveform traced by the movement of matter on the tongue, whether this waveform works because of its molecular shape or because of the vibration of this shape; the kinetic shape is what is determinate in the end. Biochemists are still in the process of cataloguing all the waveform vibrations of different taste and odorant molecules, but are explicitly aiming to demonstrate experimentally a version of Lucretius' thesis.[4]

The second part of Lucretius' thesis is that pleasant tastes are smooth and unpleasant ones rough. With respect to the waveforms of taste molecules this is a generally accurate statement. Biochemists have been able to categorise most molecular and vibrational forms of the pleasant tastes: sweet, umami, salty, and sour. All of them appear to exemplify relatively smooth or rounded waveforms. However, when the relatively smooth waveforms of non-bitter foods begin to decay and become foul, the wave patterns become increasingly distorted, irregular, and bitter, *relative to the smooth waveforms*.[5] In many, but perhaps not all cases when a given sweet waveform becomes doped with bitter compounds, the waveform undergoes a distortion or *relative irregularity* associated with a bitter taste or bad smell, sometimes irreducible to the mere shape of the molecule. Or, inversely put, if we took a molecular waveform and made it increasingly irregular or 'noisy', it would no longer be the same taste as it was, that is, one of the few pleasant tastes, but would become an unpleasant taste most often associated with bitter flavours.

This is the case because there are vastly more unpleasant or bitter-flavoured kinds of molecules than there are pleasant ones. Thus, when the molecular vibration of a pleasant taste is changed, the result is almost always unpleasant. The wormwood plant, for example, like most plants, is built from 'sweet' or 'pleasant' carbohydrate compounds produced during photosynthesis to build cell walls (cellulose) and deliver energy for growth. However, when this molecular waveform is combined with a number of other relatively irregular molecules that define wormwood, the resulting taste is bitter. In the case of honey, the bees have extracted only the carbohydrate nectar of the plant, leaving it uncontaminated by other unpleasant molecules.

In some cases this difference does not map on to any universal molecular change in shape, but can only be discerned according to the waveform. The molecular shape of sulphur atoms, for example, is not a perfect indicator of taste or smell, but the waveform or vibration of the shape is. Smell biologist Tim Jacob of Cardiff University argues that the addition of sulphur, which is part of many rotting smells and bitter tastes, does not change the shape of other molecules in a universal way, but rather adds a signature vibration to a molecule that a molecular vibration-sensitive nose or tongue might detect as a distortion or irregularity in its waveform.[6] Lucretius' thesis is not that all bitter compounds have the same shape, but that most pleasant tastes are smooth, and when their shape is changed they typically become unpleasant.

Another way to understand the difference between smooth and irregular taste flows is by their movement through saliva in the mouth. For example, non-bitter receptors on the tongue always fold together the chemical flows into two kinds of receptors at the same time (umami T1R1+T1R3; sweet T1R2+T1R3), creating a more rapid and smooth absorption of historically nutritional molecules. However, bitter receptors on the tongue are the only ones that do not fold or smooth molecular flows symmetrically into two different receptors at the same time, but instead use only one kind of receptor (30 T2Rs) to process the largest variety of different kinds of bitter-tasting foods, asymmetrically. The fact that there are more molecules that taste bitter than that taste sweet, and that only one kind of receptor does the sensing, means that bitter taste deals with the most topologically heterogeneous and thus molecularly irregular of all the tastes. Even though there are vastly more bitter molecules and bitter receptors, there is no difference in the way in which these are tasted, making bitter flows the most relatively irregularly shaped flows received by a single receptor.[7] If we looked at a saliva flow of all bitter molecules and one of all sweet molecules, the bitter flow would be much more irregularly shaped and asymmetrically received than that of non-bitter compounds (Fig. 12.1).

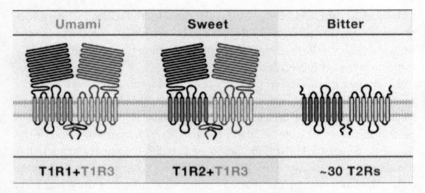

Figure 12.1 Taste Receptors. Image from D. A. Yarmolinsky, C. S. Zuker, and J. P. Ryba, 2009, 'Common Sense about taste: From Mammals to Insects', *Cell*, vol. 139, pp. 234–44.

Sound

Things also sound differently depending on the shape of their movement or waveform (2.408–13).

> *omnia postremo bona sensibus et mala tactu*
> *dissimili inter se pugnant perfecta figura;*
> *ne tu forte putes serrae stridentis acerbum*
> *horrorem constare elementis levibus aeque*
> *ac musaea mele, per chordas organici quae*
> *mobilibus digitis expergefacta figurant;*

> Finally, all things that are good and bad for the senses
> to touch fight with one another, made from different shapes;
> lest by chance you should think the sharp shudder
> of a shrieking saw is made up of figures as smooth
> as musical melodies which musicians awaken and shape
> on the strings with their agile fingers;

Sound is nothing other than the vibration or movement of matter. Atoms and molecules vibrate at different frequencies, producing different waveforms or sounds. We most often, although not universally, associate the sound of smooth or regularly periodic sine waves, such as a note played on a musical instrument, with pleasant feelings. On the other hand, we often associate the sound of rough, sawtooth, or irregular waveform sounds, such as 'noise' and 'distortion', with unpleasant

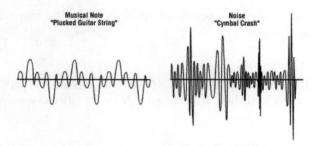

Figure 12.2 Smooth and rough sound waves. © O'Reilly.

feelings. The shapes of the two waveforms can be clearly distinguished. In one, matter quite literally moves in an irregular or rough shape and is often, like a cymbal crash, described as more chaotic and unpleasant than the pluck of a guitar string, for example (Fig. 12.2).

Smell

Similar to taste, different smells also correspond to the different molecular shapes and their vibrational waveforms (2.414–17).[8]

> *neu simili penetrare putes primordia forma*
> *in nares hominum, cum taetra cadavera torrent,*
> *et cum scena croco Cilici perfusa recens est*
> *araque Panchaeos exhalat propter odores;*

> the first beginnings penetrate people's noses
> with similar shapes when they burn foul corpses,
> as when the stage has just been sprinkled with Cilician saffron
> and the altar nearby breathes scents from Panchaea;

Foul smells often correspond to the release of toxic compounds which can be identified by the shape of their waveform. Different kinds of pleasant smells can also be formally distinguished according to their vibrational patterns and shapes: musky, floral, pepperminty, and so on. Burned bodies smell differently than saffron because the atoms in each scent vibrate in different waveforms and are shaped differently. The same contemporary biochemical research that confirms this fact for taste also confirms it for smell. Whether tasted or smelled, the topology of the molecular shapes, receptors, and waveforms all contribute to the sensation of that flow. Foul smells such as rot, for example, can be clearly seen in infrared spectroscopy images, often associated with sulphur, and appear as topologically distinct 'noises' in waveforms of more pleasant smells.[9]

Colour

Colours, like all other radiation on the electromagnetic spectrum, can also be distinguished according to different vibratory waveforms (2.419–21).

> *semine constituas, oculos qui pascere possunt,*
> *et qui conpungunt aciem lacrimareque cogunt*
> *aut foeda specie foedi turpesque videntur.*

> and lest you decide that the soothing colors of things
> which can feed the eyes are made up of seeds like those
> which sting the pupil and force it to tears,
> or appear awful and foul with a horrible appearance.

Colours with a smooth or regular waveform appear to us in their more 'pure' form. The colour red, for example, in its most red sensation is a vibrating flow of photons all moving in approximately the same smooth waveform and frequency (roughly 405–480 Thz). The rainbow gives us the most soothing series of smooth and rounded waveforms, all distinct from one another in the spectrum. However, the more distortion or irregularity there is in the waveforms, the less smooth it is; the more the image we are looking at appears choppy, noisy, and less as we would expect it to, the more unidentifiable it is. Technically speaking, if we were to do a Fourier transform of the wavelengths that compose the image of an apple, the image would become so distorted and irregular as the smoothness of the lightwave was distorted that we would not like to eat what we saw.

More phenomenologically, the sight of distorted or irregular wavelengths appears as strange or foreign images that often scare us. Rotting [*foeda*] (2.421) bodies, which have become blurred, distorted, and unfamiliar due to the decomposition of their flesh, often appear unpleasant. For example, if we took the series of wavelengths of light that compose the human face and began to distort their forms such that the wave became noisy, distorted, and discoloured, the face would become unpleasant and irregular compared to its regular and smoothed out features. The rotting body is the distorted and irregular waveform of the body. When we see things as choppy and indistinct at night because our vision is not as good, or when something is wrong with our eyes, or when we wear certain glasses that screen or distort our vision, these all introduce irregularities into the smooth waveforms of light or modify our reception of those wave flows. Most often this is unpleasant.

Today the exact mathematical and experimental details of lightwave transformation (regular and irregular waveforms) have become the focus of a multi-million-dollar photo-imaging market. Photo-imaging technicians operating under the same general idea that Lucretius had have developed a number of programmes that can add or subtract distortion, blur, and noise to the wavelengths of an image, using the method of the Fourier transform to add and subtract irregularities to the waveforms of light.[10] In other words, by changing the shape of the colour waveforms, the composition of colours can be made more or less pleasurable depending on the amount of blur, noise, and distortion in the shape (Figs 12.3 and 12.4).

Smooth, Rough, and Bent Waveforms

Across the senses, when the relatively smooth waveforms of pleasant tastes, sounds, smells, and colours become irregular in their frequency, amplitude, or periodicity, the result is an unpleasant and relatively rough waveform (2.422–5).

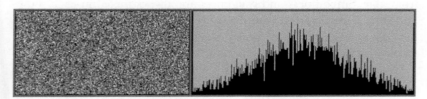

Figure 12.3 Distorted light waves.

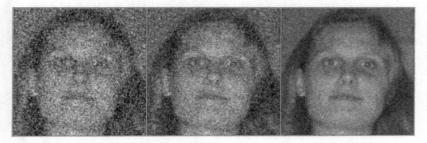

Figure 12.4 Smooth and distorted waveforms of a face. Wikimedia Commons.

omnis enim, sensus quae mulcet cumque, tibi res
haut sine principiali aliquo levore creatast;
at contra quae cumque molesta atque aspera constat,
non aliquo sine materiae squalore repertast.

For every shape that delights the senses has not
been created without some smoothness in the first beginnings.
But, in contrast, whatever shape is annoying and harsh,
has been found to be not without some roughness in its matter.

Lucretius is not suggesting that only purely smooth forms are pleasurable and that all rough [*squalore*] (2.425) forms are unpleasant, but simply that all waveforms that we find pleasurable are going to have at least some smoothness in them, and all unpleasant ones some roughness. In sensation, waveforms are always mixed.

Another implication here is that it is not necessarily the case that the smoother the waveform the more pleasant, or the rougher the waveform the less pleasant. For example, the smooth waves of the ocean are pleasant, but if they were completely smooth there would be no waves to enjoy. Some roughness of the waves could make the ocean unpleasant, but even more roughness may result in a beautiful storm viewed from afar. Smoothness and roughness are always mixed in each sense and each sense is mixed with the other senses in experience, such that the composite may be pleasurable or displeasurable with respect to the whole experience and not just because of one aspect of it.

The poetic image of turbulence from the proem can be found throughout Book II. Just as it is pleasurable to watch the turbulence of the waves from the shore, so from a distance the rough waves look smoother and therefore more pleasant to the eye. At the right distance the roughness of the roar of the ocean sounds more soothing. The question of sensual pleasure is therefore not only a question of the shape of the corporeal flows themselves, but also their shape as they touch our senses. High turbulence at a distance can actually give rise to a sensual pleasure.

In between smooth and rough waveforms there are also more angled forms, which may only tickle the senses without becoming too unpleasant (2.426–30).

Sunt etiam quae iam nec levia iure putantur
esse neque omnino flexis mucronibus unca,
sed magis angellis paulum prostantibus, ut quae

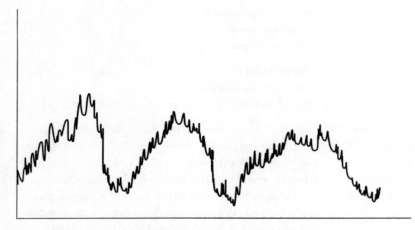

Figure 12.5 Fuzzy waveform.

titillare magis sensus quam laedere possint,
fecula iam quo de genere est inulaeque sapores.

And there are those first beginnings, too, which in their turn are thought
rightly neither to be smooth nor completely hooked with curved points,
but rather with angles projecting out a little, the sort which
would tickle the senses rather than cause them any harm.

For example, it is possible to have a waveform with regular periods and
amplitudes, but also to have between them rapid frequency changes
(Fig. 12.5).

These kinds of sharp [*mucronibus*] (2.427) little bends [*flexis*] (2.427) in
sound often produce a very low-level distortion or fuzzy sound which
many experience as pleasurable in rock 'n' roll and electronic music. In
the sensation of colour, impressionist paintings would appear fuzzy up
close and smooth-fuzzy at a distance. In taste and smell, the gastronomic
play between bitter and pleasant flavours is an important art in haute
cuisine. Wine lees, for example, have a yeasty bitter taste, but also sweetness from the grapes, as Lucretius notes.

Touch
The difference between smooth and rough material shapes may be most
evident in touch. Touching smooth things is generally more pleasurable
than touching rough things, Lucretius writes (2.431–3).

Denique iam calidos ignis gelidamque pruinam
dissimili dentata modo conpungere sensus
corporis, indicio nobis est tactus uterque.

And next, that hot fires and cold frost
are toothed in different ways to sting the senses
of the body, the touch of each of them indicates to us.

Fire and ice, for example, have 'teeth' shaped quite differently [*dissimili dentata*] (2.432) from those in our bodies. Some degree of fire and ice may be pleasurable to the body (a hot shower, a cold drink); however, once the momentum or kinetic energy of the molecules being broken apart by the fire becomes increasingly irregular in the form of a pedetic gas (in the case of fire), we are burned. When molecular momentum increases, molecules can move fast enough to break apart the molecular bonds that hold together our skin cells, causing them to become damaged. They quite literally puncture [*conpungere*] (2.432) into our skin and destroy our body's molecular bonds through collision, causing burns. The shape of the fire 'teeth' that penetrate our skin is an extremely irregular and rapidly changing figure drawn by the molecules of carbon dioxide, nitrogen, and oxygen as they fly pedetically through the air at high momentum, damaging the molecular structure of our skin by puncturing it [*conpungere*]. Fire is a high-momentum and irregularly shaped gas. Other things can be hot, but heat itself tends towards entropic radiation and evaporation.

Ice, on the other hand is shaped differently, since the figure drawn by cold things has a relatively low energy-momentum and a very regular solid shape. The shape of cold things in general is a result of the limited kinetic motion of their molecules. Increasingly cold states tend towards solid and immobile shapes. The 'teeth' of ice bite us in the inverse way that heat does. Ice damages our cells, causing pain, because the energy of our cells is transferred to the ice, slowing them down and eventually destroying them. Ice and cold physically penetrate the skin, changing its shape by making it more solid and less mobile. Human animal cells, when frozen, actually expand and burst, while the momentum of the molecules in the ice then begins to move more freely in the form of liquid water. In other words, because the shape of ice is more solid and less mobile, it bites us and moves our cells in different ways.

Both fire and ice, with respect to our body's patterns of momentum, are highly irregular in their shape and momentum as they puncture our bodies. This is consistent with Lucretius' subsequent claim that touch occurs both inside and outside the body. Fire and ice can damage us from outside, but the body can damage itself from the inside as well when it transfers its momentum outside itself in the form of heat loss (2.434–41).

One very interesting consequence of the idea that sensation occurs outside and inside the body is that sensation is not a strictly human attribute. For Lucretius, the figures and folds drawn by the *corpora* inside our bodies, what we today call cells and molecules, are effectively capable of their own sensation. They sense and react to exterior figures and interior figures without our necessarily being conscious of this. This is because matter itself is already sensitive and requires no mental substance in order to sense.

The Kinetic Theory of Matter

Related to the different shapes of fire and ice, Lucretius also puts forward a kinetic theory of matter. Thus, in addition to the waveform theory of material sensation described above, which explains how we *sense* matter's kinetic figures, Lucretius also provides a theory of why matter appears in different figurative densities in the first place. The kinetic theory of matter and the waveform theory of matter are therefore two parts of the same kinetic thesis: that the attributes of matter are defined purely by the shape of their motion. There are no pre-formed atoms (round, hooked, etc.) only wave patterns of motion (smooth, rough, etc). The kinetic theory of matter describes the *density of the waveforms*. This kinetic density is directly related to the structure of the figure traced by the motion of the *corpora*.

Solids
Hard and dense things such as rocks, for example, are hard because the corporeal vibrations or frequencies are held together very tightly or compactly [*compacta teneri*] such that their motion is relatively more constrained than that of other things. *Corpora* hold each other together with themselves [*inter sese esse*] in a compact intertwined branchlike formation (2.443–5).

> *Denique quae nobis durata ac spissa videntur,*
> *haec magis hamatis inter sese esse necessest*
> *et quasi ramosis alte compacta teneri.*

Next, the things which seem hard and dense to us
must be held together and joined deep within by first beginnings
that are more hooked to one another and branch-like.

Physically speaking, this is true. The molecular and atomic bonds of harder materials such as rocks or iron are less elastic and contain more connective bonds than less dense materials. Although molecular bonds are invisible to the eye, they form a branching network called a 'lattice' of multiple shared connections known as covalent bonds. This does not mean that *corpora* are immobile in solids, but rather, as Lucretius says, that their figurative movements are more compact and held together [*compacta teneri*] (2.445) through branching bonds. As solids are heated, their molecules vibrate faster and faster and break these bonds, so that they move increasingly further apart from one another, whereby the solid expands (Fig. 12.6).

Liquids

On the other hand, less hard or dense things such as fluids are liquid because the corporeal waveforms or vibratory frequencies are more elastic and contain fewer connective bonds between molecules (2.451–5).

illa quidem debent e levibus atque rutundis
esse magis, fluvido quae corpore liquida constant.

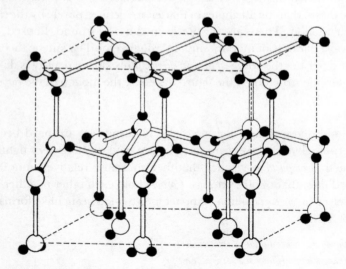

Figure 12.6 Ice crystal lattice. © Ben Best.

namque papaveris haustus itemst facilis quod aquarum;
nec retinentur enim inter se glomeramina quaeque
et perculsus item proclive volubilis exstat.

And those things ought to be made of lighter and rounder
first beginnings, which are liquid and have a fluid *corpore.*
For it is just as easy to scoop poppy seeds as water;
the individual globules are not hindered by each other,
and a poppy seed, when struck, rolls just as easily downhill.

Liquids are made from corporeal figures that are smoother [*levibus*] (2.451) and more rounded [*rutundis*] (2.451) in the sense in which liquids are composed of corporeal folds which are less densely bound to one another and move past each other more easily (smoothly) without bonding into a more fixed lattice and taking on an increasingly rigid, fixed or rough networked figure. For example, just as poppy seeds flow past each other easily without sticking to each other, so the corporeal folds also move past each other smoothly without bonding. Furthermore, just as poppy seeds fall from a scoop in a more random motion than the flows of matter in rocks, so the folds or atomic molecules in liquids move in increasingly random order as well. Fluids have fewer connections or conjunctions between them so they can more easily roll away or leak.

Gases
Finally, the least hard or dense things take the form of gases because the corporeal waveforms or vibratory frequencies are the most mobile and there are the fewest connective bonds between molecules (2.456–63).

omnia postremo quae puncto tempore cernis
diffugere ut fumum nebulas flammasque, necessest,
si minus omnia sunt e levibus atque rotundis,
at non esse tamen perplexis indupedita,
pungere uti possint corpus penetrareque saxa,
nec tamen haerere inter se; quod cumque videmus
sensibus dentatum, facile ut cognoscere possis
non e perplexis, sed acutis esse elementis.

Finally, all things which you see fly apart
in an instant, like smoke, clouds, and flames, even if they are not
composed entirely out of smooth and round first beginnings,
nevertheless must still not be hampered by entangled first beginnings,

so that they are able to sting the body and penetrate rocks,
and nevertheless not cling together.

Gases are composed of highly pedetic corporeal motions which are moving so quickly and are so unbound from one another that they break apart from one another in an instant [*puncto tempore cernis diffugere*] (2.456). However, gases are not completely unconnected; they still conjoin with one another [*perplexis*] (2.459), but not nearly as much as liquids or solids. Smoke and fire, for example, still sting the body, but the molecules are not sufficiently strongly bound together to turn fire into a solid object. Lucretius here is correct to connect fire and heat to the expansion and increased mobility of matter. The more flying motions break free, the more gaseous and the more momentum the matter. Gases therefore have the most free and irregular unbound [*perplexis*] kinetic figures.

Kinetic Sensation

The wave and kinetic theories of matter can now be combined to understand all the mixed sensory matters. Lucretius gives the example of the taste of briny seawater. Based on the two kinetic theories put forward, Lucretius now shows how obvious it is that salt water can be both fluid and unpleasant at the same time. Following the kinetic theory of matter, the corporeal folds of the liquid are mostly unbound, un-latticed [*provolvi*] (2.470), smooth [*levibus*] (2.471), or rounded [*globosa*] (2.469), making its material figure the shape of a liquid. Following the waveform theory of matter, some of the corporeal folds in the liquid also vibrate in a rough or relatively less smooth waveform compared with more pleasant tasting molecules, that is, the waveform of sodium and other bitter ocean molecules.

The fact that the shape of matter is composed of a moving mixture [*admixta*] (2.467) of different waveforms and densities is evident by the fact that we can filter out the unpleasant components of the brine through the more dense medium of the earth. Saltwater becomes freshwater through filtration. The more rough waveforms will bond to those of the earth, while those more rolling, smooth, or liquid aspects will pass through the earth without bonding in a more dense lattice.

Although still quite general in its features, Lucretius' theory of kinomorphic sensation is broadly consistent with the experimental findings of contemporary physics. This theory has a number of implications for materialism and ontology more broadly, as we will see in the next chapter.

Notes

1. Insofar as Aristotle's hylomorphism adopts any of these three aspects of Platonic formalism, Lucretius' theory is different as well.

2. Karl Marx, *The First Writings of Karl Marx*, trans. Paul M. Schafer (New York: Ig Publishers, 2006), 111. My emphasis.

3. Robert Epstein, 'The Empty Brain', *Aeon*, 18 May 2016, https://aeon. co/essays/your-brain-does-not-process-information-and-it-is-not-a-computer (accessed 29 July 2017).

4. The science of taste and smell is becoming increasingly accurate. Along the lines Lucretius proposed, scientists at IBM and elsewhere are working on mapping all the wavelengths of different tastes and scents. See https://www.dietsensor.com/technology/ (accessed 29 July 2017). IBM is currently working on a massive project to categorise all measures of wavelength for odorants. See http://www.extremetech. com/extreme/193591-ibm-seeks-the-secrets-to-the-science-of-scent (accessed 29 July 2017).

5. Shaoqing Cui, Jun Wang and Xinlei Wang, 'Fabrication and Design of a Toxic Gas Sensor Based on Polyaniline/Titanium Dioxide Nanocomposite Film by Layer-by-layer Self-assembly', *The Royal Society of Chemistry Advances*, 5 (2015), 58211–19, http://pubs.rsc.org/ En/content/articlepdf/2015/ra/c5ra06388d (accessed 29 July 2017). Toxic gases can be measured as wave number changes in the olfactory wavelengths, giving more sawtooth or sharp wave patterns compared with more regular ones.

6. See H. L. Klopping, 'Olfactory Theories and the Odors of Small Molecules', *Journal of Agricultural and Food Chemistry*, 19 (1971): 999–1004; and S.-Y. Takane and J. B. O. Mitchell 'A Structure Odour Relationship Study using EVA Descriptors and Hierarchical Clustering', *Organic & Biomolecular Chemistry*, 2 (2004): 3250. 'In similar fashion, vibration theory can successfully account for the commonality of the odor of molecules of different structures that contain the same functional groups [sulfuraceous, nitric, ethereal, etc.], a phenomenon both familiar and otherwise unexplained by shape theory. Furthermore, vibrational spectra appear to be a better predictor of odor character than shape descriptors.' Simon Gane, Dimitris Georganakis, Klio Maniati, Manolis Vamvakias, Nikitas Ragoussis, Efthimios M. C. Skoulakis, Luca Turin and Wulfila Gronenberg, 'Molecular Vibration-Sensing Component in Human Olfaction', *Plos One*, 8.1 (2013), http://journals.

plos.org/plosone/article?id=10.1371/journal.pone.0055780 (accessed 29 July 2017).

'Smell biologist Tim Jacob of Cardiff University in Wales, says that rotten egg smell is a good example of the vibration theory's appeal. Sulfur is a chemical hallmark of rotting organic material – something that is dangerous for us to eat. And molecules containing sulfur almost always smell horrible to us, he says – just as should be the case if evolution worked properly to favor our survival. But there's no single shape or simple chemical property that sulfur universally confers to every kind of odorant molecule. On the other hand, sulfur does add signature vibrations to a molecule that a molecular vibration-sensitive nose might detect. "I do all my research without needing to know which model most accurately describes what's going on," Jacob says. But, he says of the vibration theory, "from a biological point of view it has great interest."' Mark Anderson, 'Study Bolsters Quantum Vibration Scent Theory', *Scientific American*, 28 January 2013, http://www.scientificamerican.com/article/study-bolsters-quantum-vibration-scent-theory/ (accessed 29 July 2017).

7. S. Rodgers, J. Busch, H. Peters and E. Christ-Hazelhof, 'Building a Tree of Knowledge: Analysis of Bitter Molecules', *Chemical Senses*, 30.7 (2005): 547–57.
8. Luca Turin, *The Secret of Scent: Adventures in Perfume and the Science of Smell* (New York: Ecco, 2006); Jason Palmer, 'Quantum Biology: Do Weird Physics Effects Abound in Nature?', *BBC News*, 28 January 2013, http://www.bbc.co.uk/news/science-environment-21150047 (accessed 23 May 2013); C. Burr, *The Emperor of Scent: A Story of Perfume, Obsession, and the Last Mystery of the Senses* (New York: Random House, 2003).
9. Klopping, 'Olfactory Theories and the Odors of Small Molecules'.
10. 'Fourier Transform Processing with ImageMagick', http://www.fmwconcepts.com/imagemagick/fourier_transforms/fourier.html (accessed 29 July 2017).

13. Morphogenesis

The thesis that form is kinetic and material has a number of important consequences for Lucretius' broader theory of materialism, and even has its mythological equivalent in the well-known theory of the Great Mother Goddess.

Finite Forms – Infinite Morphogenesis

Matter, Lucretius argues, is infinite, but the topological figures of the motions of matter are not. This is the case because if all figures were possible then all sizes would be possible, and if all sizes were possible then there could be *corpora* which bound together a single, infinitely large body of matter [*infinito debebunt corporis auctu*] (2.481–4).

However, since nature is a non-totality, there can be no such single, infinite shape which does not already delimit itself and thus presuppose that which is beyond it. If there was an infinite figure that bound an infinity of matter, it would itself be bound by nothing, which is a contradiction. Furthermore, if a new figure or form was needed for every single thing in nature, this would also require the creation of a single form for the whole of nature. Therefore, since there is no such infinite form, the only possible conclusion is that there is an infinity of infinite combinations of finite forms.

If forms were always getting bigger and bigger they would also be getting smaller and smaller at the same time, relative to the next largest form. However, since there is no largest and no smallest figure, as argued in the previous chapters, there cannot be an infinite diversity of unique forms. However, this does not mean that there cannot be an infinite *combination* of forms.

The folds of matter are infinitely small and large composites of other folds, but the kinetic shapes or waveforms drawn by these folds are

limited by the corporeal folds in which they are vibrations (2.523–5).[1]
For example, according to Lucretius, there are at least three kinds of
figures: smooth [*levibus*] (2.402, 411), rough [*squalore*] (2.425), and sharp
[*mucronibus*] (2.427). These three figures correspond to three kinotopological regions on the waveform continuum: smooth waves, which are
gently and smoothly curved with regular frequencies; sharp waves,
which may draw regular frequencies but do so along a fuzzy curve; and
rough waves, which have relatively more irregular frequencies.

There are no absolutely or infinitely 'straight' figures or forms because
matter is fundamentally pedetic. Since matter always includes a swerve
or *clinamen*, it is always vibrating at some level of its *minima* and is never
absolutely straight. The straight line is a geometrical fiction. Matter
always moves in a curve or frequency waveform. Even a ray of light is
made of photons which vibrate at certain frequencies and whose flow is
curved around large celestial objects. There are no absolutely straight
lines, but only very low frequencies whose smoothness appears to be
relatively straight from a given perspective.

All three of these formal figurations are found mixed together in their
motion [*admixta*] (2.467). Like briny seawater, things [*rebus*] are made of a
complex assemblage of different waveforms. There may be finite figures
(smooth, sharp, and rough), but there is an infinite process of morphogenesis by which the frequencies and waveforms change, combine, and
continually modulate into the macroscopic forms we recognise as leaves,
animals, and planets. Thus, the differences between smooth, sharp, and
rough are not only differences in kind, but insofar as they are modulations or transformations of a single, continuous waveform, they are also
differences in degree.

Therefore we can say, somewhat strangely, that between every difference in degree (along the waveform) is a difference in kind (smooth,
sharp, rough), but the difference between differences of kind is a difference in degree. Since there is only constant and continuous movement
in the universe, the difference between things cannot be a merely formal
difference. The formal differences (smooth, sharp, rough) that define the
shape of things is itself a modulation of the continuous waveform: a difference in degree of modulation and frequency.

The waveform or kinotopology of the corporeal fold is therefore fundamentally limited by the limits of the fold in which it persists. Therefore,
just as there can be no single largest fold or totality, there can be no
single largest figure either. *Corpora* are infinite but *rebus* are always finite.

Insofar as shape or figure is always bound to the thing or fold whose shape it is, it is bound at both ends [*utrimque*] (2.512). The *corpora* literally bind things [*rebus*] from both sides when they produce a fold. Therefore, there is always a certain limit to things [*rebus reddita certa finis*] (2.512–14), even though there is not always a certain limit to the *corpora*. Things are by definition limited, whereas *corpora delimit* them. For Lucretius, the world is not an infinitely large thing, but rather a process of infinitely larger and smaller material *combinations*. There are thus infinite combinations or infinite sums, but not infinite things [*rebus*].

If the universe were a large, single thing with a single shape, it would be a totality and thus be frozen, immobile, and dead, as seen in the previous chapters. If, however, the universe were a single, smallest shape (like a singularity), it would also be frozen, immobile, and dead. The universe, for Lucretius, is therefore not 'an infinite thing' but an infinite sum in process and in motion.

Lucretius' kinetic theory of matter is again prescient. According to contemporary physics there are only finite kinds of particles or shapes of matter, and they have mostly been mapped by the 'standard model' of particle physics. All sensible forms in the universe are made from basic waveforms of matter along a continuum and a combination of more or less smooth, rough, or sharp figures without a single largest or smallest figure.

Thermodynamics
Correlatively, for Lucretius, there is no shape or thing which is infinitely cold or infinitely hot. The temperature of things in the universe is limited by two extremes (2.514–17).

> *denique ab ignibus ad gelidas hiemum usque pruinas*
> *finitumst retroque pari ratione remensumst.*
> *omnis enim calor ac frigus mediique tepores*
> *interutrasque iacent explentes ordine summam.*

> Next, from fires all the way up to the cold frosts of winter
> there is a limit, and it is measured back again in the same way.
> For all heat and cold and levels of warmth in the middle
> lie between two extremes, and cover the range in succession.

Although Lucretius' examples are directed at temperatures on Earth, which he is more obviously correct about, his comments at the cosmological level are also, scientifically speaking, correct. There is nothing in the universe that is zero degrees Kelvin, nor can there be. Zero degrees Kelvin would mean that a thing would have absolutely no motion at all, which is a violation of the Lucretian principle of motion and a violation of the laws of quantum physics. Even radio waves still have a temperature of 0.001 Kelvin corresponding to the length of their waveform (2.897 metres). On the other hand, there is nothing in the universe that is infinitely hot, like an infinitely dense singularity. Such a singularity would violate the laws of general relativity and quantum physics. Again, an infinitely dense energetic singularity would imply a lack of motion and thus render the universe immobile, uncreative, and dead.

The Turbulence of Form

There are finite kinds of waveforms or frequencies at which folds vibrate, but there is also an infinity of each kind of vibration. If there were not an infinity of *corpora* then the sum of matter would be finite (2.525–8). However, if there is an infinity of forms then there could be a single form of an infinite totality, and therefore only one total form. If, on the other hand, the *corpora* were finite then how would they explain the enormous variation of forms that we see (2.547–50)?

> quippe etenim sumam hoc quoque uti finita per omne
> corpora iactari unius genitalia rei,
> unde ubi qua vi et quo pacto congressa coibunt
> materiae tanto in pelago turbaque aliena?

> For indeed if I assume this, too – that the *corpora* which generate
> this one thing were finite, tossed about through the universe –
> whence, where, by what force, and how will they meet
> and congregate in such a great ocean and foreign throng of matter?

The solution is that for each kind of form (smooth, sharp, rough) there is an infinite number of *corpora* that can draw those figures. This is possible because all corporeal flows are turbulent, pedetic, and therefore capable of transforming their form in an infinity of ways as they assemble and reassemble themselves in the great collision of heterogeneous flows [*pacto congressa coibunt materiae tanto in pelago turbaque aliena*] (2.549–50). If the *corpora* that produce [*genitalia*] (2.548) things [*rei*] were finite they would not be able to modulate or assemble themselves within the turbulent motion of matter. They would fail to adapt, combine forms, and produce anything but a few limited things and not an infinite diversity of things. In order to produce an infinite universe there must be an infinity of *corpora*.

Lucretius' poetic example is absolutely fitting to the waveform theory of matter. Matter is like the 'faithless sea' of turbulent chaos, he says, upon which the ships of things float. If *corpora* were finite, they would have already fallen apart after an infinite amount of time, incapable of reordering themselves into what we see today. Just as entropy introduces disorder into closed systems, so the ocean tears apart the closed vessels of ships. However, if the universe is not a closed and finite system, but an open and infinite one, then reorder is possible from disorder.

Contemporary physics confirms precisely this: that the universe is an open and infinite system, therefore re-creative and capable of negentropy or reorder. Again, Lucretius is explicit here that the *corpora* are not discrete things at all, but flows or currents strewn or scattered [*sparsa*] into continually modulating assemblages [*concilium*] (2.560–6). The disorder, entropy, and funerals of these assemblages are mixed in motion [*admixta*] with order, negentropy, and the birth of new ones. There is not a single kind of thing [*rebus*] in the world which is composed of only one kind [*genere*] of consistently ordering *corpora* [*consistat principiorum*] (2.584). All things are made from consistently [*constet*] mixed [*permixto*] corporeal seeds [*semine*] (2.581–5). There is no purely smooth figure or purely rough figure or form. Waveforms are always composite and mixed with others at different levels and to different degrees. Form is never static, fixed, or stable. It is nothing but the kinotopology of matter itself, and therefore constantly mixed and morophogenetic.

Cybele: *mater materque*

The mythological and historical name of this morphogenetic process, according to Lucretius, is *mater materque*: Mother Earth, the Great Mother, the Mother of Mothers, the Mothering Mother, the maternal origin or source of all matter. Although this section is often read as a denunciation of pagan religion or a 'parody'[2] of allegory, I would like to show here that it is precisely the opposite: it is a mythological demonstration of Lucretius' own theory of morphogenesis befitting his previous interpretations of other goddesses (Venus and Artemis). Only in a few lines does he critique the specific dangers of treating the mother goddess as a transcendent deity. The focus, however, is actually on her poetic similarity with Lucretius' own theory. This is why he discusses her here, directly after his writings on morphogenesis, and not earlier in Book I in his rejection of *religio*.

Mater materque is the single creative source from which and within which all bodies flow [*et nostri genetrix haec dicta est corporis una*] (2.599). She is the infinite and ever-renewing source [*inmensum volventes*] (2.590) of the flows of springs [*fontes*] (2.590) and rivers [*fluvios*] (2.596), the volcanic flows of matter itself [*ignibus impetus*] (2.593), and the wild flows of plants [*arbustaque*] (2.594) and animals [*ferarum*] (2.597). She is the mythological expression of kinetic materialism.

Goddess of Mobility

Lucretius' description of *mater materque* follows closely his description of Venus from the proem of Book I, but more clearly refers to the even more original goddess Cybele, from which all other Greek and Roman goddesses are derived (2.600–3).

> *Hanc veteres Graium docti cecinere poetae*
> *sedibus in curru biiugos agitare leones,*
> *aeris in spatio magnam pendere docentes*
> *tellurem neque posse in terra sistere terram.*

> The ancient, learned poets of the Greeks sang that she
> from her throne on a chariot drives two yoked lions,
> thus teaching that the great earth hangs in a stretch
> of air and that earth cannot sit upon earth.

Cybele, the mother goddess, is also the goddess of mobility depicted in a flying chariot. She is seated on her throne, an ever-moving chariot driven by two conjoined [*biiugos*] (2.601) lions. The lion is the queen of the beasts, a symbol of corporeal vitality and endless power. Mother Nature is driven by the constant motion of the corporeal flows of strong animal bodies produced by their kinetic conjunction, just like Lucretius' *corpora*. Nature constantly moves, but as an infinite sum remains what it is, seated on her throne. The earth itself is not the centre of the universe, but rather flies through the infinite universe.

Goddess of Pedesis

Nothing comes from nothing and so the wild lions come from their mother, and in this way their pedesis is not random at all, but emergent.

Turbulence is not merely negative chaos, but a generative and creative chaos that produces order and form from initial conditions. Everything comes from something and is thus in relation to something which softens or makes supple the straight line into the curve, wave, and fold. Our universe is not the product of random fluctuations, but a pedetic unfolding from a very low entropy state: the initial state of the universe before the big bang. From this maternal or initial condition, all order and disorder emerge, not by a predetermined order but from an emergent order based on the specific maternal entropy state of the universe (2.604–5).

adiunxere feras, quia quamvis effera proles
officiis debet molliri victa parentum.

They attached the wild beasts, because however wild an offspring is,
it ought to be subdued and softened by the kindness of its parents.

The wild beasts [*feras*] (2.604) do not move randomly, but through a specifically adjoined or conjoined [*adiunxere*] (2.604) motion. No matter how wild [*effera*] (2.604) the offspring are, their movement is never random. It is always made supple [*molliri*] (2.605), held back and curved back [*debet*] (2.605) over itself into folds, nourished [*victa*] (2.605) by the love [*officiis*] (2.605) of its maternal condition or source. Nature itself is nothing other than the immanent driving, agitation, bending, and folding of material flows into order and form.

Lucretius uses the same language of driving to describe the *corpora*. Earlier in Book II, he says that the *corpora* are driven [*exercita*] (2.97) along in continuous motion and driven [*exercita*] (2.120) on by their frequent meetings and partings. Later in Book II, he says that they fly around in many ways, driven [*exercita*] (2.1055) on by eternal motion.

Goddess of Politics
Mater materque also wears a crown on her head (2.606–7).

muralique caput summum cinxere corona,
eximiis munita locis quia sustinet urbes.

They encircled the top of her head with a crown in the shape of a wall,
because she is fortified in excellent locations and upholds cities.

On the condition of her continual sustaining motion, the flow of matter not only curves, but folds back over itself into the stable form of the circle [*cinxere*] (2.606), figured by the crown [*corona*] (2.606) on her head.

Nature is therefore not only the condition of motion, form, and emergence, but is also capable of sustaining such emergences in the cycle or repetition of the circle. The form or the kinotopology of the circle, as I have shown in this book and elsewhere,[3] is the basic condition for politics in the form of the *munita* or *moenera:* the community, the debt/credit relation, social service, and so on. The circle is precisely the *munita locis* (2.607), the place where social relation occurs. In other words, Mother Nature in the form of the countryside, the *chora*, the earth itself, is the material condition for politics, but as such not reducible to it. She not only makes possible the natural disasters which destroy cities, but also the material and spatial conditions for the enclosure, protection, and stability of the basic social form: the *munita*.

The Horror

The only problem with this image of the mother goddess, according to Lucretius, is that it has been deified and personified into a weapon of fear and terror (2.608–9).

> *quo nunc insigni per magnas praedita terras*
> *horrifice fertur divinae matris imago.*

> Endowed with this emblem, the image of the divine mother
> is now carried with horrifying effect throughout the great earth.

The image [*imago*] (2.609) of the mother is now carried around as if she were an actual person in order to instil terror and demand offerings. People are sacrificing each other for her as if she were a real person. For Lucretius, it is truly horrifying and idiotic to see her turned into an image of worship as if she could reward or punish people. Nature is everything, the pure movement of matter; it makes absolutely no sense to sacrifice or pray to her.

Her History

The mother goddess, however, is also the oldest and most important figure of ancient worship in the West, from which all preceding Graeco-Romanised versions come (2.610–13).

> *hanc variae gentes antiquo more sacrorum*
> *Idaeam vocitant matrem Phrygiasque catervas*
> *dant comites, quia primum ex illis finibus edunt*
> *per terrarum orbes fruges coepisse creari.*

The different races in accordance with the ancient practice of her sacred
rites call her the Idaean mother and give her bands of Phrygians
as her attendants, because they declare that it is from these borders
that crops first began to be produced for the whole world.

The earliest recorded name of the Great Mother was Cybele, which
was adapted from the name Kubaba or Kumbaba (Kybebe in Greek),
related to the goddess Humbaba, the guardian of the forest in the Epic
of Gilgamesh.[4]

Kubaba may also mean a hollow vessel or cave, which again evokes the
imagery of the Neolithic, and her shrines, like Cybele's, were often situated
in a cave or near a rock. Kubaba or Kumbaba may be a Hittite name for
the goddess, and a statue of her at the city of Carchemish shows her wearing
a high cap embellished with roses and what appears to be a snake emerging
at the front of it, over her forehead. In her hand she holds a pomegranate.
Roses and pomegranates still belong to her in Rome 1,000 years later.[5]

Cybele, like all great goddesses, was the founder of agriculture and law,
the mother of seeds and natural generation. Cybele was the goddess
of death, fertility, and wild life. This history connects her with the
Sumerian goddess Inanna, the Egyptian goddess Isis, the Greek goddess
Demeter, and Gaia. Cybele is thus a complex figure combining Minoan-
Mycenaean goddesses with the Phrygian ones from Asia Minor.[6] In
Greece, as in Phrygia, Cybele was the goddess of animals [*potnia therōn*]
who rode a chariot driven by lions. She is the original complex from
which all the Greek and Roman goddesses come. She is the Minoan-
Greek Earth Mother Rhea, praised by ecstatic rituals. She is the grain
goddess Demeter; the mother of wild forests and animals, Artemis; and
the goddess of love, Venus.

De Rerum Natura is devoted to the many names of nature. In Book I,
Lucretius draws on Venus, Artemis, and Helen, all of whom are connected to Cybele. In Book II, Cybele unifies them all. She is the great
foreign goddess of nature, adopted by the Greeks and Romans, but
whose rituals and place among the other gods is quite different because
she is the only immanent god. She is the only god whose divinity is
nothing other than matter in motion, the *corpora sancta*. She is nature
become divine and divinity become natural. In Greek and Roman soci-
eties, Cybele was a foreign and strange goddess of the lower classes, of
migrants, strangers, of ecstatic music, and dancing.

Her Priests

Lucretius writes that people foolishly believe that the priests of Cybele are castrated as a punishment and are therefore afraid; but this is a distortion of their origins. The mother goddess and her castrated/sacrificed son-lover is a much older mythological relation that dates back to the Bronze Age worship of Innana and Ishtar. Cybele, like them, had a son-lover named Attis.

> Whatever their origin, the relationship between Cybele and Attis confirms once again the image of the sacred marriage between the goddess and the god or king who once personified the year god and was sacrificed and dismembered in person or in mime at the spring fertility ritual. Whether the son-lover is Attis, Dionysos or Zagreus, the imagery of dismemberment and death followed by resurrection is the same. The sickle used for the castration of Attis and the flint knife used by the priests of Cybele point back to the sickle of the Old European male companion of the Mother Goddess of the Neolithic era. The castrated high priest of Cybele was regarded as Attis himself, and in Rome was called Archigallus. The shadowy lineaments of the old vegetation and initiation rites come into focus: it is more than likely that castration, like circumcision, was at one time substituted for the ritual killing of the king or high priest. Originally, Cybele may have had a single high priest and king, her 'son-lover', who was at first killed but whose genitals in a later era were offered in sacrifice instead of his life because their potency was believe to fertilize the earth they fell upon.[7]

Castration is actually a symbol of fertility. Instead of the god-king being sacrificed, his fertile organ was sacrificed in order to make the world fertile again. The priests of Cybele were like her: highly mobile and wandering throughout the country. In Rome,

> On 24 March, the Day of Blood, the day of lamentation for the death of Attis, the Taurobolium, or sacrifice of the bull, took place and his genitals were offered to the goddess. This was the day when the priests flagellated and lacerated themselves, sprinkling the altar and the effigy of Attis with their blood, and when devotees castrated themselves. These rites represented the dismemberment of the god, the life-force of the earth, similarly enacted in the Dionysian and Orphic rituals, and most probably also in the Canaanite rituals detested by the prophets.[8]

Generation and creation are thus associated with the flow of vital fluids: blood, the *sangre semita*, the creative flow of seeds that gives life to the earth. Attis is depicted as a shepherd like Dumuzi, the son-lover of Innana.

> Sun-rays or ears of corn or fruit emerge from his cap, proclaiming him both a solar god and a god of regeneration; this imagery is shared with the rites of Eleusis. In his rituals he was called 'the cornstalk' or 'the ear of wheat', and his symbols were the pine-cone and the pomegranate. Like Dumuzi and Tammuz, he was lord of cattle, sheep and plants.[9]

Cybele and Attis are thus linked to the Oracle of Delphi by their engraved images at the site, their connection with Dionysus, the sacrifice of the bull, the pine-cone *thyrsus*, the oracular prophecy of Gaia, and feminine knowledge through bodily transformation and intoxication. In fact, in order to decide whether to adopt Cybele as a Roman goddess, the Romans consulted the Oracle of Delphi, which said, unsurprisingly, 'yes'.

The *corpora* have a similar status in *De Rerum Natura*. Matter is a flow of generative seeds, but there is no reason to fear their punishment. The flow of their vital fluids or blood is the creative condition of all things [*rerum*]. Through death and destruction life is created. Things are castrated in order to release yet more abundant corporeal flows.

Rhea, Metis, and Chora

In addition to the priests that castrate and flagellate themselves, there were also Cybele's followers who, Lucretius reports, travelled, danced, and wildly played the tympana (drums), cymbals, and horns. This too has a resonance with Lucretius' material kinetic philosophy (2.633–9).

> *Dictaeos referunt Curetas, qui Iovis illum*
> *vagitum in Creta quondam occultasse feruntur,*
> *cum pueri circum puerum pernice chorea*
> *armat et in numerum pernice chorea*
> *armati in numerum pulsarent aeribus aera,*
> *ne Saturnus eum malis mandaret adeptus*
> *aeternumque daret matri sub pectore volnus.*

> recall to mind the Dictaean Curetes, who are said
> to have concealed once the famous wailing of Jupiter on Crete,
> when as boys around a baby boy with agile dance
> in armor they beat bronze against bronze in measured time,
> so that Saturn might not get him and chew him in his jaws,
> and produce an everlasting wound in his Mother's heart.

The followers of Cybele were called Corybantes, but the Greeks identified or confused them with the Curetes or earth sprites who helped to hide the crying of Zeus from his father Cronos. Lucretius recounts this philosophically important myth connected with yet another major earth goddess, Rhea.

Rhea is the Earth Mother consort of Cronos. Out of fear that one of his children would become more powerful and overthrow him, as he did to his father Ouranos, Cronos ate each of his children as soon as they were born. Rhea consulted with Gaia and together they conspired to deceive Cronos by giving him a swaddled rock instead of a baby. The baby Zeus was then hidden in a cave on the island of Crete where Gaia's earth sprites danced and played loud music to cover up the sound of the baby's crying.

Ovid, in the *Metamorphoses*, says the Curetes were born from rainwater. For Lucretius, the children of nature, the *corpora*, are similarly described as corporeal seeds falling/flying around pedetically. A similar flow of creative matter is recounted in the birth of Venus through Ouranos' seed falling from the sky into the ocean. Cronos eats his children precisely because of the masculine anxiety about the feminine power of creation: that Rhea will create something more powerful than himself. Nature is capable of destroying the most powerful structures and creating something new. Rhea's power is not the empirical power of an object or physical strength that she wields over him, but the power of what the Greeks call *metis* or 'creative cunning'. Rhea's power is in her productivity and in her feminine knowledge of craft and weaving.[10]

As Lucretius writes, Jupiter (Zeus) was invaginated in a cave on Crete [*vagitum in Creta*] (2.634) where he was raised by a goat and protected by the dancing [*chorea*] (2.635) of the Curetes. The *chora* is not only the creative 'space' [*loci, spatium, inane*] of the cave from which things emerge, but it is also the fundamentally hidden [*occultasse*] (2.634) space produced by the insensible *corpora*. The *chora* covers, obscures, and folds the flows of life together in its enclosure. But the *chora* is not simply passive fecundity, it is the creative and pedetic movement of matter itself exemplified in the dancing [*chorea*] of the Curetes. They conceal therefore not by negativity, but by an excess of noise and motion. The chaotic dancing and noise of the Curetes mirrors the battles of the corporeal flows as they clash wildly on the open sea, but not randomly, since they are also connected to their mother [Gaia/Rhea]. The battle of the Curetes is the deathless battle of creation.

Cronos, however, seeks to complete the *moeneric* cycle of exchange. A baby is produced, then consumed and returned to where it started: inside Cronos. In his way he retains power, unity and totality. Rhea's wisdom and weave disrupts the circle of exchange and opens it to the outside, to nature, to the pedesis of the Curetes and the flows of divine milk from the goat, Amalthea. Into the cycle of production and consumption, Rhea thus introduces an entropy or disorder from which a new order can be born. Within the circle, however, Rhea is reduced to a negativity, an everlasting wound [*pectore volnus*] (2.639), through which children pass, only to be consumed again by their father. The theft of Zeus breaks the cycle and transforms Rhea into a true creatrix.

Rhea serves as a perfect poetic exemplar of Lucretian materialism. Matter is born from its mother and keenly woven in the dark, noisy, and pedetic *chora* or void. Through its own rhythm, dancing and music, and the nourishing liquid flows of milk, the *corpora* fold themselves up into the complex patterns of things. The *moenera* is evaded, but returns again in Zeus, the father of all the gods, whose own masculine anxiety is satisfied only by eating the more powerful morphogenetic goddess *Metis* herself.

The strange dancing of strangers (Cybele's Curetes) is akin to the 'turbulent movement of matter [*materiae tanto in pelago turbaque aliena*]', described by Lucretius early in Book II in line 550. Pedesis is the first and original music, writing, and inscription. As Elias Canetti writes,

> Rhythm is originally the rhythm of the feet. Every human being walks, and, since he walks on two legs with which he strikes the ground in turn and since he only moves if he continues to do this, whether intentionally or not, a rhythmic sound ensues . . . The earliest writing he learnt to read was that of their tracks; it was a kind of rhythmic notation imprinted on the soft ground and as he read it, he connected it with the sound of its formation.[11]

Religio

It is fine, Lucretius concludes, if anyone wants to use the idea of the mother goddess to poetically describe the immanent nature of nature and related mythologies, but only as long as this does not make us think that nature is a person or subject to whom sacrifices could be made or from whom rewards could be received. Nature does not care about us, nor should we be afraid of it. For Lucretius, mythology is just another way of describing nature, nothing more (2.659–60).

The Multiplicity of Forms

All the individual forms of matter emerge through the morphogensis of a single and infinitely diverse nature. Just as all the different animals drink from a single stream of water, so all the *corpora* flow from the 'single' stream of nature (2.663–5).

> . . . *sub tegmine caeli*
> *ex unoque sitim sedantes flumine aquai*
> *dissimili vivont specie retinentque parentum*

> . . . beneath the same expanse of sky,
> slaking their thirst from a single stream of water,
> live their lives with different appearances and retain their parents'
> nature

All of life comes to rest, folding up in the single stream of nature [*unoque sitim sedantes flumine aquai*] (2.664), but each life is figured differently [*dissimili vivont specie*] (2.665). The single stream or flow of nature is, as discussed in previous chapters, not total, but a simplex which is nothing other than the infinite multiplicity from which the infinity of material differences are formed. For example, every bit of matter contains in itself an infinite multiplicity of formal differences (2.666–71).

> *tanta est in quovis genere herbae materiai*
> *dissimilis ratio, tanta est in flumine quoque.*
> *Hinc porro quamvis animantem ex omnibus unam*
> *ossa cruor venae calor umor viscera nervi*
> *constituunt, quae sunt porro distantia longe,*
> *dissimili perfecta figura principiorum.*

> So great is the difference of matter in whatever
> type of grass, so great in every stream.
> So too each living creature of them all
> is composed of bones, blood, veins, warmth, moisture,
> flesh, and sinews, which are also all very different,
> formed by different shapes of the first beginnings.

There are just as many formal differences in a blade of grass as there are in a stream of water, an infinite multiplicity. For each component form we might discover in the blade of grass, such as its cells, its molecules, its atoms, its particles, for example, there are component forms of these forms produced by infinitely modulating and superpositional quantum fields, or, in Lucretius' terminology, coporeal flows.

The conclusion here is dramatic: all form is already composite form. There is no pure form of grass, only an infinite multiplicity of composite forms within the grass. In other words, the grass is infinitely different than itself! The grass which we see is only its form *at a certain macroscopic level*, and not its 'true essential form'. Since it is composite, it has no single true form. Furthermore, the blade of grass is constantly in process or in motion such that its composite form is constantly changing at different levels, even if we cannot see it. There is no stable form at all, but an infinity of continual, minute, formal *trans*formations. Streams, animals, and everything else follow suit. Again, this does not mean that there is an infinity of types of forms, but simply an infinity of formal combinations.

Different shapes are agglomerated [*formae glomeramen*] (2.686) and mixed by motion [*permixto semine constant*] (2.687) into infinitely diverse composite waveforms. The forms and patterns of the mixing are not *ex nihilo*, but have to do with the initial conditions or *parentum* (2.698) from which the flows come. For example, there are currently no centaurs because such an animal would have to come from a long line of patronage of successive mutations, each imitating the waveform patterns of those before and making small modifications, and so on. Not all things can be connected in all ways [*Nec tamen omnimodis conecti posse putandum est omnia*] (2.700–1). Human bodies do not sprout from horses' bodies *ex nihilo*, nor do goat heads sprout from lions, like chimera *ex nihilo*. Goats come from goats and horses from horses precisely because the form and shape of these animals are natural composites transformed through relations of successive parentage [*parentum*] and direct material connection. All organisms have a certain seed [*seminibus certis*] (2.708) and a certain mother [*certa genetrice*] (2.708) from which they grow, but also a pedesis which allows them to mutate.

Conclusion

We can now clearly state in the final line of this section Lucretius' position on the question of form: the forms drawn by corporeal flows are not the shapes of particles or discrete atoms but rather the shapes or figures traced by the waveform of the corporeal flows (2.725–9).

semina cum porro distent, differre necessust
intervalla vias conexus pondera plagas
concursus motus; quae non animalia solum
corpora seiungunt, sed terras ac mare totum
secernunt caelumque a terris omne retentant.

Since, furthermore, the seeds are different, there must be differences in
spacings, paths, connections, weight, blows,
meetings, and motions. These things not only separate
living *corpora*, but sunder the earth and the entire sea
and keep the whole sky away from the earth.

The form of *corpora* or *semina* is differentiated over a distance [*cum porro
distent*] (2.725). Their form is thus defined, not by discrete geometrical
shapes, but by the continuous patterns they draw out over those distances: their waveforms. This is precisely why Lucretius says that the
form or figure of things is defined by the interval [*intervalla*], path [*vias*],
connection [*conexus*], weight [*pondera*], collision [*plagas*], convergence
[*concursus*], and motion [*motus*] of the *semina* (2.726–8).

If the shape of things were given in advance as an eternal essence,
the above kinetic factors would be irrelevant to the form of matter.
Furthermore, if the shape of things were determined by the shape of the
corpora themselves as discrete particles, then again these kinetic factors
would be irrelevant. All that would be relevant would be the shape
produced by the combination of the shapes; a simple matter of combi-
natorial geometry. However, this is not at all what Lucretius describes
in these lines. Form and figure are the product of nothing other than the
intervallic paths of connection, collision, and convergence of corporeal
matter in motion. *Corpora* draw or trace out waveforms, which all move
at a certain frequency.

The material kinetics of form developed here thus provides the foundation for a more complex theory of sensation and life, which we will
look at more closely in the next chapter.

Notes

1. There are infinite *corpora* with the same kind of *figura* (regular, irregular,
   and fuzzy).
2. Monica Gale, *Myth and Poetry in Lucretius* (Cambridge: Cambridge
   University Press, 2007), 28.

3. See Thomas Nail, *The Figure of the Migrant* (Stanford: Stanford University Press, 2015); Thomas Nail, *Theory of the Border* (Oxford: Oxford University Press, 2016); and Thomas Nail, *Being and Motion* (Oxford: Oxford University Press, under review).
4. Anne Baring and Jules Cashford, *The Myth of the Goddess: Evolution of an Image* (London: Viking Arkana, 1991), 395.
5. Baring and Cashford, *The Myth of the Goddess*, 395.
6. Walter Burkert, *Greek Religion* (Cambridge, MA: Harvard University Press, 1985), 177.
7. Baring and Cashford, *The Myth of the Goddess*, 407.
8. Baring and Cashford, *The Myth of the Goddess*, 410.
9. Baring and Cashford, *The Myth of the Goddess*, 408.
10. Ann Bergren, *Weaving Truth: Essays on Language and the Female in Greek Thought* (Washington, DC: Center for Hellenic Studies, Trustees for Harvard University, 2008).
11. Elias Canetti, *Crowds and Power* (New York: Viking Press, 1962), 31.

14. The Sensation of Matter

Corporeal flows are insensible and insensate. *Corpora* are insensible, and they become sensible only when their flows have folded back over themselves and have produced a relatively stable loop or thing [*rebus*]. Things are junctions [*iuncta*] or folds [*plex*] that can be joined together [*coniuncta*] (1.449) into different kinotopological patterns [*contextum*] (1.243) whose figures [*figura*] (2.341), positions [*positura*] (1.685), and kinetic circulations [*dent motus accipiantque*] (1.819) give rise to different sensible waveforms we call taste, touch, sight, sound, and smell. In this way, *corpora* are the material conditions of sensation but themselves do not have sensation. They are the condition of sensation and thus are incapable of sensation, or they would require yet another condition other than themselves for such sensation, and so on to infinity. Sensibility and sensation are thus emergent products of motion like everything else, and not fundamental features of an inert matter.

In lines 730–1022 of Book II, Lucretius introduces a material kinetic framework for the theories of sensation and sensibility, which he further develops in later books. In the course of doing so, he introduces a material kinetic theory of optics consistent with contemporary notions, and a new theory of kinetic emergence, rivalling those of more recent theories. The aim of this chapter is to draw out his kinetic theories of sensation and life through a close reading of the Latin text and its comparison with contemporary theories.

Sensation

Corporeal motions, positions, figures, and mixtures are the material conditions under which all sensation occurs. The fold of matter gives sensation to the fold so that the fold may experience a self-affection or sensation of itself. Things can produce a quality or sensation only on the condition that they create at least one point of intersection of a flow with itself: an affect. This point of intersection is then identified with the sense *of the fold* in which it occurs. However, since unfolded *corpora* do not have such a point of intersection, but are rather the conditions by which the affect or intersection are produced, they cannot be sensed in any way. If they were, it would presuppose that something smaller must be folded within them, and so on to infinity. This is clear from an examination of the different senses, Lucretius writes, particularly vision.

Kinoptics

Kinoptics is the kinetic theory of light. For Lucretius, colour is a series of conjunctions [*coniuncta colore*] (2.743) of folds that touch our eyes in specific waveforms. *Corpora* in themselves have no colour, but rather draw, give, or provide colour through the folded waveforms [*praedita formis*] (2.758). The quality [*quali*] (2.761) of the colour that appears in each case depends entirely on the interposition [*positura*] (2.761) of the folds that enclose, hold, and surround [*contineantur*] (2.761) the point of intersection or affection of the flow with itself, and how those motions circulate [*inter se dent motus accipiantque*] (2.819) or give and receive motion back to itself. The relative positions of these folds as they move and circulate produce a specific waveform. This allows for the same corporeal flows to change their colours in an infinite number of ways. If the *corpora* had colour, all their motions would look the same colour.

For example, Lucretius says, the same ocean can quickly change from dark-coloured to marbled [*marmore*] (2.765) with white-capped waves precisely because the position, momentum, and figure of the flow has changed (2.763–7). Again, it is not random that Lucretius provides yet another fluid dynamic image to describe the nature of sensation. Matter is continuous, but only appears discrete or differently coloured at different topological regions depending on how the waveform is folded and arranged. The waveform of the ocean wave, for example, is the perfect poetic image to describe the waveform of sensation of light that hits our eyes at different wavelengths, giving us a sensation of different colours. As soon as the ordered waveforms produced by the corporeal change, so do our sensations of colour [*permixta est illius et ordo principiis mutatus*] (2.769–70).

Lucretius presciently defines colour as the waveform of light. Colours, he says, cannot exist without light [*sine luce colores esse neque*] (2.795). Following the recurring poetic image of the 'shores of light' [*luminis* oras] (1.20, 1.170, 1.179, 2.577, 2.617) Lucretius says that *corpora* never emerge into the light. This is the case precisely because the corporeal flows are also flows of light itself. Light does not emerge into the light without something else illuminating this light. Just as light is the material condition of visibility which itself is not visible to the eye as a thing, so the *corpora* are the material conditions of sensation and are therefore nothing sensible.

According to Lucretius then, colour and optics are produced by the reflection of light off objects and into our eyes. Colour is the waveform or shape [*figura*] of the flows of light that touch our eyes. As the object moves and the light changes, so the colours change as they reflect off the object and hit our eye differently.

For example, we see the colours of a peacock's feathers change and shimmer as the peacock moves. This indicates that colour is produced by different collisions of light in motion [*gignuntur luminis ictu*] (2.810–16).

> *Et quoniam plagae quoddam genus excipit in se*
> *pupula, cum sentire colorem dicitur album,*
> *atque aliud porro, nigrum cum et cetera sentit,*
> *nec refert ea quae tangas quo forte colore*
> *praedita sint, verum quali magis apta figura,*
> *scire licet nihil principiis opus esse colore,*
> *sed variis formis variantes edere tactus.*

> And since the pupil of the eye receives into itself a certain type
> of blow when it is said to perceive white color,
> and yet another type, when it perceives black and other colors,
> and since it makes no difference what color the things you touch happen
> to be, but rather with what sort of shape they are furnished,
> you can be certain that the first beginnings have no need of colors,
> but by their different shapes they produce different kinds of touch.

Different waveforms produce different kinds of touch on the pupil: colour. As such, the nature of colour, like other sensations, is not fixed. *Corpora* are always capable of moving otherwise and changing their waveform into any colour. *Corpora*, as argued in the previous chapter, are morphogenetic. Lucretius even creates a new Latin word to describe the morphogenetic mutability of kinetic forms: *formamenta* (2.819), the process by which the waveforms of matter continuously change their shape, thus producing different sensations. For Lucretius, as we also saw in the previous chapter, there are no fixed shapes of *corpora* [*non certis certa figuris*] (2.817), but only continuous flows in the process of morphogensis or *formamenta*.

Physically speaking, this is pretty consistent with contemporary optics. Optics today shows us that light itself is made of colourless photons which vibrate in different waveforms that produce different colours on the electromagnetic spectrum. It is precisely the motion, position, and collision of matter on our eyes that produces different sensations of colour. However, even more relevant to Lucretius' theory is the problem in the quantum sciences of trying to observe photons and subatomic particles without introducing additional photons through spectroscopy or some other photon-emitting light source that would render certain particles visible. The problem of quantum observation is that by introducing photons in order to observe, we change the situation of what we observe. The introduction of photons actually changes the subatomic position, momentum, and relations of that which we are observing. In other words, Lucretius was more right than he realised about this problem in fundamental physics. Light allows us to observe but does not allow us to observe our observation independent of the light used to observe. *Corpora* thus remain insensible.

All other waveforms of sensation follow suit. For the same reasons that the *corpora* have no colour, they also have no taste, smell, touch, or sound. They are not hot or cold, or wet or dry. The flows of *corpora*, Lucretius says, are like the flows of a scentless olive oil, which only takes on scent after folding in other oils such as marjoram (2.846–58).

In physics, quantum fields follow much the same description. They are the fundamentally insensible material conditions for sensibility. They have no colour, texture, smell, taste, or sound. Only once they have folded and woven themselves into more stable folds can these folds be said to produce a sensible quality.

Sensibility

Sensibility is the flip side of sensation. Corporeal motions, positions, figures, and mixtures are also the material conditions under which all sensibility occurs. The fold of matter gives sensation to the fold so that the fold may experience a self-affection or sensation of itself. Things sense themselves in a number of ways: rocks touch themselves, plants respond to light, animals respond to sound and taste, and so on.

However, before the *corpora* have folded themselves into a 'self' that can sense its 'self', there is no self to sense or be sensed. Since the flow of matter is the condition for sensibility, it cannot itself have sensation. This will be clear from an examination of different levels of sensibility.

Emergence

The qualities or sensations that emerge as products of the corporeal process of folding are mutable and therefore perishable, but the *corpora* themselves are not. Lucretius defines *corpora* as matter which has been disjoined [*seiuncta*] (2.861) completely from its qualities or folds. Thus, for Lucretius, the transcendental difference is that the fundamental [*fundamenta*] (2.863) condition of things [*subiungere rebus*] (2.862) cannot itself be a thing. The conditions of transcendental materialism do not resemble in any way that which they condition. Therefore sensibility cannot be composed of anything which itself has sensibility. Sensibility, like sensation, is an emergent process, irreducible to what it is composed of. All living creatures emerge from non-living processes (2.870).

> *ex insensilibus, quod dico, animalia gigni.*

> living creatures arise, as I say, from things that lack sensation.

All of life is made from non-living matter. Worms are made from cells, which are made from molecules, which are made of atoms, which are made of quantum fields, none of which are alive. This does not mean that worms or any other animal are not alive. It simply means that every thing is made of smaller things, which are not identical to their larger composition. This is demonstrated by the fact that more complex organisms have abilities and capacities that the component parts do not have on their own. Organisms get hungry, breathe, and metabolise, but molecules, atoms, fields, or *corpora* do not.

Matter Recycles Matter. Corpora compose, decompose, and recompose again and again into all the varieties of life, which have the capacity for sensation (2.875–8).

> *vertunt se fluvii in frondes et pabula laeta*
> *in pecudes, vertunt pecudes in corpora nostra*
> *naturam, et nostro de corpore saepe ferarum*
> *augescunt vires et corpora pennipotentum.*

> Brooks, branches, and glad pastures turn themselves
> into cattle, and cattle change their nature into our bodies,

and from our body often the living force of wild
animals and the bodies of the powerful-of-wing increase.

Flows of water [*fluvii*] (2.875), plants [*frondes*] (2.875), and nourishing
earth [*pabula*] (2.875), by turning back over themselves [*vertunt*] (2.876),
fold into animals, which then fold into our own bodies, and when our
bodies die or unfold, they will be in turn [*vertunt*] folded into the wild
animals and birds that will gain strength from our bodies. In each different body the capacity for sensation (sensibility) occurs differently
because the flows of matter have been arranged and folded differently.
It is not the same sensibility in each body, river, plant, and animal.
Matter is capable of this affective morphogenesis precisely because it has
no fixed or essential qualities. Similarly, matter is capable of so many
different forms of sensibility because it has no fixed or essential sensibility of its own.

The capacities for sensation in any given organism are different not
because the kind of *corpora* is different, but because the same *corpora* are
mixed, arranged, and circulated [*et commixta quibus dent motus accipiantque*]
(2.885) differently. Not all relations of motion produce sensibility, only
certain ones.[1]

The Paradox of Emergence

This theory of sensation and life, however, also gives birth to a strange
philosophical paradox of emergence: that new capacities, like sensibility,
seem to emerge from things which themselves lack sensibility (2.910–13).

> *at nequeant per se partes sentire necesse est:*
> *namque animus sensus membrorum respuit omnis,*
> *nec manus a nobis potis est secreta neque ulla*
> *corporis omnino sensum pars sola tenere.*

> But it is impossible that parts are able to have sensation by themselves,
> for every sensation of the parts looks to something else,
> and neither can the hand nor any other part of the body, when separated
> from us, maintain any hold on sensation by itself.

The hand separated from our body has no sensibility, but as part of our
body it does. According to Lucretius, either there is no sensibility at all,
because none of the parts have sensibility, or everything has sensibility, because everything is its own whole. Neither of these, however, is
correct. Philosophically, therefore, we are confronted with two equally

unsatisfying solutions to the problem of emergence: reductionism and holism.

Reductionism. In the first solution, higher order systems are completely reducible to their lower order systems and could hypothetically be calculated by a very powerful computer. For example, if organisms, cells, and molecules are all made of atoms then as long as we knew the initial position and momentum of those atoms, we could, through classical mechanical models, predict how the organism would respond to a certain stimulus at the macroscopic level. Such a theory was explicitly put forward by the eighteenth-century French atomist Pierre-Simon Laplace.[2] Life, consciousness, cells, sensibility, and every other macroscopic effect would simply be an illusion or deterministic effect of a more fundamental process of atomic motion. No real novelty or new capacity emerges at higher orders of motion that is not completely explainable at the lowest level.

Holism. In the second solution, higher order systems are not reducible to their lower order systems but rather introduce true novelty and new capacities into being. No computer, or Laplacean demon, no matter how powerful, could calculate the behaviour of larger order systems based on the movement of their component parts. The macroscopic system works according to completely different laws and patterns that only work on that level. In this account, sensibility, consciousness, and social systems are truly novel phenomena with their own laws.

However, the problem with this solution to the problem of emergence is that it does not answer the question of where such new capacities come from. Presumably, sensibility, consciousness, and social systems are all made up of smaller parts and should obey the laws of physics. If they don't, the physical laws are profoundly wrong, which they do not seem to be in all other regards. Or else, there is some mystical substance animating them which has not been discovered. Either the laws of particle physics are wrong or something new and mystical has been introduced *ex nihilo* which is not subject to its laws. Both options are deeply unsatisfying.[3] The paradox of emergence remains a contemporary problem in philosophy and science.

Pedetic Emergence

Lucretius puts forward a third theory of emergence in *De Rerum Natura*: pedetic emergence. The perceived gap or leap between the capacity of the parts and those of the whole seems insurmountable because it leaves out one crucial aspect of nature, which is at the heart of Lucretian materialism: pedesis. The movement of matter, both classical and quantum, does not always obey fixed patterns or laws of motion. Laplace was wrong. If we knew the position and momentum of every atom in the universe we could not predict its behaviour, because the movement of matter is turbulent at every level of reality – fundamentally. The movement of quantum fields is indeterminate; the movement of electrons is stochastic; atoms and molecules move and vibrate pedetically; cells and living organisms take novel actions and adopt mutations; social systems rise and fall in highly unpredictable ways based on the pedesis of social motions.[4]

Pedesis is why weather patterns are not completely predictable; it is why the motion of water molecules is not predictable; and it is why we cannot predict the behaviour of organisms. It is, as Richard Feynman says, 'the most important unsolved problem of classical physics'.[5] At each level the pedesis of the component parts is compounded, producing novel effects at higher levels, which in turn have a 'downward' or feedback effect on the motion of the lower levels. Although the pedesis of matter is quite small compared to that of organisms, and retracing the vast interconnection and feedback mechanisms would be almost impossible, there is none the less *some kind of connection*.

This is not a matter of simply not knowing all the variables in a weather system or in the matrices of human behaviour. Even if we knew all the variables, matter would still have a degree of stochastic motion that makes any prediction about how it will behave fundamentally undecidable in advance.[6] This is one of the great insights of the third revolution in physics in the twentieth century: non-linear dynamics.

For Lucretius, the parts and the whole are not ontologically different kinds of things. The problem of emergence has been plagued by reification [*res*]. For reductionists, parts are things and wholes are *composites* of things, not things in their own right. For holists, however, both parts and wholes are things, just different kinds of things. The emergence of metastable systems appears to us today as a problem precisely because the *movement* of things has not been sufficiently theorised. Movement is not a thing.

For Lucretius, however, matter is pedetic at every level, because the *corpora* are themselves pedetic. Things [*rerum*] are com*plicated* products of matter and are therefore defined purely according to their relations of motion, which are different at each level. The relations of motion make 'things' different than the sum of their parts because each thing is not only a composite of other *rerum* but, more importantly, is a specific distribution of pedetic motion that gives it its features.

A weather system, for example, is strictly the sum of its parts, but a sum of *pedetic parts* whose collective motion produces fundamentally new, unpredictable motions at a higher level. This turbulence results in genuinely new forms and capacities, such as storm systems and sensibility in organisms, not reducible to atomic motions. In other words, the sensibility of organisms only looks like an *ex nihilo* emergence or an illusion if one thinks of matter as reducible to a bunch of discrete things moving according to fixed laws of motion. For example, Lucretius asks us to consider the example of biological life.

Life

Lucretius' thesis that life emerged from non-living matter is entirely consistent with modern evolutionary biology. Life, for Lucretius, is a very specific kind of assembly of matter that has been folded in just the right way so as to circulate a living breath [*vitalis animae*] (2.950). Before the flows of matter fold together from their scattered locations in the air, water, and earth, life does not emerge (2.941–3).

> *nec congressa modo vitalis convenientes*
> *contulit inter se motus, quibus omnituentes*
> *accensi sensus animantem quamque tuentur.*

> nor has it come together yet and assembled the appropriate
> interactive live-giving motions, by means of which the all-watching
> senses, once kindled, watch over every living creature.

Life emerges only when a certain circulation of vital motions [*modo vitalis*] (2.941) are gathered together in a relatively stable pattern of exchange and specific self-relation: respiration [*animae*]. All life respires. Once respiring life emerges it kindles [*accensi*] (2.943) the animate [*animantem*] (2.943) senses. *Corpora* are not alive, but are the matter that composes the metabolic [*inter se motus*] (2.942) and respirating [*animantem*] motions of life that animate the senses of living creatures. Non-living things also have the capacity for some sensation. Even rocks touch. However, in living creatures life is a prerequisite for the animation of their senses. In short, life emerges as a truly novel relation of non-living matter in motion.

Death

Death, for Lucretius, occurs when the flows, folds, and circulations that produce life unfold and scatter (2.947–51).

dissoluuntur enim positurae principiorum
et penitus motus vitales inpediuntur,
donec materies omnis concussa per artus
vitalis animae nodos a corpore solvit
dispersamque foras per caulas eiecit omnis;

For the arrangements of the first beginnings are dissolved
and deep within the life-giving motions are obstructed,
until the substance is shaken throughout every limb,
releases the life-giving knots of the soul from the body,
and scatters and expels the soul outside through every pore.

Since matter is not alive but life is a *relation of motion* endowed with certain metastable capacities due to pedesis, it loses these capacities when those relations are changed. Since life is not a type of thing but a kinetic relation, matter is not destroyed, but simply unfolded and refolded elsewhere. Life is the vital knot of matter [*vitalis animae nodos*] (2.950) that makes possible respiration and the metabolic circulation of motions.

A knot [*nodos*], for Lucretius, is the intersection of two or more corporeal circulations at two or more of the same junctions. Knots make it possible for circulatory patterns of motion to morph or change their patterns of motion without changing the number of shared junctions or crossings. As long as the morphisms or movements in the circulations do not disjoin from the shared junctions, the two circulations remain knotted. However, as circulatory or woven [*contextum*] systems change and move, their flows and junctions may move closer to or further away from one another, forming different topological 'neighbourhoods', or proximities. Topological neighbourhoods may change but the number of shared junctions will remain the same in the knot. In other words, knots are what allow composite sensations and things to persist in their composition without dissipating, even when they are moved around or morphed.

The soul [*animae*] (2.950) is nothing other than a big knot of flows that all share a series of interconnected affects within the body. The soul is therefore immanent to the body as a living breath [*vitalis animae nodos*], like the oxygen that moves through all our blood and body and allows it to do work. Without oxygen, without breath, which suffuses all the other circulatory processes, the circulatory connections unknot and the junctions [*iuncta*] unfold. The death of a living organism occurs when enough knots of life are unknotted. However, an organism may have many of its vital knots destroyed but still be able to quiet the disturbances and return the flows back to their previous circulatory patterns (2.954–8). For Lucretius, death is not a type of thing, but a 'threshold' after which the kinetic relations are no longer capable of returning to their previous state of metabolic respiration.

Pain and Pleasure

Furthermore, since corporeal flows have no sensibility, they have no pain or pleasure either. Pain, for Lucretius, is the disjunction of the flows from their relatively stable circulations, while pleasure is the conjunction of the flows into relatively stable circulations (2.963–72).

> *Praeterea, quoniam dolor est, ubi materiai*
> *corpora vi quadam per viscera viva per artus*
> *sollicitata suis trepidant in sedibus intus,*
> *inque locum quando remigrant, fit blanda voluptas,*
> *scire licet nullo primordia posse dolore*
> *temptari nullamque voluptatem capere ex se;*
> *quandoquidem non sunt ex ullis principiorum*
> *corporibus, quorum motus novitate laborent*
> *aut aliquem fructum capiant dulcedinis almae.*
> *haut igitur debent esse ullo praedita sensu.*

> Moreover, since there is pain when the bodies of matter
> are disturbed by some force throughout the living flesh
> and limbs and they shake within in their dwelling places,
> and when they return to their place, alluring pleasure arises,
> one can realize that the primary bodies cannot be assailed
> by any pain, nor can they take any pleasure from themselves,
> since they are not composed of any bodies of first beginnings,
> by the strangeness of whose motion they might be afflicted
> or take any enjoyment of refreshing sweetness.

Following his account of pleasant and unpleasant sensations, developed in Chapter 12, Lucretius further clarifies their general differences. Pain [*dolor*] (2.963) occurs when there is a disturbance [*sollicitata*] (2.965) or irregular motion [*trepidant*] (2.965) in a previously existing and relatively smooth, stable [*sedibus*] (2.965) relation of motion. When the relations of motion return [*remigrant*] (2.966) back to their stable places [*locum*] (2.966), it produces pleasure [*voluptas*] (2.966).

The first ordering matters [*principiorum corporibus*] (2.991–2) cannot take [*laborent*] (2.970) any pain or pleasure for themselves because they are the active [*laborem*] (2.1160) matter which produces the conditions of pain and pleasure in the first place. Pain and pleasure are relations of motion (conjunction and disjunction) only possible for *rerum*, since only things can become joined or disjoined. Corporeal flows are not products of previous conjunctions nor can they be disjoined from themselves.

In the proem of Book I, Lucretius says that corporeal flows are driven by *voluptas* or desire, but pleasure and desire are not strictly identical; they are two sides of the same process of folding. Corporeal flows are driven by *voluptas* but they cannot 'take pleasure from themselves' [*voluptatem capere ex se*] (2.968). Through desire [*voluptas*] the *corpora* produce pleasure [*voluptas*], but only through the folds or *iuncta* which consume it. In other words, the fold of things can be understood from two sides, implied in the first line of *De Rerum Natura* with respect to the double genitive *voluptas* of Venus. From the perspective of the constituting flows, *voluptas* appears as a purely positive excess without subject or object. However, from the perspective of the subject constituted by this folded flow of desire, the constituting flow appears as a source or object of pleasure *for the subject*. The pleasure of the subject is only a retroactive pleasure of that which constitutes it, but now as an 'object'.

Since the corporeal flows precede the subject and the object, they cannot be an object or subject of pleasure. From a third perspective, the process as a whole thus describes a kind of triple genitive by which the corporeal flows of desire are all three dimensions at once: the subject who receives pleasure, the object of pleasure, and the process of desire that produces them. Pleasure is something that can only be held [*capere*] (2.968) by the fold, junction, or thing that holds it. The fold 'holds' its pleasure inside, but the corporeal flow remains the pure exteriority that produces the difference between interior and exterior in the fold itself. Corporeal flows produce the fruits of enjoyment [*fructum*] (2.971) in one sense, but can only consume or lay hold of them [*capiant*] (2.971) in another qua fold. Things are nourished [*almae*] (2.971) by a continuous flow of matter, but *corpora* themselves need no nourishing because they are the nourishment.

Conclusion

Lucretius describes the whole process of kinetic materialisation and the emergence of sensation and sensibility as a great mytho-hydraulic cycle (2.999–1003).

> *cedit item retro, de terra quod fuit ante,*
> *in terras, et quod missumst ex aetheris oris,*
> *id rursum caeli rellatum templa receptant.*
> *nec sic interemit mors res ut materiai*
> *corpora conficiat, sed coetum dissupat ollis;*

> Likewise what was from the earth before falls back again
> into the earth, and what was sent from the shores of heaven
> the regions of sky take back again when it is given back.
> Nor does death destroy things so much that it does
> away with the bodies of matter, but it disperses their union.

Water falls, like the *corpora* themselves, the seeds of Ouranos, into the curved bosom of Mother Earth [Gaia] where it is folded into life and sensation, only to be disjoined by death and returned through evaporation to the sky so it may fall and fold again (2.1004–6).

> *inde aliis aliud coniungit et efficit, omnis*
> *res ut convertant formas mutentque colores*
> *et capiant sensus et puncto tempore reddant;*

> Then it joins one thing to others and brings it about
> that all things transpose shapes and change colors
> and experience sensations and lose them in an instant of time;

Sensations and sensibility emerge from this process based on the relations of motion (including form, position, path, interval, and so on), only to lose them in an instant [*puncto tempore*] (2.1006). Just as the flows from the sky pool up on the surface of the earth, so things [*rerum*] float up to the surface [*quod in summis fluitare*] (2.1011) and on to the shores of light.

Notes

1. This is dealt with in greater detail in *De Rerum Natura*, Book V.
2. Pierre Simon Laplace, *A Philosophical Essay on Probabilities*, trans. F. W.

Truscott and F. L. Emory, 6th edn (New York: Dover Publications, 1951), 4.

3. There is an ongoing discussion in philosophical literature on the relation between emergence and downward causation – also called macro-determinism. See, for example, Mark Bedau and Paul Humphreys, *Emergence: Contemporary Readings in Philosophy and Science* (Cambridge, MA: MIT Press, 2008), and Evan Thompson, *Mind in Life: Biology, Phenomenology, and the Sciences of Mind* (Cambridge, MA: Belknap Press of Harvard University Press, 2010).

4. This last claim is large and is defended at length in Thomas Nail, *The Figure of the Migrant* (Stanford: Stanford University Press, 2015).

5. Dan Vergano, 'Turbulence Theory Gets A Bit Choppy', *USA Today*, 10 September 2006, http://usatoday30.usatoday.com/tech/science/columnist/vergano/2006-09-10-turbulence_x.htm (accessed 29 July 2017).

6. In 2009 Gu et al. presented a class of physical systems that exhibits non-computable macroscopic properties. Mile Gu et al., 'More Really Is Different', *Physica D: Nonlinear Phenomena*, 238.9 (2009): 835–9; P.-M. Binder, 'Computation: The Edge of Reductionism', *Nature*, 459.7245 (2009): 332–4.

15. The Multiverse

Lucretius' argument for the multiverse is perhaps one of his most radical, unsettling, and unbelievable arguments. However, the more we discover about contemporary quantum physics, the less unbelievable this argument has become. Unfortunately, the reception of Lucretius' theory of the multiverse, just like his theory of matter, has been constrained by the historical limitations of prevailing scientific knowledge. In particular, the historical interpretation of Lucretius' theory of the multiverse has been limited by the pre-quantum mechanical belief that there is only one universe. Debates in cosmology have historically been over whether the one universe is finite or infinite; but it was not until 1952 that the theory of the multiverse was introduced by Erwin Schrödinger as a conclusion of quantum physics.

As we have seen, Lucretius describes a number of natural phenomena with an astounding level of descriptive accuracy: turbulence, optics, the insensibility of matter, and others, in ways generally consistent with our contemporary understanding. His poetic descriptions are about as accurate as one could get without the use of modern experimental and mathematical methods. His thesis on the multiverse is another case in point. Only now, after the insights of quantum physics, are we in a position to be able to finally appreciate the philosophical prescience of his theory of the multiverse.

In short, the argument of this chapter is that, for Lucretius, the universe is not only infinite, as he has been previously interpreted as saying, but that there are also *an infinite number of infinite universes*: the multiverse.

Quantum *corpora*

Lucretius begins his argument for the multiverse by encouraging his readers not to be scared off by the newness of his argument alone. In this regard, things have not changed much. It probably took just as much bravery for Lucretius as it did for Erwin Schrödinger to put forward the same idea in 1952. In fact, Schrödinger similarly warned his Dublin audience that what he was about to say might 'seem lunatic'. The multiple quantum equations describing different histories are 'not alternatives but all really happen simultaneously'.[1]

The idea of multiple universes, Lucretius writes, sounds just as fantastic as it would be to describe a single universe with all its wandering plants and stars to someone who had not seen it before. The idea of the multiverse follows directly from the theory of *corpora*. If *corpora* compose an infinity of infinities (see Chapter 9), are irreducible to space and time [*incerto tempore / incertisque locis*] (1.218–19), and are productive of space and time themselves through folding (see Chapter 7), then it follows that *corpora* are capable of producing an infinite infinity of real space-times or universes (2.1052–7).

> *nullo iam pacto veri simile esse putandumst,*
> *undique cum vorsum spatium vacet infinitum*
> *seminaque innumero numero summaque profunda*
> *multimodis volitent aeterno percita motu,*
> *hunc unum terrarum orbem caelumque creatum,*
> *nil agere illa foris tot corpora materiai;*

> Now in no way must it be thought to be like the truth –
> since everywhere infinite space lies empty
> and seeds numberless in their number in the totality of the heavenly
> depths fly around in many ways driven on by eternal motion –
> that this was the only world and heavens created,
> and that beyond it those many bodies of matter do nothing at all;

If matter is infinite [*innumero numero*] (2.1054) and capable of flowing [*voliteni*] (2.1055) and composing itself in an infinite number of ways [*multimodis*] (2.1055), then it follows that it can produce an infinite number of spaces [*spatium vacet infinitum*] (2.1053), earths [*terrarum*] (2.1056), and heavens [*caelumque*] (2.1056). Because *corpora* are insensible and flow infinitely in all directions, we must apply this thesis to both micro and macro domains at the same time. *Corpora* are insensible on the macro level because their motion extends beyond our vision into the space beyond our planet. Our universe is infinitely large. However, *corpora* are also insensible on the micro level because their motions occur infinitely below our level of sensation. Therefore, it follows that if matter creates in the domain of the insensible, then it creates both *beyond* our sensation and *below* our sensation as well. Therefore, at the macro level there is a movement of matter without beginning or end, which creates, over an infinite amount of time, an infinite number of *successive universes* using every possible combination of infinite matter.

The universe expands and collapses again and again in a series of big bounces without the creation or destruction of new matter. There is also, at the micro level, an infinite number of *simultaneous universes* which produce multiple coexisting space-times in superposition. This is possible because space and time are *not ontologically fundamental*, but are products of corporeal motion itself. This follows by necessity: if *corpora* are infinite and creative of space-time itself, then they are capable of producing infinite different but simultaneous space-times. Just because we do not see this process happening does not mean that it does not logically follow from the natural conditions of what we do see.

Other Worlds: *alios alibi*

The *corpora* spontaneously create by themselves [*sponte sua forte offensando*] (2.1059) in an infinite number of ways [*multimodis*] (2.1060). If *corpora* can create in an infinite number of ways, why did they create in the way the world is now, as opposed to some other way? If the actual world in all its infinite expanse were the only way in which the corpora could create, this would contradict the claim that the *corpora* were truly and infinitely creative because the actuality of the existing world would limit the infinite creativity of the *corpora*.

The only way to remain consistent with Lucretius' realist theory of the *corpora* is that they must be *actually* creative in an infinity of ways [*multimodis*]. This is possible only if there is an infinity of simultaneous but different worlds. If there were only one world, then the *corpora* would only be potentially creative in an infinite number of ways and not actually so. Since there is no such thing as possible or hypothetical *corpora*, then they and their creations must be real and actual ones. Therefore, there must be infinite actual, but non-intersecting, universes (2.1064–6).

quare etiam atque etiam talis fateare necesse est
esse alios alibi congressus materiai,
qualis hic est, avido complexu quem tenet aether.

> Wherefore again and again it is necessary to admit
> that there are other directions of matter in other locations
> like the one here which the aether holds in its greedy embrace.

The Latin phrase *alios alibi congressus* (2.1065) is important here. The words *alios* and *alibi* come from the Latin root *alius*, meaning 'other'. Depending on the conjugation, the root takes on different inflections. For example, according to the OLD, *alias* means 'another time', *alibi* means 'another place', and *alios* means 'another course of action or direction'. Based on this, we should translate the above passage as 'there are other worlds which follow completely different courses of action or direction [*alios*] in other places [*alibi*] which are created by the other world trajectories, and not reducible to a single-world trajectory'.

In the case of a single-world trajectory, the other worlds are just regions of the same world, and thus not truly other courses of action [*alios*]. This would presume the fundamental and pre-given nature of a single homogeneous space-time. The fact that other worlds have radically other space-time trajectories of their own implies that the *corpora* can create space-time in many ways [*multimodis*] concurrently [*congressus*].

For Lucretius, *corpora* are explicitly not spatio-temporal; thus, the concurrent-courses-of-action interpretation put forward here is theoretically more consistent with his theory of *corpora*. However, if one interprets space and time as pre-given fundamental backgrounds within which *corpora* move, one contradicts two Lucretian theses: the thesis against *ex nihilo* creation and the thesis on the non-spatio-temporal nature of the *corpora*. If the immateriality of pure space-time comes first without any matter and then produces matter, we are guilty of *ex nihilo* creation. Further, if the *corpora* are derived from the immaterial they cannot themselves be material. Therefore, the only interpretation consistent with the universal creativity of matter is that multiple concurrent space-times emerge from matter and not the other way around.

Many Actual Worlds

Since *corpora* are infinite, there is no prior limit on what the *corpora* can create and no restriction on their creation of an infinity of infinite worlds, each with their own different distribution or course of action [*alios*] and different space-time [*alibi-alias*]. Over an infinite amount of time, an infinity of different courses of action are possible. Being infinite and productive of space-time itself, *corpora* actually create all these different courses of action concurrently. Each new direction or trajectory of action produces a new branch or bifurcation in a single flow of matter. If the *corpora* could not produce many actual concurrent worlds, then these would only be 'possible' worlds, which would indicate an *a priori* limitation or hindrance [*debent*] (2.1022) on the infinite creativity of matter, which is impossible (2.1067–9) (Fig. 15.1).

> *Praeterea cum materies est multa parata,*
> *cum locus est praesto nec res nec causa moratur*
> *ulla, geri debent ni mirum et confieri res.*

> Moreover, when much matter is on hand,
> and when space is present and neither substance nor any cause is a
> hindrance, things ought of course to be carried out and created.

If there is infinite matter and thus the creation of infinite space, then all things [*res*] will be created at the same time, since matter and space produce time and time does not produce matter or space. Contemporary physicists call this phenomenon 'superposition', meaning that many worlds or spatio-temporal waveforms are created simultaneously.

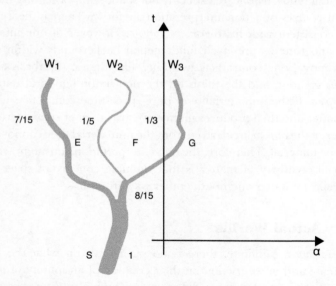

Figure 15.1 Branching worlds in Everett interpretation. Image from Simon Saunders, *Many Worlds?: Everett, Quantum Theory, and Reality* (Oxford: Oxford University Press, 2010), 199.

Quantum Interpretations

There are, however, a number of different quantum interpretations of the status of the superposition of quantum fields, known in physics as the 'measurement problem'. There is still no consensus in physics on how to interpret it, however. One approach argues that while the wave function predicts experimental outcomes, it does not actually represent physical reality. The reason quantum fields are so unpredictable is that we are still missing some 'hidden variables' which, when known, would render matter completely predictable.

Another approach denies the existence of quantum reality altogether. Quantum waveforms, it argues, are just experimentally useful for human observers to predict events, but reality is not actually a superposition of vibrating fields. This position is expressed by Niels Bohr when he writes that 'There is no quantum world. There is only an abstract physical description. It is wrong to think that the task of physics is to find out how nature *is*. Physics concerns what we can *say* about nature.'[2]

In both the 'hidden variables' theories and the 'antirealist' theories, quantum waves are interpreted as purely mathematical probability models or 'wave functions'. Wave functions are non-local superpositions but when they are observed they 'collapse' into a single discrete particle or thing in a single place. The mathematical wave function 'collapses' into a simple local coordinate matrix.

A third interpretation, however, was put forward by Hugh Everett in 1957, not long after Schrödinger suggested a multiverse as the conclusion of quantum physics. For Everett, the entire universe is a single superpositional wave function, evolving according to the Schrödinger equation. For Everett, reality is actually made of a superposition of non-local vibrating quantum fields. It never collapses and there is no fundamental division between system and observer because the observer is also composed of quantum fields. Things continue to persist as discrete particles in space-time because their quantum fields have become *entangled* such that the determination of one instantaneously produces the determination of others in specific interlocking patterns or networks which we call 'things'.[3]

One conclusion of the Everett interpretation is that if each of the superpositioned quantum waveforms of the universe is actually real, then that means there is an infinity of simultaneous universes or worlds. Each waveform is one actual world, but it does not communicate to any of the other worlds. Each 'branch' of the waveform is another world in the single/multiple material world. In every situation, every degree of freedom actually, and not possibly, occurs. Possibility only has meaning from the perspective of one of the degrees of freedom.

If *corpora* create along every degree of freedom at once without hindrance from any outside power, as Lucretius says, the conclusion is consistent with that of the Everett many-worlds interpretation.

Dimensions

If *corpora* are non-localisable [*incerto tempore / incertisque locis*], just like quantum fields, they can actually be in different space-times simultaneously, like dimensions or branches of a single-multiple world (2.1072–6).

> *quis eadem natura manet, quae semina rerum*
> *conicere in loca quaeque queat simili ratione*
> *atque huc sunt coniecta, necesse est confiteare*
> *esse alios aliis terrarum in partibus orbis*
> *et varias hominum gentis et saecla ferarum.*

> the seeds of things each into its place in the same way
> as they have been thrown together in this world it must
> be admitted that there are other worlds in other regions,
> as well as different races of men and breeds of wild beasts.

If the *corpora* are capable of creating our world according to similar conditions [*simili ratione*] (2.1073), they must be able to do so along alternate directions or courses of action [*alios*] (2.1075) in other [*aliis*] (2.1075) worlds [*terrarum*] (2.1075) as dimensions or aspects [*in partibus*] of the world [*orbis*] (2.1075). Recall that the Latin word *partibus* can also mean 'dimension or aspect' and does not necessarily presuppose the division of the whole into 'parts'. Therefore, not only is the universe itself infinite, but it also simultaneously creates an infinity of other alternate dimensions such that every possible creation is actually created. Logically this entails not only spatial infinity in the same universe, but a temporal infinity of branched universes.

This means that no type of thing is singular but it exists multiply across all its branching universes. 'Both the earth and sun, the moon, these and others that exist are not unique, but rather innumerable in number' (2.1085). For every earth there is an infinity of other earths, both within the space of our universe and within each of those in their own alternative timelines. There are an infinity of *alibis* (places) and *alias* (times). All permutations or degrees of freedom on our earth therefore are not possible, but actual, although inaccessible to us.

Nature creates all this by its own motion without the help of gods [*ipsa sua per se sponte omnia dis agere expers*] (2.1092). What god or gods could possibly rule over such a multiverse? A single god would be scattered into an infinity of non-communicating gods.

The Heat Death of the Universe

Our earth is sustained by the constant addition of new *corpora* from outside in the form of meteors and radiation. The entire biosphere of the earth originally came from the addition of outside energy that produced and sustained it. Just like every other material system, its corporeal flows were distributed or spread out [*corpora distribuuntur*] (2.1113) and then folded back on themselves in stable junctions [*et ad sua saecla recedunt*] (2.1113), continually supplied by exterior flows.

The universe is a network of junctions connected together by flows of energy. However, all closed systems or junctions are subject to entropy. Ultimately, all junctions will unfold when the flows that support them unfold. There will therefore be a chain reaction of unfolding through which the entire universe will ultimately unfold itself (2.1116–17).

> *donique ad extremum crescendi perfica finem*
> *omnia perduxit rerum natura creatrix;*

> until nature, the perfecting and creative mother of things,
> has led all to the final limit of growth.

Nature conducts [*perduxit*] (2.1117) all junctions to their completed limit [*perfica finem*] (2.1116), after which they can no longer be sustained. 'When nothing more is put into the life-giving veins than what flows out and draws back' (2.1118–19), then the junctions begin to die and flow away. The corporeal flows of matter that sustained them are not destroyed, but simply flow away without refolding into something else. Such an outflow presumes that the flows become so dispersed that they no longer intersect or fold with themselves at a limit of total disbursement (2.1120–1).

> *omnibus hic aetas debet consistere rebus,*
> *hic natura suis refrenat viribus auctum.*

Here development ought to stop for all things,
here nature forcefully reins in growth.

At this point, nature bridles all forms of enlargement, junction, and order. All things [*rebus*] disjoin back into their corporeal flows. The universe is capable of producing order or negentropy, but only on the condition of increasing entropy elsewhere. One by one the process of negentropy or order exhausts its external sources and order can no longer be maintained. The larger the body is, Lucretius writes, 'the more bodies it scatters everywhere in all directions and sends out from itself' (2.1131–5). The earth's sun, for example, is dying with the release of great energy, which we redirect into order.

Eventually, Lucretius says at the very limits of the corporeal flows of the universe, the walls of the world will crumble into ruins (2.1144–5).

Sic igitur magni quoque circum moenia mundi
expugnata dabunt labem putrisque ruinas;

So too, therefore, will the walls of the wide world be assailed
on all sides and sink into crumbling ruins.

All the planets, stars, and celestial bodies, and the regional limits or walls that hold them together in a relatively enclosed circulation [*moenia*] (2.1144), will fall [*labem*] (2.1145) into ruins. We can even see evidence for this process on Earth when we extract minerals from the earth through agriculture. Through agriculture, we exhaust the mineral energy of the soil without replenishing it, and disperse its corporeal flows in wider and wider distribution. Year after year, the earth cannot yield the same minerals unless they are returned into the soil by other means. Human civilisation is a high-entropy system which produces complexity, but always at the cost of the entropy of the earth. Civilisation is wasting the earth's and sun's energy faster than any other life form. The more things are ordered, the more flows are required to sustain them, the more the regional source of these flows is depleted, and so on throughout the universe (2.1173–4).

nec tenet omnia paulatim tabescere et ire
ad capulum spatio aetatis defessa vetusto.

He does not grasp that all things gradually waste away
and go to the grave, exhausted by the long space of time.

All things [*omnia*] (2.1173) flow away, dissolve, or melt [*tabescere*] (2.1173) in time. Things melt away, but the corporeal flows that produce time and space do not. They simply become so dispersed that it is increasingly difficult for them to fold and collide into something else.

However, no matter how dispersed the pedetic flows of matter become, they can never rule out the collisions or folds that would initiate the formation of a new universe. This brings Book II of *De Rerum Natura* full circle to the infinite pedesis of matter and the creative power of its pedetic swerving. Read in light of the opening proem of Book II, it is thus possible that a swerve or *clinamen* will occur and begin to produce another universe. This new universe will repeat the same process as the previous one in a new combination, which will also end in heat death, and so on infinitely.

The Quantum Crunch

Lucretius' theory of the infinite expansion, death, and recreation of the universe is remarkably close to a theory in contemporary cosmology dubbed 'The Big Crunch'. According to everything we currently know about the universe, Lucretius is correct that it will ultimately unfold itself faster and faster in all directions until every atom is unravelled back into the constitutive vibrating quantum fields that composed it all in the first place, often referred to as 'vacuum energy' or the 'cosmological constant'.

> Astronomers estimate that the last dim star will wink out around 1 quadrillion (10^{15}) years from now. By then the other galaxies will have moved far away, and our local group of galaxies will be populated by planets, dead stars and black holes. One by one, those planets and stars will fall into the black holes, which in turn will join into one supermassive black hole. Ultimately, as Stephen Hawking taught us, even those black holes will evaporate. After about 1 googol (10^{100}) years, all of the black holes in our observable universe will have evaporated into a thin mist of particles, which will grow more and more dilute as space continues to expand. The end result of this, our most likely scenario for the future of our universe, is nothing but cold, empty space, which will last literally forever.[4]

However, cosmologists also estimate that after roughly $10^{10^{10^{56}}}$ years another universe could be created by random quantum fluctuations or quantum tunnelling.[5] According to the Poincaré recurrence theorem, thermal fluctuations, and fluctuation theorem,[6] over an infinite amount of time there would be a spontaneous entropy decrease. Even at the smallest level, just a little bit of order would produce enough gravitation relative to the surrounding fields to gather all the fields back together in spontaneous inflation.

Just as quantum fields never stop vibrating, so *corpora* never stop flowing. Unlike things [*rerum*], *corpora* have energy without it being supplied from elsewhere. They are the fundamental producers of it. It is precisely this matter/energy that is responsible for both the big bang, heat death, and the big crunch, and their endless cycle of composition and recomposition. If there were only 'things' or folds, they would have unfolded long ago and nothing would be left. There would be no universe now. The fact that there is a multiverse now, for Lucretius, is demonstration that there must be some indestructible matter from which all other things are made.

Conclusion

Poetically, our final chapter ends with the end of all worlds and the beginning of all worlds at the same time. The beginning and the end are therefore not absolute, but simply different distributions of the same indestructible matter. The condition of the destruction of all worlds is also the condition of their rebirth: the corporeal flows of matter.

Notes

1. David Deutsch, *The Beginning of Infinity: Explanations that Transform the World* (New York: Viking, 2011), 310.
2. As quoted in Paul McEvoy, *Niels Bohr: Reflections on Subject and Object* (San Francisco: Microanalytix, 2001), 291.
3. Sean Carroll, *The Big Picture: On the Origins of Life, Meaning, and the Universe Itself* (New York: Penguin Random House, 2016), 168–9.
4. Carroll, *The Big Picture*, 52–3.
5. Sean M. Carroll and Jennifer Chen, 'Spontaneous Inflation and Origin of the Arrow of Time', *Preprint* (2004), https://arxiv.org/abs/hep-th/0410270 (accessed 29 July 2017).
6. Xiu-San Xing, 'Spontaneous Entropy Decrease and its Statistical Formula', *Research Gate*, 1 November 2007, http://arxiv.org/abs/0710.4624 (accessed 29 July 2017).

Lucretius: Our Contemporary

Lucretius was less the revolutionary harbinger of modern science than he was its greatest victim. After five hundred years of abuse by modern atomists and mechanists, it is now time to return to *De Rerum Natura* from a new perspective. In the light of contemporary philosophy and physics it now appears that some of the most important contributions of Lucretius' poem have been historically overlooked or misunderstood.

By interpreting *De Rerum Natura* as a poem about discrete particles (atoms), human freedom, laws of nature, rationalism, random swerves, and so on, the poem has been treated with the same violence as nature itself was during the scientific revolution. Just as the wild flows of water were hydraulically forced into the mechanical fountains of Versailles, so the corporeal flows of matter were interpretively forced into the discrete globules of atoms.

Modern science did the same thing to nature as it did to *The Nature of Things*. Instead of being open to the radically different worldview of *De Rerum Natura* – pedetic naturalism, goddess mythology, the ontology of motion, and the multiverse – Lucretius' ideas were forced to fit the deistic and mechanistic philosophies of the age. Among other things, this resulted in a complete distortion of ancient materialism into modern mechanism. The modern interpretation of *De Rerum Natura* is therefore no anomaly. It is part of a larger systematic worldview of patriarchy, rationalism, mechanism, and quantification that was on the rise during the time that Poggio recovered Lucretius' great work.

Thanks to the last fifty years of critical philosophy and quantum physics, however, we now have ample cause to reject the so-called fundamental nature of humanism, classical physics, and patriarchy that formed the basis of the modern interpretation of *De Rerum Natura*. Only on this condition is it now possible to locate within *De Rerum Natura* a minor literature of kinetic materialism ignored and mutilated by its modern historical appropriation. If it is at all possible to think a 'new materialism' today, distinct from mechanism, then it is fitting that it should begin with a volcanic eruption from within the founding document of Western materialism itself and from which the entire history of an error began: *De Rerum Natura*.

The Consequences

There are three important consequences of this new interpretation. The first is that modern mechanistic materialism is based on a mistaken, and by no means universal, interpretation of *De Rerum Natura*, limited by its own historical and mechanistic worldview. The consequence of this revelation is that a new theory of kinetic materialism is possible today for philosophy and the sciences that is no longer tied fundamentally to this old definition.

The second consequence of this book is to have shown that this 'new' kinetic materialism is actually quite old. It was in fact put forward by Lucretius almost two thousand years ago. *De Rerum Natura* is not a complete theory, but it can offer us a good place to start working out a more robust materialism today. It offers us a new materialism, which is also a much older materialism.

The third consequence of this book is that its findings and method can provide a useful tool and inspiration for similar studies on the primary texts of other thinkers, artists, and scientists, which might reveal further precursors to this sort of kinetic materialism lying hidden in the past.

Limitations

However, this study is also limited in some sense by the empirical and mathematical constraints of the ancient sciences with which Lucretius was familiar. Lacking more precise and experimental methods, Lucretius relies on poetic, mythological, empirical, and conceptual vocabulary as the basis of his philosophy. He gives the best descriptive account of nature he can, given the tools he has to work with. The aim of this book is therefore not to supplement Lucretius, but rather first to show the internal coherence of his theories in Books I and II, and only afterwards to cross-check them with contemporary physics to see if there are any glaring conceptual contradictions.

Thus, this book is not a projection of quantum field theory on to

Lucretius' natural philosophy. This is the case, first, because the book deals with more than merely issues of physics: it also considers mythology, politics, art, philosophy, and ontology. Secondly, the argument of this book is not that Lucretius discovered quantum physics before contemporary science did. Obviously, Lucretius' account remains at only the most general conceptual level and is no substitute for the mathematical and experimental rigour of contemporary physics.

My interpretive thesis with regard to the sciences is much more minimal: that Books I and II of *De Rerum Natura* do not contradict any of the basic conceptual frameworks of contemporary physics, as atomism clearly does. To be clear, contemporary physics not only has a much more accurate description but also has much more robust predictive and descriptive tools to work with than Lucretius. This book has not shown that Lucretius' description *matches* that of contemporary science, but simply that it is *not inconsistent* with it. Even this minimal gesture is quite impressive: there are no assertions in Books I and II that we currently know with certainty to be absolutely false.

This is not the upper limit of what *De Rerum Natura* has to offer, of course, but only a minimal limit that any materialist philosophy should take seriously: that it should not violate the well-tested outcomes of experimental physics without just cause. In addition to this minimal limit, Books I and II of *De Rerum Natura* offer incredibly sophisticated and poetically beautiful speculative theories of materiality, politics, transcendental philosophy, and the multiverse, which are not empirically verifiable or which at present remain at the very limits of scientific and philosophical knowledge. In this way, Lucretius gives us much more than physics can.

The method of this book is therefore not a projection of the present on to the past, but rather an unfolding of a dimension of the past which had always been there but has remained hidden until the present.

Future Work

The most immediate future work to be completed is the extension of this study to Books III–VI of *De Rerum Natura*. The current volume is thus only the first in a projected three-volume work. This first volume has focused on issues of ontology, cosmology, and physics because these are the main issues of Books I and II. The next volume on Books III and IV, however, will focus on issues of epistemology, aesthetics, and ethics.

After this, volume III on Books V and VI will focus on astronomy, history, and natural science. Both subsequent volumes will draw on the conceptual framework developed in Books I and II and are already underway. Once these volumes are completed, similar kinetic studies are planned for a number of other major figures in Western history who have prioritised motion in their work, in philosophy, politics, the arts, and sciences.

Index

Note: Page number in *italics* indicate figures and page numbers followed by 'n' refer to end-of-chapter notes.